PSYCHOPATHY
WITHIN

Eve Maram

ᑭ CHIRON PUBLICATIONS • ASHEVILLE, NORTH CAROLINA

www.ChironPublicatons.com

Cover design and typesetting by Nelly Murariu
Printed in the United States of America.

Library of Congress Cataloging-in-Publication Data

Names: Maram, Eve, author.
Title: Psychopathy within / Eve Maram.
Description: Asheville, North Carolina : Chiron Publications, [2016] |
  Includes bibliographical references and index.
Identifiers: LCCN 2016011749 (print) | LCCN 2016012267 (ebook) | ISBN
  9781630513757 (pbk.) | ISBN 9781630513764 (hardcover) | ISBN 9781630513771 (E-book)
Subjects: | MESH: Antisocial Personality Disorder | Psychopathology--methods
  | Psychoanalytic Theory
Classification: LCC RC555 (print) | LCC RC555 (ebook) | NLM WM 190.5.A2 | DDC
  616.85/82--dc23
LC record available at http://lccn.loc.gov/2016011749

For Albert Bodinger
1924–2009

Acknowledgments

There is not room on the page to give due recognition to everyone (and every experience) that birthed this book. Even determining a correct order leaves me stymied, so the following represents a wild gesture in the general direction of focusing my gratitude, with the caveat that it is incomplete and insufficient.

The omnipresence, skill, and guidance of Margaret Ryan, my editor extraordinaire, muse, and fairy god sister, has been insurmountable.

My Swiss friend, Robert Hinshaw, was the earliest inspiration and support who sparked the big dream of making this into a book.

I will remain forever grateful to all the people at Chiron Publications for believing in me and giving this project life.

The ever-present bedrock of love and ongoing encouragement from my husband, Wesley Maram, my children, Evan Fields and Nierika Gilbert, and my dog, Moki, has been invaluable.

Contents

Author's Note

Case histories and stories presented in this text are true, but details have been altered to protect privacy. In some instances, similar cases have been consolidated into one example.

But how about this empty space in our soul? How can anyone be interested in an empty space in our soul? How can anyone be concerned with a vacuum? Nature has a "horror *vaccui*;" we, as part of nature, always shy away from any vacuum. However that may be, I think the existing deficiencies in our soul, even the empty spaces, are important for psychology. It is important that we see them in our fellow human beings and react accordingly to avoid being fooled by the charm, not denying them, but taking them into account. But it is even more important to see these empty spaces in ourselves and not fool ourselves by denying them.[1]

—The Emptied Soul, *On the Nature of the Psychopath*, Adolf Guggenbühl-Craig

"I'm now in this phase where I'm looking back and things matter less than ever. The problem was, I never had a conscience. I was ego-driven and self-focused on my career. I've finally decided there's no need to look further. I was solipsistic."

—Albert Bodinger, August 26, 2009

---

1 Guggenbühl-Craig, Emptied Soul, ix.

Preface

The concept of a gradated definition of psychopathy, which is the central theme of this book, emerged through a confluence of my personal and professional experiences. The spark that ignited that process was my experience of my father's death, when I began to realize the connection between aspects of his personality and my work. Specifically, my job as a forensic psychologist working in the prisons and providing therapy for criminals represented my introduction to psychopathy from that perspective. With my father's passing, my curiosity about psychopathy became personal, which gave birth to a broader inquiry and deeper understanding of this intriguing and complex trait.

In this book, I am focusing on the phenomenological, qualitative aspect of psychopathy—the sense that something deep within is simply missing, as first conceptualized by Jungian analyst and author, Adolf Guggenbühl-Craig. This approach is distinctly different from a causal emphasis, as well represented by numerous theories, and instead invites exploring an archetypal dimension to the idea and our understanding of the character trait.

I struggled with using detailed personal information for what arguably constitutes case study purposes. My final decision to do so involved at least two reasons. The fact that something was missing in my father's personality and in our relationship—Adolf Guggenbühl-Craig's psychopathic gaps, as it were—actually released me to be able to share details with candor that I would otherwise have been more guarded about. Although my father, Albert, and I somehow forged our own version of an intimate relationship, at least at the end of his life, I was forever unable to feel the safe connection with my father for which I yearned. As a result of his resolute abstinence from a traditional parental bond, I can analyze and discuss his personality with objectivity in a way I could not regarding my mother, for example, because with her I would feel protective. This reality is both painful and freeing, in terms of being able to examine and share details of my father's history—toward the greater good. With all due respect to him and to the ancestors, submitting the story of Albert's character to scrutiny at this point, when he can no longer argue, feels somehow appropriate—perhaps even compensatory—with the overriding goal of contributing positively to our understanding of psychopathy. I hope that the end will justify the means.

I hesitate to say this book is all about my father, but in some regard, it is. The bare truth of the world is that at some level, the personal is always at the core of our life experience, how we assemble and understand it. There is just such an expansive dimensionality in us all, spanning personal, professional, and collective.

CHAPTER 1

Psychopathy: Professional, Personal, and Collective Perspectives

This book integrates several different approaches to the concept of psychopathy in response to several fairly distinct aspects of my own personal and professional life that began to appear related: forensic psychology concepts, my father and our relationship, Jungian concepts, clinical references, mythological material, and cultural observations. Interweaving these contents revealed the possibility of an expanded meaning and potential application of *psychopathy* through conceptualizing the term along a gradient.

The juxtaposition of my life experiences, both professional and otherwise, generated this gradated perception of psychopathy. My enthusiasm for the idea of a continuum of psychopathy began to emerge even before I realized the link to my father, Albert. My recognition that the topic of psychopathy, which had been forefront in my forensic work and studies for decades, was so much about my father as well (and by extension, myself) came to me upon reflection after he died—a fortuitous discovery, which gained momentum in the context of my earlier forensic work in this area.

As a psychologist, I straddle an unusual combination of theoretical perspectives and practice. Jung and the world of depth psychology have always felt like hearth and home to me. I never envisioned myself interviewing prison inmates on their turf, conducting risk assessments, or writing clinical evaluations for the courtroom, let alone testifying about my conclusions. However, my husband is an exclusively forensic psychologist, so through him I became familiar with that area, so divergent from my own primary orientation, and then became professionally active in that capacity. This work has involved visiting state prisons to interview inmates and conduct psychological assessments to determine their risk for sexually violent reoffense, then writing reports that may be used in court, contingent upon my findings.

The psychic atmosphere of that whole forensic psychology process is a maelstrom of shadow contents, from the pressures inherent within the patriarchal structure of the correctional institutions and the courtrooms, to the odd context and framework for contact with these individuals—our involuntary clients—who appear for an interview no one in their right mind wants, sometimes in shackles, anxious and wary involuntary hosts to our intrusive, snapshot visits. I do not mind the clinical interviews inside the institutions; in fact, I enjoy them. Although the labyrinthine bureaucratic process of gaining permission to enter is frustrating, there is something satisfying about completing the entry requirements and then navigating the locked, heavily guarded facilities themselves—from the ominously barred gates and massive stretches of coiled barbed wire to the ever-present security cameras and periodic identification screens—to finally meet with my carefully barricaded (sometimes handcuffed) client, about whom I have read in the thick reams of documentation that constitute his correctional files.

With some imagination (and amplification) my experience of visiting these inmates where they live reminds me of Persephone tromping through Hades. Once we meet, however, and despite the harsh circumstances and the setting, I have found these diverse, beleaguered souls to be as receptive to my presence as anyone else. It is a mutual arrangement of sorts that brings us together; we each have a job to do and we both perform our respective duties as assigned. I approach them to complete the task I have been sent to accomplish, but despite the confines of the structured interview, I bring with me my depth orientation and my awareness of psyche, so that, too, is part of our meeting.

Although my job includes trying to coax the truth out of them, these inmates' statements about the crimes for which they have been convicted are so consistently fabricated that my acknowledging that factor as a given caveat ironically frees us both to communicate genuinely. As the saying goes, the prisons are packed with innocents. The stories these inmates tell once they begin to open up, however, are a uniquely poignant genre of tragic poetry, their lives being rich and twisted dramas of downfall, provoking repulsion—and at least from my perspective—often inspiring pathos.

In addition to forensic work in the prisons, I have also done considerable individual therapy with patients who have criminal histories of various kinds. I have always experienced some degree of affinity with this population that I never quite understood. I have no criminal record or conscious propensities myself. I spent years under the assumption (delusion) that the reason for my fit with this clientele was simply logistics—contracts and referral panels affiliated with probation and parole, the luck of the draw, and the constraints of my other jobs and scheduling demands. However, the convergence of this forensic work, reflections about my father after his death, and my Jungian studies made me realize that there was more to this "coincidence" than mere logistics. My awareness slowly evolved and deepened into a recognition of my long-standing identification with the *prisoner archetype*—a realization that formed an important piece of the puzzle as I gradually conceptualized a new understanding about psychopathy.

I found that my experience of this strange identification with the prisoner archetype changed following my father's death. Only its sudden and relative absence called my attention to the subtle power of the prisoner archetype's presence in him—and in me.

Almost as an afterthought, I noticed that prisons were less compelling and the inmates I was sent to interview were only men, lacking the luster of fantasy. At that point I began to realize the magnitude of my own projections around this prisoner archetype, and the inner shift I felt as my complex began to dissolve. I was integrating my own inner criminal, the wounded animus figure who had so consistently haunted my dreams and beyond. The outer representations of this creature were just less interesting, did not carry the same powerful charge. I had never before associated my father in any way with my draw to prisoners or criminals; even the idea seemed strange. He was neither.

My father was not a criminal in the legal sense, but he was certainly adept at committing crimes of the heart. Albert abandoned five wives, three biological children, and two adoptive children, leaving one marriage of 27 years abruptly, without a note or a backward glance. He created a lengthy trail of broken hearts, and when he finally departed from the world, he left on his own terms—as he had always lived. In the grand finale of his life, despite his physical discomfort, he once again managed to escape relatively unscathed, this time into an eternal sunset he seemed to have painted himself. He provided no explanations for his lifetime of blatant self-absorption, and the final conversation that seemed glaringly imperative to me, in order for him to make peace with his past (or was it mine?), was left forever unspoken. His approach to his own death was as unilateral as his chosen lifestyle; he ceased eating and drinking, refused all medication or intervention for his Parkinson's disease, irregular heartbeat, and advanced prostate cancer, and donated his withered body to the University of California, San Diego School of Medicine. He thus executed this last chapter of his life with characteristic austerity and one-sidedness, with as close to a complete absence of sentimentality as could possibly be achieved under his circumstances.

Before Albert became ill, I had already begun studying and writing about psychopathy. What struck me initially was how adamantly most of my forensic colleagues identified this concept as describing a category of behavior that *unequivocally* did not apply to them. From a

Jungian perspective owning one's own shadow—each individual's inner unclaimed, undesirable attitudes, traits, behaviors, and inclinations—is fundamental to becoming a more whole, individuated, true self. Psychopathy seemed to belong to the realm of shadow contents, but with a distinction I understood as explained by Jungian analyst and author Guggenbühl-Craig, who described psychopathy as *lacunae*: empty pockets or gaps in the soul. This Jungian viewpoint began to influence my perceptions about psychopathy, which I had been studying primarily in forensic terms, helping me to understand my father and to find meaning and value in the harshest of my own life experiences. Although I saw the value of forensic research on the topic, that perspective seemed incomplete to me. Guggenbühl-Craig's definition of psychopathy broadened the scope of my understanding and felt more resonant with the range of my life experiences, both personal and professional.[1]

In some forensic circles there appeared to be heightened enthusiasm about identifying a select group of individuals as *psychopaths*, with some qualifications subject to debate, but ultimately bearing absolutely no resemblance to the experts themselves or to most of the rest of us. Corresponding research neatly explained this sharp dichotomy, identifying various characteristics—including the propensity for horrendously callous violence—of this essentially separate subspecies. Based upon my experience in conducting prison interviews and working with forensic therapy clients, I was not convinced of such a neat either/or division between psychopathic character qualities in those individuals and the rest of us. Rather, I perceived a spectrum of human characteristics, even among the criminal population.

Although there are the obvious, rare characters at the extreme end of the psychopathy scale, I had most often noticed a combination of humane and inhumane qualities in people, both in my professional life and beyond it. From a young age (perhaps even originating when my father left me at age 2), I had been sensitized to the duality within

---

1   Guggenbühl-Craig, Emptied Soul, x, xi.

people, which also seemed to fluctuate—at least for most of us humans. Because psychopathy seemed to me to be inherently as fluid as human nature itself, I found the forensic experts' definitive theorizing to be suspicious (although admittedly reassuring in its very exactitude). Further, proponents of this either/or perspective exuded a transparent and exaggerated comfort about being on the safe end of the witch hunt, which led me to distrust their findings as less than objective. From what little I knew informally, as well as what I understood from Guggen- bühl-Craig's writing, these individuals were not without *lacunae* of their own—any more than the rest of us. As Guggenbühl-Craig wrote: "We all have psychopathic sides which we attempt to compensate. My chief concern is that we recognize *how* we compensate our psychopathy, *how* we compensate our *lacunae*, since I am taking it for granted that none of my readers consider themselves one of the saints."[2]

Once Albert passed away, I began to realize, with new poignancy, the association between my father and my interest in psychopathy, and to consider that the stories of both might have something to teach me, to serve my psyche in some broad way, to generate healing, or to prove useful in helping others. I envisioned that this rather grandiose devel- opment might become part of his legacy, as he became larger than life by leaving it. In hindsight, I realize that this magnanimous perspective also suggests inflation on my part (ironically resonant with his)—but it also helped me to start writing.

This writing about Albert, about psychopathy, offered a healing compensation that emerged with the creative process, potentially salvaging my optimistic memory of him with the hope that I would be able to mid-wife something good from the totality of his existence, including his obvious character flaws. Writing was a blessedly familiar task with needed structure to hold my wild grief and organize my reflec- tions about his life and our relationship. Although the subject matter of

---

2 Guggenbühl-Craig, *Emptied Soul*, 133.

my father was personal, a soothing objectivity was essential to convey the glaring opposites within his personality: how his inconsistencies both charmed and wounded me, and how my relationship with him helped to inform and broaden my understanding of psychopathy, especially as I reflected upon the nearly four decades of our lives that we shared and as I mourned his passing. The catharsis of writing made me feel that there was a dimension of meaning and utility to the suffering he caused, while it helped to ease the pain of losing him forever. It would have been nearly impossible to undertake this project while he was still alive, and not just because of his acerbic presence. His death brought a gift of insight I could only have gained in retrospect—from a safe distance.

The perspective of hindsight presumably yields a unique opportunity to examine the opposites contained within our life experiences with unprecedented clarity and awareness. After I began writing, I reviewed dozens of family albums to cull pictures of my father. In the process I rediscovered his playful, loving connection to my children throughout their growing-up years, in ways I had all but forgotten in the harsh context of the end of his life, during which he struggled with devastating Parkinson's. This positive impression was radically different from his psychopathic gaps. Both were true. My experience of the dual reality of Albert's personality, together with my professional experiences and Jungian studies, began to coalesce into a theory about psychopathy, a definition revised from my forensic introduction to the concept.

There is a common thread of meaning in the radically diverse content presented in this book, from a brief biography of my father, to personal anecdotal material, timeless mythological references, and examples from current culture and psychology. All offer ideas on psychopathy that invite us to question our language and perspective on the subject and to improve our understanding and response to those characteristics, both in others and within ourselves, whether for diagnostic and clinical purposes or for our own inner work and relationships.

My thoughts about the concept of psychopathy were most strongly influenced initially by my impressions of the courtroom process. I noticed the resonance between public reactions to sex offenders and my ideas about polarized thinking. I did not connect my conceptualization of psychopathy in any specific way with my father until after he died, when I was able to reflect upon and review the curious gaps in our relationship, in his character and mine, and the wounded love that somehow survived anyway. After Albert's death, as I struggled to process his behavior over a lifetime and integrate his impact on me, my awareness of what I had learned about psychopathy in academic and professional environments began to merge with its meaning to me personally. From there, my perceptions broadened about how psychopathy played out collectively. One clue about this common thread was the similarity of my intense inner response, at a visceral level, to the lack of eros—which I came to perceive as signifying psychopathy—wherever I experienced it. This response was triggered in me across a wide range of settings and situations. For example, I realized that my feeling of desperate frustration when dealing with the callous, cut-off aspect of my father was strikingly akin to the way I felt waiting to testify in the courtroom: powerless and unseen. The story of Albert's life and death thus provided a bridge for me between an individual and a collective definition of psychopathy. Once I began thinking about psychopathy as a characteristic whose valence falls along a continuum, I began to notice polarized thinking and feeling more universally, not only within myself, but in my work and in the world.

As I noted in the Preface, in this book I am focusing on the phenomenology, the qualitative aspect of psychopathy, which is a sense that something deep within is simply missing. This is different from examining the cause of psychopathy. Any numbers of theories overlap with some of these observations, but the archetypal piece is a different matter. Attachment theory, for example, tells the story of how this gap happens in early childhood. Perhaps it is easier to say that we had a traumatic childhood than to acknowledge that there is just something in the human heart that is dark—which is one of Jung's premises. As he stated in *Memories, Dreams, Reflections*: "As far as we can discern, the sole purpose of human existence is to kindle a light in the darkness of mere being."[3] We experience this phenomenon of psychopathy in widely variant ways, and it affects us to varying degrees. My goal is less to create a new theory than to describe psychopathy from my experience and perspective, subjectively and objectively, in others and myself: to explore what it is like when I am in that space within myself or when I experience it with others. When I encounter psychopathy, it is as though I could pour love in forever and nothing would fill the hole.

The sequence of topics in this book follows the order in which different levels in my perceptions of psychopathy emerged. My introduction to the concept occurred in a forensic context. I began to question that forensic perspective, informed by the specifics of my work with criminals, including sex offenders, after my father died, and I identified undeniably psychopathic traits in him. I then saw a resonance with many Jungian concepts I had been studying for decades. My thinking, my studies, and this writing thus evolved from forensic, to personal, to Jungian/academic, and developed from there to include examples of the new continuum conceptualization and how we deal with psychopathy personally and culturally, across time and context. My focus then progressed to consider how we might heal this gap in the psyche—and why it behooves us to do so, individually and collectively.

I realize the potential hazards of presenting personal material for case study. My overriding purpose in doing so is to illustrate psychopathy from the genesis of an inside viewpoint. My personal experience is the core from which the main thesis of this writing emerged: *psychopathy* extends beyond the purely pathological realm and exists along a continuum. Some degree of unassimilated psychopathy is dormant in all of us.

---

3   C. G. Jung, *Memories, Dreams, Reflections*, 326.

CHAPTER 2

Questioning the Forensic Approach to Psychopathy

As I learned about the forensic measurement of psychopathy, I began to feel increasingly confused, instead of less so, and to suspect that my difficulties identifying them (psychopaths) were associated with the lack of a clearly definable category. Further, thinking about the concept of psychopathy was polarized and seemed to miss an important dimension of meaning that drew my interest and motivated me to question prevailing psychological ideas about it, such as the theory of an evolutionary subspecies of humans carrying it, which is popular in forensic circles. The creation of a finite target group called *psychopaths* appeared to represent an understandable but flawed attempt to safely differentiate the rest of us from this unwanted pool of human traits.

The Forensic Approach

My initial associations with the term *psychopath* were of serial murderers and sexually violent predators—embodiments of dreaded, dramatic extremes well designed to draw and hold our collective projections of evil. As a forensic evaluator, with every mandatory training and conference, I was immersed in a statistically validated attitude that promised to keep me at a safe distance from any personal identification with psychopathy. Although I respected my colleagues (who included my husband) on the state panel, and was duly impressed—even intimidated—by the international plethora of sophisticated research on measuring criminal propensities and risk assessment, I found that Guggenbühl-Craig's definition of psychopathy struck a deeper chord in me that felt fundamentally true and that I simply could neither forget nor ignore:

> I am not speaking of "us" and of "them," of us as integrated, balanced, or whole and of the others who are missing something—the psychopaths. . . . It seems to me far more important that, in speaking of psychopathy, we strive to realize in what way we are psychopaths. The notion that there are *lacunae*— empty places—where each and every one of us is lacking in something is of significance. . . . It is of utmost importance to apply the question of *lacunae* to ourselves: where are my *lacunae*? Where am I missing something? . . .
>
> An appreciation for psychopathy can help each of us to reduce the damage we do to our own psychopathic side. Finally confronting and dealing with psychopathy gives us a fuller appreciation for what it means to be human.[1]

On the basis of my own experience with my father as well as my Jungian studies, I came to believe that psychopathy has a subtler dimension that is more elusive than the most elaborate forensic research can capture. The common human propensity is to polarize what makes us uncomfortable into an identifiable outer entity that can be ostracized and avoided, since to consider having such aspects within feels unpleasant. Some of us are duly blessed or cursed with a persistent psyche that disallows or at least discourages that maneuver. In contrast, as far as I could determine, my father's psyche did not appear to host a similar inner whistleblower.

---

1 Guggenbühl-Craig, Emptied Soul, 79, 80, 85.

Years ago I attended a mandatory training with about 40 other psychologists on how to administer and interpret the results of the Psychopathy Checklist—Revised (PCL-R), the hallmark checklist of psychopathy developed by criminal psychology researcher Robert Hare.[2] I dreaded going because I hate violence, including discussing or watching it. For me, any kind of sex is much easier to discuss. But to serve on a panel of psychologists assessing the risk of reoffense for potential sexually *violent* predators, I had to be trained to administer and interpret the PCL-R.

We spent two seemingly endless days figuratively drenched in gore, viewing up-close-and-personal, uncut documentaries of the worst known modern serial killers, from the infamous Hillside Strangler to Richard Speck, who systematically murdered eight young student nurses. By the end of each training day, I felt contaminated and nauseous, as though I had come to know these frightening characters intimately against my will and had been poisoned by them. I concluded that perhaps this was what it felt like to have an encounter with a full-blown psychopath. These were people even I would choose to stringently avoid, although I had an almost poetic attitude toward criminals in general. My father was still alive and annoying at that point, and I had not yet begun to put the pieces together about why I might feel a psychological affinity with a prisoner archetype or what that had to do with his personality or mine.

It would have been convenient if the tool had actually worked, which in my simple way of thinking would mean that these monsters would score off the chart, making it possible to identify and stop the true carriers of evil in our midst—the lethal psychopaths. I was hopeful. Following each film clip, we were to score these individuals using the psychopathy risk assessment checklist and then compare our level of consensus. We were all close in our scoring, but what became eerily obvious was that *none* of these most dangerous, violent killers

---

2   Robert D. Hare, Hare Psychopathy Checklist—Revised (PCL-R) (New York: Multi-Health Systems, 2007).

actually qualified as a psychopath on the PCL-R! In fact, most of their scores fell in the midrange. Reasons for this shocking finding may have included that many of them had no criminal records or that they frequently exhibited the characteristics of a stable lifestyle, such as steady employment or relationships. In fact, often they were charismatic or at least appeared almost picture-book benign—until they went on serial killing sprees.

What arose for me, other than nausea at having to watch these nonstop repulsive narratives, was confusion about what we were actually measuring. I doubted how helpful this so-called *state-of-the-art* tool was for measuring extreme psychopathy, if it did not isolate these most severe psychopaths, who would obviously comprise the group we would be most interested in differentiating from the rest. I wondered about the categories, although of course they had all been statistically validated, which did not make much sense to me. I managed to frame my question aloud in the training, in a politically correct way: "How is this tool helping us if these prototypical psychopaths are earning moderate scores?" The instructor's only response was: "That's a good question!"

The problem with the tool seemed to affirm what I had been thinking all along: that even as forensic psychology was attempting to define it in relation to a relatively small subset of people, psychopathy is actually a human characteristic whose manifestation occurs on a continuum that eludes finite measurement, as suggested by Guggenbühl-Craig's view. My father would have earned a low score on this tool; he had some of the affective characteristics, which was unsettling to me, but nothing else in common with this gruesome group. The fact that Jack the Ripper also had a low score did not help to resolve my confusion.

The breakthrough idea that shaped the PCL-R was purportedly identifying and itemizing the *combination* of affective, interpersonal, and socially deviant lifestyle factors that comprise psychopathy, rather than just criminal traits or acts—but that never felt like a landmark distinction to me. I was introduced to Hare's trademark set of diagnostic criteria on the PCL-R because it was a required tool for psychological testing and assessment in my forensic work, but regrettably it did not, after all, prove to me that such a human characteristic could be unequivocally reduced to a finite measurement with a convenient cutoff score; in fact, my illusion had to be sacrificed. This also meant the sacrifice of another illusion: the kind of neatly defined thinking about psychopathy that justified my (politely unexpressed) righteous indignation when my stepmothers and siblings referred to my father as a *psychopath*—since he surely did not fit the diagnostic profile of one as I understood it at that point in my forensic career.

Albert and the PCL-R

What became disturbingly apparent to me during the training on the PCL-R, however, was that although certainly Albert was no criminal, *some* of those PCL-R checklist traits sounded undeniably familiar as I thought about his personality: lack of remorse or empathy, egocentricity, glibness, episodic relationships, and persistent violation of (some) social norms—at least regarding marriage, family, and religion. An argument could have been made either way regarding grandiosity, (emotional) dominance, shallow emotions, manipulativeness, and lying. It was difficult for me to concede that my father was cold-hearted, simply because I knew with certainty that he was not always that way. He was able to form lasting bonds with people, principles, and goals. However, he was also able to abandon marriages and children without forewarning or communication of any kind, which reflected a serious— even breathtaking—lack of empathy. If he felt guilt or remorse, I never knew about it. It did not matter to my father how many once-significant others pointed out to him that his behavior was unfair and hurtful; to him, his actions made perfect sense, or so he declared. He was highly resistant to fulfilling social obligations and responsibilities on anyone else's terms, but also could be downright tenacious about doing so on his own—if *he* so chose.

Perhaps most blatantly confounding in terms of Albert fitting the forensic definition of a psychopath was that he did not have the lifestyle or antisocial characteristics found in standard measures of psychopathy. He did not have a pronounced need for stimulation or a proneness to boredom, nor did he lead a parasitic lifestyle or lack realistic long-term goals. He was not impulsive, although his treatment of his families and children was gravely irresponsible at times. He did not have poor behavioral controls or early behavioral issues. He had no history of criminality at any age and never suffered from substance abuse or legal problems. Low frustration tolerance, impulsivity, force, and parasitic lifestyle did not seem to apply to Albert at all. There were no close matches in the behavioral dimension for him on the classic psychopathy checklist. He achieved academic and professional success. He was not sensation seeking, criminal, or substance abusing.

Albert's likely overall scores on clinical or forensic measures of psychopathy across the PCL-R content areas—interpersonal, affective, lifestyle, and antisocial—would grant him a low profile (i.e., normal/ not a psychopath). Interpersonally, he could be glib and charming, and he seemed to have a grandiose sense of his self-worth. He lied, although not pathologically. Affectively, he seemed to lack remorse or guilt for his hurtful conduct, to lack empathy, and to deny responsibility for this behavior.

Yet his many positive qualities were undeniably as real as his serious gaps. He clearly presented with *some* of the trademark psychopathic characteristics but not most of them, and not the most obvious ones in any public way, such that he would never have been identified by the world at large as a psychopath—only by some of those individuals involved in intimate relationships with him, whom he abandoned— usually very suddenly. The sting of his abrupt, dispassionate departure was magnified by the sharp contrast between this behavior and the engaging intensity of his apparent devotion during his periods of apparent involvement.

Although my father never fit the common description of a psychopath in terms of criminal orientation, his prevailing capacity for relentless and unexpected callous conduct in his closest relationships does suggest a kind of psychopathic inner void—a gap deep in his psyche, a sometimes shocking absence of eros—undisrupted by any calling from within demanding that he question himself. His radical inconsistencies remained a painful enigma to others, and any inner conflict he may have suffered as a result was insufficient to change him. Any need he might have had to fill the gap in his psyche apparently remained unconscious and unmet; he never acknowledged or integrated his inner psychopathy, and his potential to do so consciously remained untapped. At the end of his life, though, I believe there was some healing, an influx of eros energy, albeit not deliberately sought on his part.

I am a less-than-objective observer, clearly, and cannot know what was going on inside Albert. I realize that my perceptions are colored by my own projections and introjections. With that caveat, my father's radical mix of character traits posed a compelling dilemma to me—and an invitation to investigate psychopathy further—both as his daughter and as a forensic and clinical psychologist. At the very least, I was forced to acknowledge that there was nothing simple about defining psychopathy as it applied to Albert—and perhaps to most of us.

Psychopaths and the "Rest of Us"

A plethora of scientific research about psychopathy is designed to delineate and confirm the differences between psychopaths and the rest of us. A colleague of mine contributed research to support one such theory posited by a recognized forensic expert: that psychopathy is not a mental disorder but an evolutionary adaptation, a *genetic aberration* initially designed to further the species' survival. The main idea is that the same characteristics that were helpful in ancient times continue to be genetically transmitted but with negative implications in modern society. According to this theory, evolution designed a *subgroup of humans* to use aggression and deception to obtain resources from others. Such people would need to have skill at deception, a lack of concern for others, a willingness to use violence, ease and flexibility in the exploitation of others, a lack of concern for the opinions of others, and extreme reluctance to be responsible for others (including, for males, their own offspring).[3]

When I realized that my forensic colleague, a proponent of this "subgroup" theory, came from such a fundamentally different school of thought regarding psychopathy, I was shocked and disappointed. The notion of a "subgroup of humans" was indigestible to me. Admittedly, part of me also wondered, a bit nervously, if perhaps my father and I had this genetic propensity—if in fact there were such a genetic predisposition. More objectively, I viewed this construct as another way to sharply discriminate between those who carry this trait and those who do not—an appealing concept to researchers because traits that are discrete can be measured. What this conceptualization leaves out is that these characteristics cannot be neatly assigned to a finite group—many of our modern, most dangerous serial killers would not be recognized as part of this subgroup, based on our measurement tools! Furthermore, some of these characteristics are not only common but also collectively touted as admirable, at least covertly. In fact, having such psychopathy genes would probably promote success in politics, business, and other competitive venues.

I was not alone in my confusion about psychopathy, even among those who supposedly shared the same theoretical perspective. The evolutionary subgroup proponents argued about exactly *who* comprises this subgroup of humans. The lead forensic researchers argued about whether a history of violence and criminality is a vital qualifier, or whether psychopathy is a personality disorder that does not necessarily manifest in criminal acts, especially violent ones. Psychopaths as a group are a shifty, nebulous entity to differentiate, all the more elusive

---

3   G. Harris, "Psychopathy Might Be an Adaptation, Not a Disorder," Entre Nous, MHCP Newsletter, n.d., 1.

because those at the extreme end of the spectrum often appear the most benign. It seemed uncomfortably clear to me that our difficulty with identifying them definitively is that *there was no them*. For me, narrow thinking about the concept was not enough; it was missing an important dimension of meaning.

The continuum definition of psychopathy is not a safe, easy one. It means sacrificing the satisfaction of confidently identifying myself as *not* one. A major benefit of the creation of *them* is that it safely differentiates *us*. Jung put it this way:

> All gaps in our actual knowledge are still filled out with projections. We are still so sure what other people think or what their true character is. We are convinced that certain people have all the bad qualities we do not know in ourselves or that they practice all those vices which could, of course, never be our own. We must still be exceedingly careful not to project our own shadows too shamelessly; we are still swamped with projected illusions. If you imagine someone who is brave enough to withdraw all these projections, then you get an individual who is conscious of a pretty thick shadow. Such a man has saddled himself with new problems and conflicts. He has become a serious problem to himself, as he is now unable to say that *they* do this or that, *they* are wrong, and *they* must be fought against. He lives in the "House of the Gathering." Such a man knows that whatever is wrong in the world is in himself, and if he only learns to deal with his own shadow he has done something real for the world. He has succeeded in shouldering at least an infinitesimal part of the gigantic, unsolved social problems of our day.[4]

The real and fictional psychopaths well known to us in popular media—from Ted Bundy to Hannibal Lecter—represent the proto-

---

4   C. G. Jung, Psychology and Religion: West and East. Vol. 11. The Collected Works of C .G. Jung, 2d ed. (Princeton, NJ: Princeton University Press, 1958/1938), 83.

typical character identified by forensic professionals. These human monsters are egotistic, impulsive, irresponsible, shallow, unfeeling, cold, merciless, lying, manipulative, ruthlessly criminal—and capable of extreme violence.[5] Because violent psychopaths constitute an extreme form of dangerousness, forensic professionals are often called upon to isolate this relatively rare kind of personality in the much larger context of general criminality, usually by using tests designed to measure factors research has shown are representative of the trait.

Even often cited forensic research acknowledges that there are many expressions and forms of psychopathy. From a medical or forensic model, when identifying and treating psychopathy, the practical focus is understandably behavioral, since the overriding goal is controlling or (if possible) eliminating deviant behavior to protect society.[6] That focus requires either/or thinking. I do not disagree with such an approach for practical reasons, certainly including public safety, but the broader, deeper application of the concept of *psychopathy* is what intrigues me, given my personal history.

Some individuals, particularly violent criminals, deserve a category of their own because their crimes against humanity demonstrate extreme, pathological manifestations of psychopathy. As traditionally defined, psychopathy would always be pathological, but my point here, consistent with the ideas of Adolf Guggenbühl-Craig, is that there are characteristics of psychopathy that are simply human. As he stated, "We are all, as I will repeatedly insist, partially psychopaths."[7] That being said, it is important to hold both notions simultaneously: (1) We are all partially psychopaths, *and* (2) identification of extreme and dangerous forms of the behavior is essential. However, even within the rare population of extreme psychopaths, vulnerabilities such as hidden

---

5 Hervey Cleckley, The Mask of Sanity (St. Louis, MO: Mosby Co., 1988/1976); Hare, Hare Psychopathy Checklist—Revised.

6 Robert D. Hare, "Psychopathy: A Clinical Construct Whose Time Has Come," Criminal Justice and Behavior 23 (1996): 25–54.

7 Guggenbühl-Craig, Emptied Soul, 127.

suffering, loneliness, and lack of self-esteem, rather than mere callous indifference, have been identified by some researchers as risk factors for violent criminal conduct. For example, forensic psychiatrist Willem H. J. Martens suggests that studying the statements of violent criminal psychopaths illuminates their striking and specific vulnerability and emotional pain.[8] Martens further posits that the current prevailing picture of the psychopath, reflected in the leading diagnostic criteria of psychopathy offered by Cleckley and Hare et al. is incomplete because emotional suffering and loneliness are ignored.[9] Martens urges consideration of these dimensions to ensure that our conception of the psychopath "goes beyond heartless and becomes more human"[10]—a controversial point worthy of consideration. Granted, the idea of generating compassion for psychopaths sounds counterintuitive if not absurd. The implication, however, is consistent with our gradated definition, because it suggests that psychopathy is not a definitive condemnation but a character trait that does not necessarily preclude the essential humanity of an individual in other ways.

There are multitudes of reasons why the idea of having compassion toward this population, or perceiving these individuals as being vulnerable or suffering emotional pain, is ego dystonic for us as individuals and as a culture. Not only is this dissonance obvious and understandable—because those we label as psychopaths are typically individuals who have caused others great pain—but also because we reject those uncomfortably similar aspects within ourselves that are insensitive or lacking in moral integrity.

There may be some modification of our typical associations with the term *psychopathy*. Even the second edition of Hare's PCL-R defines

---

8   Willem H. J. Martens, "The Hidden Suffering of the Psychopath," Psychiatric Times XIX (2002): Issue 1.

9   Cleckley, Mask of Sanity; Robert D. Hare, Without Conscience: The Disturbing World of the Psychopaths Among Us (New York: Guilford Press, 1999).

10 Willem H. J. Martens, "The Hidden Suffering of the Psychopath," Psychiatric Times 1 (2001): 3.

the condition in terms of broad characterological manifestations that are *not* exclusively violent or criminal in nature. Hare describes psychopathy in terms of early-onset, chronic symptoms that characterize the individual's long-term functioning and result in social dysfunction or disability: a spectrum of outer and inner characteristics, including unstable interpersonal relations, poor occupational functioning, and increased risk of involvement in criminal activity.

The idea of psychopathy as a societal problem confined to an identifiable population also makes it finite, although there has been some tempering of our collective definition. The term *psychopathy* is often juxtaposed with *sociopathy*, even using the words interchangeably. Sociopathy has less pejorative implications, focusing on the nonviolent dimension of crimes against society, as demonstrated in the heartless behaviors of some politicians and business professionals, for example. Sociopathy refers to antisocial behavior against society that is usually attributed to social and environmental factors in an individual's early life. The concept of psychopathy is broader in scope, describing a condition of the soul, mind, and spirit. Psychopathy is associated with a lack of moral conscience that manifests in traits such as callousness and lack of empathy or remorse. This may result in a range of personality characteristics and behaviors, from heartlessness to gruesome, violent, and bizarre acts towards others. One appeal of this reductive definition is that it sounds more manageable.

As a forensic psychologist, I am tasked with measuring psychopathy by looking for descriptive indicators, such as an antisocial lifestyle and interpersonal problems, and then adding up the score on a risk assessment tool to conclude whether or not an individual makes the cutoff as a psychopath. This dry, concrete approach serves a purpose. With the paramount concern of community safety, legal and criminal justice systems need to be able to unequivocally define who belongs in this dangerous category in order to make clear decisions and justify consequences; thus the category must be finite.

Reassuring though it may seem, however, either/or thinking may miss the mark on a personal, intrapsychic level. Darker dimensions of our existence and experience are inherently fraught with ambiguities, as fluid as human nature. Polarized thinking about psychopathy is helpful and necessary—even a survival instinct—in the courtroom, but it can lead us astray even in that milieu, where recognizing the nuances of human personality and behavior may determine momentous consequences for individuals facing judgment in those chambers.

Psychopathy and the Courtroom

Our criminal justice system provides an apt collective illustration of the problems inherent in a formulaic dichotomous thinking that is often fraught with glaring inconsistencies, despite the omnipotent display of reassuring equity and absolute judgment. My involvement in the courtroom and associated activities led me to believe that there is often nothing particularly sensible or impartial about what goes on there, contrary to my impressions before any real-life exposure. I have seen life-and-death verdicts determined by which attorney is able to create a better argument to devastate the opposing side, intimidate witnesses, or emotionally manipulate jurors. Professionals who appear regularly as expert witnesses are in an impressive league, to which I never belonged. The best I could do was to impress jurors with my fervent efforts to make myself clear to them; after one jury trial, the attorney who subpoenaed me told me I did a good job being "genuine."

The best expert witnesses are savvy court strategists who can effectively focus their preparation and presentation upon escaping the wrath of a temperamental judge or supporting the bias of an attorney. This process may occur almost autonomously in these experts, artfully compartmentalized from their actual knowledge of the subject area, their rapport with clients, or the specifics of their various cases—a specialization unto itself. The courtroom, as I experience it, is like a drama with a life of its own beyond the ostensible presentation of its righteous purpose. An unpredictable, potentially lethal game plays out repeatedly there, and achieving a desired outcome by whatever means necessary may subordinate any other values or considerations—not always, but enough to make me wary, attentive, and disinclined to be part of it.

Courtroom life is loaded with political power plays; it is a cult-like culture with its own personality and script. Ongoing subplots include the constant interweaving of multiple layers of obvious and ulterior motives, like a deadly serious, complicated soap opera. Everybody has to wait, seemingly interminably and without recourse. The hierarchy is crystal clear, and so are the stakes in the competition to win. There is an almost magical attribution of importance surrounding decisions that are made, those who make them, and the legal system itself. The mystique and the mind games are fundamental to this aura of omnipotence. The famous scene from *The Wizard of Oz* comes to mind, when Dorothy and her friends discover that the intimidating image of the wizard is, in fact, a projection operated by a small man behind a curtain.[11]

Among its other attributes, the courtroom is a collective incubator for polarization: for all-or-nothing, either/or thought and judgment. There are times when we need that kind of black-and-white decision-making, when we need the finality of the gavel and the verdict. We have constructed an entire system to take care of our collective needs for retribution, punishment, and justice; I imagine the uncivilized alternative would be much worse. However, the dimension I find frightening and unsettling is that sometimes decisions that are of crucial importance to defendants, victims, and society appear arbitrary. Deals or bargains that may free or destroy lives are wagered, negotiated, contested, and finalized between competing attorneys, while their clients wait to see the result of the match like passive spectators at a sporting event.

After I had been studying Jungian psychology for years, and then became more involved in forensic work, I suddenly noticed our court-

---

11   L. Frank Baum, The Wonderful Wizard of Oz (Chicago: HarperTrophy, 1987/1900), 209.

room symbol carrying the scales with a revised perspective, and the irony struck me: the blindfold on Lady Justice is intended to symbolize objectivity and fairness, but given the inconsistent reality of the legal system, her sightless eyes also seemed to represent lack of vision or awareness—maybe even a disabled feminine aspect, a disconnection from the feeling function or an absence of eros—that had certainly characterized aspects of my experience in the courtroom.

CHAPTER 3

Collective Psychopathy, the Media, Sex Offenders . . . and Jung

Psychopathic dynamics are pervasive far beyond the courtroom and the high-security prison yard. Projecting our most unwanted aspects onto a definable category of miscreants to represent them is one way we collectively contain not only those individuals but also those gaps within ourselves. Our collective fondness for all-or-nothing thinking is artfully nurtured by the media, an entity with the instantaneous power to incite extreme reactions, via a plethora of venues from social networking gadgetry to broader categories of news and information. Generally I regard this media power as an incontrovertible reality that often seems pointless to question.

The Internet is a superb resource, but the coexistence of horrifically underfunded education and nearly universal access to sophisticated high-tech communication venues is concerning. Individuals who cannot afford food, housing, education, or transportation will often still have cell phones so they can text and use the Internet. Intuitively, I associate the flatness of electronic media, like the flatness of a TV screen, for all of its tremendous positive communication potential, with a parallel flatness in terms of psychological depth, insight, or perspective. The information industry has such incredible power and influence. Profuse information conveyed with limited dimensionality to a random audience can be a recipe for disaster and public hysteria: a virtual tsunami of fierce but under-informed opinions. Such a combination can create as many problems as it identifies.

Psychopathic dynamics are widespread in our culture. White-collar crime and government or corporate scams conspiring for money or power at the expense of fairness or integrity draw frequent major media attention. These represent a different dimension of psychopathy than the violent variety. Over half a century ago, Dr. Hervey Milton Cleckley (1903-1984), an American psychiatrist and early pioneer in the field of psychopathy, made a resounding impact on American culture with his classic book, *The Mask of Sanity*, originally published in 1941. He was touted as providing the most influential clinical descrip-tion of psychopathy in the 20th century.[1] In a personal communication to Hervey Cleckley in 1986, a colleague of his observed: "There are psychopathic personalities in the highest echelons of government, and even within religious hierarchies in America. You can't just assume that a person with the title 'judge' or 'hospital orderly' got there honestly and won't manipulate the hell out of you."[2] This observation seems representative of a broadening perspective about psychopathy and certainly triggered increased public interest.

In 1993, Robert Hare published a huge best seller, *Without Conscience*, the purpose of which was to alert us to the reality of those predators who walk among us—not only violent perpetrators, but callous, manipulative individuals who take advantage of others in a multitude of ways. Hare provided a way of coping for those whose lives are shattered by encounters with such psychopaths. This book was clearly a call to identify psychopaths in our midst, inviting the public to join in the satisfying differentiation between psychopaths and the "rest of us." Along with its more serious application, it also armed the

---

1   Cleckley, *Mask of Sanity.*
2   Personal communication from psychologist Walter Schreibman to Hervey Cleckley, Feb-ruary 10, 1986

masses to trust their own judgment about who might be a psychopath, providing titillating entertainment and verbal ammunition in problematic relationships. This popularization of the concept of psychopathy affected our collective definition of the term.

Psychopathy and Sex Offenders

A prime example of this phenomenon in action—how the public perceives and responds to psychopathy among us, if not within us—is the media coverage that resulted in the passage of current legislation regarding sex offenders. Crimes against children automatically summon the fierce protector within us. I readily identify with that sentiment; I worked with child abuse victims for decades and have children of my own. The way the news covers sex offenders affects me deeply because of my work. I have spent many hours interviewing sex offenders in the prisons for forensic evaluations, as well as in private treatment, so I have a finely tuned sense of the very broad range of individuals included in this growing category, simplified by the media into monsters without variation.

Sex offender legislation is understandably motivated by outrage at violent sexual crimes against children. Justified outrage can be triggered and manipulated, however, and in the case of these laws, amplified and convoluted to create a vague scapegoat of such epic proportions that the label *sex offender* becomes nearly meaningless. The large downside to misplaced efforts is that they not only risk failure because they are not focused or preventive, but they also produce other problems that affect the entire community and, ultimately, our quality of life. The mass of individuals caught in the ever-expanding category becomes increasingly unwieldy. Concurrently, the rare, extremely dangerous and sexually violent child predators become even harder to differentiate. They deserve special consequences, and getting them off the streets makes irrefutable sense—however, at this point, isolating those heinous characters is more elusive than ever.

I joined the State of California forensic panel evaluating sex offenders around the time the radical legislation went into effect. This coincided with a wide range of individuals being convicted for an even wider variety of sexual offenses, both historical and recent. They were all targeted for registration as sex offenders, residency restrictions, global tracking devices, and screening for potential involuntary commitment. I was aware of the associated astronomical legal and logistical costs. It seemed to me that as a culture we were engaged in a passionate effort that was amorphous and allegorical—and yet still fundamentally logical, although perhaps not in the way that was consciously intended: We were spending billions hoping to catch, contain, and ostracize *one* form of evil.

News broadcasts and entertainment media are replete with stories of misdirected attempts at vigilante justice, bringing to mind an old film image of the unruly mob of townspeople going after the local vampire wielding their flaming broomsticks. To wit, neighbors threaten or assault registered sex offenders they locate on the Internet, post signs and posters with their addresses and photos on the block where they live, assuming and announcing that they are pedophiles who molest children—when in fact they might have been convicted at the age of 18 for having sex with an adoring 14-year-old girlfriend whose parents got angry. A little knowledge is a dangerous thing.

As a collective culture these days, we seem seriously confused and conflicted about sex. Our preoccupation with nailing sexual deviance occurs at the very time when media incessantly, radically promote and exploit sexuality, using increasingly younger and more explicit images. During prime-time TV hours, fully graphic nude sex can be viewed even inadvertently on readily accessible channels. This also means increased potential that anyone of any age in the home can be exposed to the uncut material.

Meanwhile, efforts to ferret out deviance have become increasingly flamboyant, even hyperbolic. A recent "reality" TV program on entrapping suspected sex offenders featured the camera crew and police officers hiding in the bushes by the suspect's garage and then jumping out to dramatically wrestle him to the pavement, handcuff him, and loudly announce his arrest for viewing underage pornography, film rolling. All the while there were probably ads in the newspaper lying in the same driveway featuring suggestively posed half-clad preteens advertising Calvin Klein underwear. Whether or not consciously driven, the fact that we simultaneously exploit sex and respond with such amplified outrage against sexual victimization suggests an unstated, perhaps somewhat desperate agenda. That agenda is to identify a finite, immoral subspecies to hold our collective projections of sexual deviance, implicitly absolving the rest of us from our own questionable urges and behaviors. This kind of scapegoating and projection of unwanted inner contents is reminiscent of how we collectively respond to our inner psychopathy.

One dimension of the current public outcry against sex offenders I find dubious is the unwieldy ramifications of the now toxic label, including public registration, residency restrictions, and tracking/monitoring devices such as global positioning system (GPS) electronic anklets contributing to an incomparable stigma—consequences that engulf virtually every aspect of the lives of those unfortunate enough to get caught up in the broad net. I agree wholeheartedly that sex offending is deeply concerning, but the scope of this reaction seems disproportionate in comparison to how we respond to any other criminal category; the message is that sex offenses of any kind trump even *murder* as a public menace. Our collective reactions to both kinds of crimes represent some obvious duality anyway, since our most popular advertising and entertainment flaunt—even celebrate—graphic violence, along with sex, often deviant.

The recent legislation to promote public safety that aimed at an extremely broad range of different kinds of sex offenders, but not other dangerous categories of criminals, also created a community wherein constitutional rights may be compromised. As a hypothetical example to illustrate my concern, given a choice between being alerted to the fact that someone convicted of a sex offense was living in my neighborhood or that a convicted killer was staying on the block, I think I would opt to know about the murderer's proximity to me and my home, but no such comparable registry exists. In either case, I would be uncomfortable with the human rights implications of posting their faces and addresses publicly. Such an action would undermine the possibility of productive reintegration for the individual—at least ostensibly the purpose of serving time in our correctional/"rehabilitation" institutions. In addition, it would effectively nullify any kind of preventive education in the community.

Preventive education is not titillating or fear-based; it does not emphasize the differences between *us* and *them*, and it does not typically generate news stories that appeal to the masses. As a public safety strategy it costs far less overall in terms of money and suffering than our most elaborate efforts to catch and punish perpetrators *after* the damage has been done. When I did field social work in the 1980s, I trained professional and community groups in schools, law enforcement, and hospitals to identify and report child abuse. Similarly, community outreach programs taught schoolchildren about how to avoid sexual perpetrators and protect themselves if they were approached by someone trying to touch them in a "bad" way. Most often the perpetrators were not strangers in dark raincoats offering unsuspecting children a ride home from school, luring them with candy, or accosting them in a van parked at the local mall, but known, trusted family members or friends. Children came forward with their stories during those presentations in their classrooms; the emphasis was to make them feel safe and understood enough to do so, and innumerable dangerous situations were averted.

Our response to the criminal category of sex offenders in general provides a broad example of well-intended pretzel logic, as increasingly extreme legislation is passed to promote community safety by targeting a nebulous group that becomes ever harder to accurately define. The purported goals of preventing sexually violent crimes and protecting children are obviously beyond question, but the methodological strategies employed are often impractical, not cost-effective in the long run, and less successful than desired.

Ultimately, in some ways, the consequences of these measures may potentially compromise the quality of life they claim to protect, creating a classic Catch-22, a problematic situation for which the only solution is denied by a circumstance inherent in the problem or by a rule.[3] For example, a recent newspaper article described how Los Angeles County developed a strategy to build "parks"—which were actually small strips of greenbelt that would meet the minimum legal definition—in order to oust registered sex offenders from living anywhere in the surrounding area; no effort was made to conceal the motivation. The convoluted reasoning seems to be that by making sure sex offenders are homeless and unemployed, in addition to their other problems, we will somehow improve public safety. This is a specific example of pretzel logic: the kind of response that prevails when the unconscious takes over, driven by blind fear. Our collective fears result in a growing, generic blacklist of individuals for whom consequences are unending, creating obstacles that inadvertently invite the most desperate measures on the part of these registered offenders, while preventive efforts diminish.

There are certainly sex offenders who cannot live in the community at all because the severity of their psychopathy is too dangerous. Those include the one-in-a-million child sexual murderers who inevitably make the news, whose crimes clearly warrant our most radical

---

3   Joseph Heller, *Catch-22* (New York: Simon & Schuster, 1961). Title of novel in which the main character feigns madness in order to avoid dangerous combat missions, but his desire to avoid them is taken to prove his sanity

responses. There are certainly professionals within law, psychology, and the government who approach the problem of psychopathic, sexually violent predators with objectivity and integrity. However, collective bureaucratic strategies cast an ever-widening net to locate these rare individual criminals at the extreme end of a spectrum that includes a vast preponderance of offenders who have committed lesser (and even *far* lesser) crimes.

Our elaborate research to predict risk is often well intentioned and reasonable, but produces findings that may also become a convoluted end unto themselves: absolute-sounding, complicated calculations about future behavior for courtroom contests to impress jurors. Although such predictions can be helpful, they are inevitably not an exact science; the most reliable and valid tools produce educated guesses that are little better than chance, than flipping a coin.[4] Competing attorneys frequently use this risk assessment information as ammunition. They struggle to entrap each other on statistical details while balancing mitigating factors we are uncertain how to measure, apply, or describe, such as individual differences and clinical considerations.

Meanwhile, public fears drive broad-based legislative actions that cannot adequately differentiate the thousands of individuals whose crimes share only the qualification that they are sexual in nature, from those individuals who commit the most severe, violent, dangerous sexual offenses: those brutal, gut-wrenching child sexual murder cases featured in media headlines for whom the laws like Chelsea's Law (2010), Jessica's Law (2006), and Megan's Law (2004) are named. This selective focus mobilizes and intensifies community hysteria against

---

4   Brian R. Abbott, "Throwing the Baby Out with the Bath Water: Is It Time for Clinical Judgment to Supplement Actuarial Risk Assessment?" *Journal of the American Academy of Psychiatry and the Law Online* 39/Issue 2 (2011): 222–230

the entire category of sexual criminals.[5] Information about these three laws is provided below to give a basic idea of how they work to protect the community and how they affect those convicted of sex offenses. I offer this level of detail to help illustrate the difficulties we encounter collectively in our efforts to contain—and eliminate—the worst of human propensities: our psychopathy. Essentially, our collective fears trigger absolutist judgments that can create new problems.

California's Megan's Law expanded accessible information to the public on the whereabouts of sex offenders, allowing individuals to use their personal computers to view detailed information on registered sex offenders, often including their photographs and addresses. In addition, juveniles adjudicated of certain offenses are required to

---

5   AB1844, known as *Chelsea's Law*, grew out of twin tragedies. In February 2010, 17-year-old Chelsea King was abducted while jogging through a San Diego County park, where her body was later found. The next month, the remains of 14-year-old Amber Dubois, who had disappeared a year earlier, were found in another park. Registered sex offender John Albert Gardner III admitted killing both girls and struck a deal with prosecutors to spare his life. On September 9, 2010, standing with their parents, California Governor Arnold Schwarzenegger signed a bill into law "that will keep dangerous sexual predators in prison for life and provide treatment and more oversight for paroled sex offenders" (*San Francisco Chronicle*, September 10, 2010). Internet source: http://www.sfgate.com/bayarea/article/Chelsea-s-Law-signed-by-governor-3253601.php
Proposition 83, also known as *Jessica's Law*, was passed by California voters on November 7, 2006. Jessica's Law is named after Jessica Lunsford, a young Florida girl who was sexually battered and murdered in February 2005 by John Couey, a previously convicted sex offender. The law enhances the state's ability to detect, track, and apprehend sexual offenders; it prohibits sex offenders released from prison from living within 2,000 feet of parks and schools, as well as other restrictions. The constitutionality of various versions of Jessica's Law is sometimes criticized by the courts.
Assembly Bill 488, also known as *Megan's Law*, was passed by the California Legislature on August 24, 2004, and signed by the governor on September 24, 2004. Megan's Law is named after 7-year-old Megan Kanka, a New Jersey girl who was raped and killed by a known child molester who had moved across the street from the family without their knowledge. In the wake of the tragedy, the Kankas sought to have local communities warned about sex offenders in the area. All states now have a form of Megan's Law. California's Megan's Law grants expanded, accessible information on the whereabouts of sex offenders, providing the public with Internet access to detailed information on registered sex offenders. This expanded access allows the public to use their personal computers to view information on sex offenders required to register with local law enforcement under California's Megan's Law. Previously, the information was available only by personally visiting police stations and sheriff offices or by calling a 900 toll number.

register as sex offenders upon release from the California Department of Corrections and Rehabilitation, Division of Juvenile Facilities (Pen. Code § 290.008).

Florida's Jessica's Law deals with proximity and tracking, enhancing the state's ability to detect, track, and apprehend sexual offenders by prohibiting those who have served their time and are released from prison from living within 2,000 feet of parks and schools, as well as other restrictions, including requiring them to wear monitoring devices for 24-hour GPS tracking. The constitutionality of various versions of Jessica's Law is sometimes criticized by the courts.

California's Chelsea's Law legalized life prison sentences for those offenders deemed most dangerous and further increased parole supervision requirements for all sex offenders, including creating the possibility of lifetime GPS monitoring.

Being objective is challenging when considering such laws, as is thoughtfully questioning anything about their passage or potential impact on a broad scale, because the horrifying child sexual murder cases for which they are named represent the epitome of evil and invoke an automatic, intense emotional reaction of nausea, heartbreak for the parents, and wild protectiveness of children. However, my dealing with individuals affected by these laws, who have been convicted of such very different offenses that share only the characteristic that they involve sex in some way, has made it impossible for me to ignore what may be distorted here.

Individuals convicted of a vast range of sexual crimes, including the viewing of underage pornography on the Internet, lewd conduct, adult rape, and child sexual murder, are all required to register as sex offenders. A married 60-year-old man who was convicted of rape against a teen on one occasion over 40 years ago, when he was *16 years old*, may be a registered sex offender, along with a man who has one sex offense arrest and conviction for looking at underage teen pornography on the Internet and a 35-year-old sadistic, violent pedophile with child

36

victims, who was convicted of a sexual crime against a toddler last year, after multiple similar arrests and convictions.

Differentiating the potential danger of sex offenders is rarely a matter of easy judgment, although our current legislation is aimed at *sexually violent predators*. Further complicating accurate identification of truly dangerous predators and suggesting that our preventive efforts are missing the mark are several prevailing misconceptions capitalized upon by the media: (1) that most sexual offenses are committed by strangers; (2) that most sex offenders are among the prison or parole population; and (3) that most go on to reoffend. *All* of these assumptions are incorrect. In fact, most sex offenses against children or adults are committed by *someone known to the victim or family*; most sex offenders are not caught or incarcerated; and most do not go on to reoffend.[6]

California's Welfare and Institutions Code 6600.1 statute states that if a sex offense victim is under the age of 14, the offense constitutes a "sexually violent offense," whether or not the crime actually involved physical violence. For example, an incident of fondling would qualify as a sexually violent offense if the victim were under the age of 14. Although purportedly motivated by the inarguable goal of protecting children from sexual abuse of any kind, the broadening of this category of perpetrators actually makes it more difficult to differentiate the most dangerous among them: those who are actually sexually violent and predatory.

Such an approach can make it impossible for those caught in the edges of this broad net to rebuild their lives or live and work anywhere, given the extreme requirements of this statute that eliminate privacy and curtail basic freedoms. Measures making the specific addresses and photos of registered sex offenders accessible on the Internet, and residency restrictions precluding such individuals from living within

6   Center for Sex Offender Management (CSOM), A Project of the Office of Justice Programs, U.S. Department of Justice, *Myths & Facts about Sex Offenders*, August 2000.

specified broad proximity of public parks or schools, as well as other provisions, force many who once had jobs and families into homelessness, isolation, and unemployment.

A recent article from the *San Diego City Beat* illustrates this point: "As a result of the lack of affordable housing options, homelessness among sex offenders statewide skyrocketed—by *5,700 percent* between 2007 and August 2011"[7] (emphasis added). This circumstance increases the likelihood that impacted offenders released to the community will resort to their most desperate propensities, since they are barred from constructive alternatives, resources, and support that might help them to rebuild their lives. This situation creates a drifting community of pariahs, at best simply an ineffective strategy and at worst a violation of human rights in a culture that still at least calls its state prison system the Department of Corrections and *Rehabilitation*. Serious violent offenders convicted for other types of crimes can move back to their homes and families, more readily return to work, and not have to register anywhere or contend with their neighbors locating them for what may become an Internet witch hunt.

There is something compelling about adamantly condemning known sexual perpetrators, as though in loudly doing so we declare ourselves part of a winning team. However, since such a motley range of individuals has been discovered using child pornography or molesting minors, it is apparent that such misconduct is not confined to any particular demographic. Rather, it is, after all, a human problem, reflecting propensities with a scope and definition that are about as difficult to isolate as the elusory continuum of psychopathy. Known sexual perpetrators include those who represent society's official condemners of sexual abuse: judges, law enforcement officers, educators, Boy Scout leaders, and clergy. At a collective level these mixed messages reflect unconsciousness, confusion, and the inability to consciously contain

---

7   Kelly Davis, January 3, 2013, "State Supreme Court to hear Jessica's Law challenge," *San Diego City Beat, www.sdcitybeat.com.*

dichotomous aspects of reality within us as individuals. This struggle is inevitably manifested through projection in the world we create around us as well.

I try to notice my own inflammatory reactions as well as those of the public. When I am overly impassioned about a client, a stance on something, a cause, or an opinion, I am cued to consider the intensity of my response as possibly representing a complex or something I am trying to avoid. In my forensic work, for example, if I catch myself feeling overly identified with the prisoner archetype, with one of the characters I am assigned to evaluate, I know that such a reaction is potentially as dangerous as its opposite: the attitude held by some of my colleagues that offenders referred for evaluation are, per force, sexually violent predators and warrant involuntary commitment, sight unseen, rendering an interview pointless. In my case, when I have a strong countertransference reaction of sympathy to one of my forensic clients, I know that this person has somehow triggered a recognition in me of some aspect of my own inner criminal that I feel inclined to defend—or perhaps some aspect of my father, his personality, or our relationship about which I feel possessive and protective. Evaluating my own reactions this way helps me activate the objectivity to respond more consciously. Jung makes this compelling point:

> Every psychological extreme secretly contains its own oppo-
> site or stands in some sort of intimate and essential relation
> to it. Indeed, it is from this tension that it derives its peculiar
> dynamism. There is no hallowed custom that cannot on
> occasion turn into its opposite, and the more extreme a posi-
> tion is, the more easily may we expect . . . a conversion of
> something into its opposite. The best is the most threatened
> with some devilish perversion just because it has done the
> most to suppress evil.[8]

---

8   C. G. Jung, *Symbols of Transformation. Vol. 5. The Collected Works of C. G. Jung,* 2d ed. (Princeton, NJ: Princeton University Press, 1990/1956), 375.

And:

> The psychological rule says that when an inner situation is
> not made conscious, it happens outside, as fate. That is to say,
> when the individual remains undivided and does not become
> conscious of his inner opposite, the world must perforce act
> out the conflict and be torn into opposing halves.[9]

Jung's reference to *holding the tension of opposites* and to the way in
which inner reality is inevitably reflected in the external world resonates
deeply with my own perceptions, formed over my lifetime. I discovered
Jung anew in the desert of my forensic career, and his concepts helped
me to find meaning and perspective. His impressive voice came from
such a distant time and place, and yet I have repeatedly experienced
a sense of immediate recognition and affirmation through his words.
My innermost thoughts and feelings found a kind of home in Jung's
writings, and these in turn further shaped and cultivated my field of
thoughts about polarized systems of belief, inner psychopathy, and
my father, whose death unloosed a deluge of related reflections and
unavoidable insights.

---

9   C. G. Jung, *Aion. Vol. 9ii. The Collected Works of C. G. Jung*, 2d ed. (Princeton, NJ: Princeton
    University Press, 1978/1959), 71.

CHAPTER 4

The Story of Albert

I<small>N THE COMPLICATED PUZZLE</small> of this writing, Albert is actually the center point, because he is the inner reference that constellated my thinking about the subtle nuances of psychopathy on a continuum and generated the idea of expanding the definition accordingly. His behavior compelled me to question my understanding of the concept psychopathy by merging my professional background with my firsthand experience. This chapter presents a personal perspective, including details of family history, to portray the context of my life with this beguiling character and his impact upon others. He was an unsolicited model who triggered my main thesis: that psychopathy extends beyond the purely pathological realm.

Albert personified coexisting contradictions. He was capable of captivating charm and stinging callousness. He invited emotional immersion and radically severed his closest relationships. He inspired intense adoration and caused devastating pain. In retrospect, this is the story of an enduring love—against all odds—for a father whom I could never really like. I loved my father, even when I hated his behavior. The meaning of that dual experience emerged as fundamental to the core of this writing after he died, and it continues to unfold.

My father's death ended a reign of gentle tyranny over my heart that spanned my life for more than half a century. In its aftermath, I was left feeling lighter but exhausted and fragile, as though some giant mantle had been lifted—a presence of which I was suddenly aware only after it was gone.

I somewhat arbitrarily turned to *The Tibetan Book of Living and Dying* shortly after Albert passed away; in retrospect, I think I was trying to contain my grief by at least conceptualizing a benevolent structure for it, complete with directions to follow, so that I could put him and my sorrow to rest. This was essentially a solitary mind game, since Albert was forever unavailable to participate, and if he had been around for this option, would have refused anyway. My father's dying included no formal ceremony or ritual, at his request—unsurprising given the adamantly unconventional way he lived his life. As we made meager preparations for the inevitable, his priority appeared to be keeping things simple and on his own terms, while mine involved meager attempts to find peace and order in the context of what felt like a broad range of irreconcilable differences, including how we disagreed about having some kind of ceremony to honor his spirit's ascent. (He was disinclined to acknowledge that he had a spirit or a soul. I can vividly imagine his exaggerated grimace if confronted about the subject.)

The Tibetan Book of Living and Dying describes the process of death and the importance of awareness to cultivate order in that final chapter of life by intentionally creating a purposeful, peaceful environment to contain the monumental change.[1] It suggests that ceremony is particularly important in facilitating a smooth transition to the next realm for the deceased individual, and describes some detailed, specific instructions to follow. For example, the day of the week when the death occurred has special significance for guiding commemoration and healing, and the timed positioning of the body is prescribed during certain stages.

---

1   Sogyal Rinpoche, The Tibetan Book of Living and Dying (New York: HarperCollins, 2002), 255–260.

Despite enthusiastic intentions, I felt unable to genuinely relate to this Tibetan proposal in a literal fashion, although I found reading about the concepts comforting. This was akin to my wistful, inevitably ill-fated hope that I would find a sense of easy fit belonging to an organized religion, which I had experienced on so many occasions in the past.

There was something too neatly packaged for me about this beautiful Tibetan spiritual vision. Part of my inherited struggle is that whenever things are too ecclesiastical, I have a difficult time believing that they are valid—or at least that they might pertain to me. Ironically, in the context of trying to process my father's death with respect and depth, my innate resistance to most organized approaches to spirituality emerged with renewed vigor—like part of his legacy, even a genetic predisposition. My father was sarcastic. I could say he was sacrilegious, but that almost sounds as though he belonged to a group, which he would adamantly resist. He would surely have argued with any analysis I came up with anyway.

As time passed, I discovered that the process of adjusting to Albert's death was neither predictable nor finite. Our relationship was complicated. Many of my perceptions about his true personality and his feelings toward me were intricately formed through my own desires and projections—a deep weaving. Even now it is nearly impossible to differentiate my treasured pictures from the truth, relatively speaking. My experience of him was as much my own creation as it was based upon the reality of our interaction.

The gradual shift within me is fundamental as I continue to realize the depth of impact he had on me and to cope with his final departure. Visions of our lives flood my memory, often uninvited. Some are sweet and touching, which I can typically embrace and release, but others I continue to deliberate over, unresolved or unwilling to let go. These more troubled reflections on my history with him demand my conscious attention, despite inevitable resistance to the discomfort. On some instinctual level I know not to ignore what I would rather let slip by, convinced that the purpose of this tension holds the potential for healing and that to disregard such unwanted material invites more problems than it avoids. As Jung stated, "The psychological rule says that when an inner situation is not made conscious, it happens outside, as fate."[2]

Now follows the story of Albert, or more specifically, of my personal relationship with this man to whom others referred as "a psychopath."

Albert's Story

How might my father's life experience have influenced the development of his psychopathic characteristics? Although this speculation concerns one individual, my intention is to create a bridge from his story to a more general application of the ideas that emerge in its telling.

Albert was the middle child of an intact Jewish family in New York, with an older brother and a younger sister. His parents were born in Austria and Russia; both immigrated to America as young adults. My aunt once commented that my father never quite fit in with his family of origin because he was an intellectual, and they were "on a different wavelength." His parents were intelligent, hardworking, and financially solvent, but more concerned with acculturation than demonstrating independence—and independence became my father's signature quality.

Albert loved jazz. He played the drums. He joined the Army when he was 18 years old, at which point he left home for the last time and subsequently saw a lot of frontline combat in Germany and France during World War II. This combat exposure may have been a powerful influence on him, but he never talked about his military experience. My presumption comes from impressions in hindsight after he died: a combination of the nature of his horrific hallucinations toward the end, which included corpses and other battlefield imagery, and the observ-

---

2   Jung, Aion, 70.

able difference between his old photographs from the period before the war and afterward. He came back to the United States in his 20s and attended the University of Michigan, Ann Arbor, on the GI Bill. The photos of him from that postwar period reflect an uncharacteristic somber countenance.

He later attended the Massachusetts Institute of Technology (MIT) and earned his graduate degree in architecture, which became his lifetime career. He was successful as an architect and belonged to the American Institute of Architects (AIA). He would often leave jobs when things seemed to be going well, over conflicts with others with whom he had to collaborate or to whom he was subordinate, so he held many different jobs throughout his professional life, both employed by various architectural firms and periodically forming his own businesses with partners or as an independent contractor. I remember his fine artistic style and the intricate, neatly drawn and configured miniature pasteboard models in his various studios. He designed many private homes and corporate projects, including a national chain of large retail stores and the bicycle paths for a major California university. Albert minimized his talents but not his strident opinions and critiques of other professionals, their decisions, and styles different from his own, to such an extent that it occurred to me only as an afterthought that he was a truly gifted artist and architect.

My father met my first-generation Swedish-American mother after she had graduated from Brown University and was working at Harvard. At 25 years old, she was socially inexperienced and living alone. Albert was a graduate student at MIT and married to his first wife, whom he had met while still an undergraduate at the University of Michigan. The stories I heard growing up were that his family disapproved of his first wife because she was not Jewish. However, later my father told me this was not accurate: They liked her, there was a big wedding back in New Jersey where his family all lived, and his wife even went through some attempt to convert to Judaism, steered by his maternal aunt. As with other details, the veracity of this one detail remains unclear, since Albert's primary objective in rendering information was often at least as much about manipulating a reaction and making his point, as it was about telling the truth.

Albert and his first wife met my mother because she was living upstairs in the same rooming house near the Harvard campus. The three of them would go out to movies together and discuss them afterward. My mother was enthralled by Albert's intellectual and Bohemian charm. He participated in book review club meetings and poetry readings. Within about six months of the friendship between them and my mother, Albert and his first wife divorced (they had no children), she returned to Ann Arbor where they had met, and he married my mother. My parents unexpectedly encountered his ex-wife once in a movie theater when my mother was pregnant with me. Without hesitation, he approached and chatted with her, and a potentially emotional meeting was apparently uneventful.

Albert's characteristic manner was charming and cocksure about his decisions and actions, even in situations that were blatantly outrageous to others. People generally responded to him on his own terms, which involved feeling no guilt or remorse about anything, or they stopped speaking to him altogether, about which he expressed no dismay.

My mother was pregnant with me within my parents' first year of marriage. Albert had graduated from MIT and had a job offer as an architect in Arizona, where they relocated when my mother was about eight months along. He subsequently found fault with the firm that hired him, quit his architectural job, and began working as a jazz drummer, another of his favorite vocations, and probably the passion of his life. Very shortly after I was born, they again relocated, this time to California. He told me shortly before he died that I was born on the date of one of his marriages, only he could not recall which one.

Albert had strong opinions about personal and lifestyle choices, including hair, clothing, makeup, food, music, and household furnishings. For example, he forbade my mother to wear hairpins. He pressured her to burn her deceased mother's letters, because he felt she was too sentimental and overly attached to her mother. He had clear, detailed expectations in many regards, and typically required a steady stream of attention and devotion from those closest to him. He garnered this esteem primarily through charm and emotional manipulation, powered by the fact that his approval was contingent upon compliance with his preferences, not by rage or aggression. On one occasion, he got so irritated with my mother that he poked her arm with the point of a pencil, but this is the only physically violent act I have ever heard attributed to him, toward anyone. Producing the right answer to assuage him could be a conundrum. Before I was born, when my parents were newly married, my father asked my mother what she wanted to do with her life and how she envisioned using her degree. He asked her what she had planned for her career; at that point, her plan was to support him in his. He was displeased by this answer and let her know as much. She was left wondering what the correct response would have been—presuming there was one.

During my parents' brief marriage, Albert had a motto he made into an acronym and posted over the doorway: "ESI," which stood for "Enlightened Self-Interest." This clever slogan manifests his talent for disguising the darker dimensions of self-focus in a deceptively benign, philosophical, intellectual frame: a maneuver suggestive of psychopathy with the secondary gain of avoiding responsibility for his own behavior.

Albert denied infidelity at all points during his life. Soon after I was born, my mother received a phone call from a female stranger who told her that Albert was having an affair. She thought it was a prank call at the time.

When I was 2 years old, my parents divorced. My mother took me back to the East Coast, and my father stayed in California. He never paid child support, but he did send me letters—very clever and artistic letters—regularly—for a while.

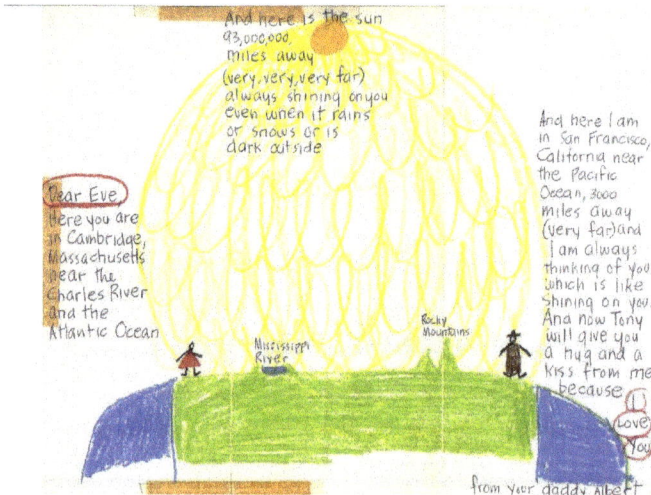

He drew me colorful, beautifully designed pictures for each letter of the alphabet, which he sent one by one. My mother put them in a book that I still have.

By the end of the alphabet, he was remarried to my first step-mother and they had a baby son.

Albert visited my mother and me in Cambridge, MA, only once, when I was 3 years old. I still have the pictures, black-and-white photos from the old Brownie camera. I remember what I felt when those photographs were taken: unsure how to behave or what age to act. With my mother I felt like a colleague. He was such a rare and lovely stranger. I yearned for some sort of traditional fantasized father– daughter relationship, but I had no idea how to make that happen. I remember mugging away with my father prompted by my mother in front of that camera, happy and sad simultaneously, at no point relaxed enough to stop performing, while my mother commented on how much we looked alike.

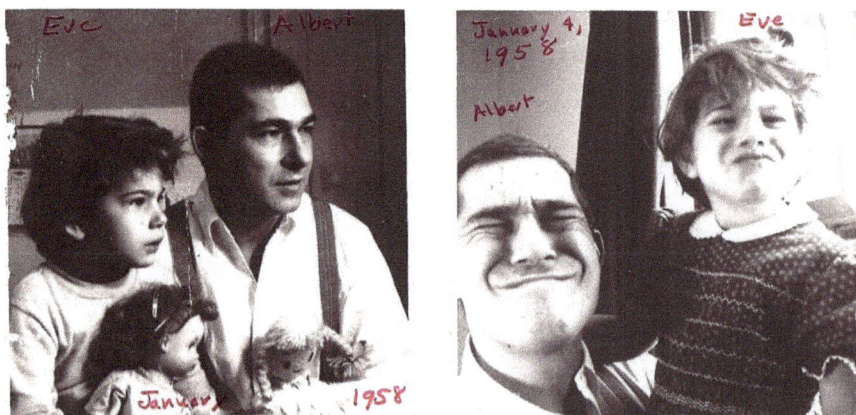

Even then I felt as though I had to be guarded with him. I already loved him almost desperately, and his letters kindled my hope-filled imagination—but in reality, I did not know him or have any memory of his ever being around. He was soon gone again anyway.

He and my first stepmother lived in Berkeley at that time. They conceived two children in those first years: my half-brother, then my half-sister, who are my only two biological siblings. When I was around 5 years old, my father located a place in Berkeley for my mother and me to live, and we moved back there. I recall going with my mother to celebrate Thanksgiving at the home of my father and his then-wife, playing with my little brother on random occasions, and my stepmother babysitting me soon after my half-sister was born. Within a year of her birth, when my half-sister was still an infant and my half-brother was about 3 years old, my father suddenly abandoned his second family. Apparently he said nothing to announce his departure, but silently climbed out a window of their home during the night, leaving a note.

He moved to his architectural studio across town, and he and his third wife divorced. According to Albert, unlike my mother, this ex-wife remained angry. Fairly soon after her marriage to my father ended, she married a professor at the university, who later adopted my two half-siblings. I saw that stepmother and the two children once more that year. My mother and I were walking home from the laundromat one day and we spotted her driving by in her sports car. She invited us to visit their new home in the hills, and I played with my siblings one last time. That was the last I saw of any of them for about 35 years.

Also around then, my father completely ceased any communication with me. He later told me that this was because he had experienced a sudden epiphany, wherein he realized that staying in touch with me felt like too much trouble and it would be better if he just stopped—so he did. The next contact we had was 14 years later. Obviously, on many levels my father's capacity for radical severance imposed a challenge to my own capacity to process and absorb such stark literal and emotional disengagement, absent eros: Psychopathy within presented itself in my personal experience early on.

At some point during the interim years, an attorney contacted my first stepmother and my mother requesting that they provide feedback about Albert's capacity to parent appropriately because he and his next wife were trying to adopt a child. Whatever both ex-wives communicated apparently did not obstruct the adoption process. He and his fourth wife subsequently adopted two children.

When I was a senior at Berkeley High School, Albert wrote a letter to me. I first wrote him a lengthy response, enthusiastically detailing all of my activities and accomplishments: scholarship, student government, and cheerleading. My mother read it and commented that I would do better to keep it short and simple, that it was likely he had reached out to me because he was having problems in a current love relationship, and that it would be best to have contact with him when I did not need anything from him. The latter cautionary phrase remained in my mind ever afterward; it was not bad advice. So I wrote a revised short letter, and that was the end of that overture for the time being.

Three years later, when I was a junior at the University of California, Santa Barbara, I responded to another letter Albert sent and this time went to meet him, my second stepmother, and their two adoptive children, who were then 10 and 6 years old. They had a lovely home in San Diego. I loved that family easily and felt accepted by this stepmother and both children. We developed an ongoing relationship. They became consistently present in my life, including when my son was born nine years later. My stepmother became my lifelong friend. My father and his fourth wife were married for 27 years—until he abruptly left that family too.

Ironically, given the adamancy with which my father consistently criticized my Jungian orientation, it was he and my stepmother who actually introduced me to the writing and ideas of Jung, giving me my first copy of *Man and His Symbols*[3] when I was still an undergraduate. I remember that they were involved with a Jungian analyst, attending private sessions and lectures. Years afterward I recognized their analyst's name and realized that he was the well-known analyst and author, John ("Jack") Sanford. For quite a prolonged period, my father and stepmother were journaling about their dreams and discussing them regularly. Apparently, all of Albert's life he experienced strong, vivid dreams, which he remembered upon waking—a trait we shared and a characteristic relevant to Jungian analysis or therapy. I later learned the origins of their analytic experience. My stepmother gave Albert an ultimatum that if their marriage were to continue, he would have to enter therapy with her. He complied but stopped before she did.

---

3   C.G. Jung, Man and His Symbols (New York: Dell, 1964).

One day when their adoptive son was a college student around 22 years old and their adoptive daughter was still living at home, Albert left. My stepmother later told me that she and Albert had gone out for dinner and had an uneventful, pleasant evening the night before. Apparently, he made a solitary decision to abruptly exit his family after nearly three decades, fueled by private reasons. My half-sister unexpectedly came home that weekday midmorning to find him packing his clothes. She was the only one present to witness his silent, sudden departure.

My father never told his wife why he left after 27 years—and he never returned. Within the months following his leaving, in a brief and rare telephone communication between them, she expressed her bewilderment, exacerbated by her perception that this past year of marriage had actually been their best. He agreed with her that it had been and then added: "But now I have to go," without further comment. They soon lost contact altogether, about which he was uncompromising, and she was left alone to process the brutally sudden end of their shared lives.

Her struggle to somehow reconcile the glaring contrasts in Albert's behavior was intensified by her recollection of his endearing qualities and their history of positive family experiences. They had lived a comfortable life in a beautiful home he had designed, in a beach community with pleasant neighbors. They gave and went to parties with friends. They both loved cooking. They had frequent family barbecues on the back patio by the hot tub and at the local bay. They owned and adored three generations of pedigreed standard poodles. Together they went to parent–teacher conferences and family church camp. Only years after his abrupt exit, my stepmother found some relief in realizing that she simply had to accept the way he was, although she would never understand the mysterious underpinnings that motivated him in the end of their relationship, deep or otherwise, despite having spent nearly three decades of her life with him.

They had made an agreement that they would not tell their two children they were adopted and had not done so. However, soon after Albert left, without consulting their mother, he sent letters to these now-adult children telling them they were adopted, apparently undeterred by any sensitivity to the emotional fallout this information would inevitably precipitate for them. His relationships with them both were forever damaged. His daughter did not speak to him for years. His son's contact with him became, and remained, minimal. Further fallout included that both of these siblings became distanced from me, although I consistently maintained contact with my stepmother and later reunited with my half-sister.

I stayed in touch with my father, who was part of my life for the rest of his. He was there when my daughter was born later the same year he left my stepmother, but this time he came to see his new grandchild alone.

Albert maintained a marriage and family for 27 years. He demonstrated caring, constancy, and shared joy. He was also unequivocally callous. He abandoned his most intimate relationships without warning or interaction—an action he later described, if at all, with arrogant philosophical detachment. The harm he caused others was magnified by the unpredictable sharp contrasts in his behavior, suggesting a dual reality within him—including an inner psychopathy that left psychic casualties.

My continued relationship with him simply manifested how I was made. I resolutely loved my father, even when I hated his behavior. At least in part, this unearned but adamant attachment reflected my desire to avoid the unacceptable reality of having such an inaccessible father. A harsher possibility is that my unswerving loyalty to him evidenced some less dramatically expressed but similar qualities of my own. His unavailability to me at a deep level created a quandary in terms of my genuine connection with him, which was stymied. I could never rely on him, so for self-protection, there was always background distrust, despite my desire to connect with him and my ongoing contact with him as an adult.

After he left his fourth wife, Albert lived alone in a downtown San Diego apartment. He dated one woman after another, most of whom he met through the artsy *San Diego Reader* newspaper. He amused himself by creating entertaining and catchy ads, some of which he would proudly recite for me. One of his female companions commented to me, "Women fall out of the trees for your father." She was one of three consecutive partners I regarded as a chronological trio. She was the only girlfriend who ever moved in with him. He was adamantly opposed to living with a woman without the formality of marriage, which seemed hypocritical or at least confusing, considering his history. The trial run with this exception to his rule was unsuccessful in the end. She moved into his place for a brief period until he tried to persuade her to move out because by then, he wanted to separate from her, but she refused to go and wanted more of a commitment from him. So finally he left her alone in his apartment, sold it, and rented another one elsewhere in the area. She called me once afterward, wanting to join my family for one of my son's basketball games, but the gesture felt contrived and manipulative. Caught between falsely accommodating her and feeling uncomfortably ensnared in the breakup, I declined her politely and never saw her again.

He married the next girlfriend after the trio. She was a Midwestern type, she shared his appreciation of jazz, and they bought a beach city duplex, which he renovated in his singular style. She had been in recovery from cancer. She had an adult son, whom I never met and Albert never mentioned in any detail. A few years later, Albert left her, ending his fifth marriage, and he relocated to a rented studio apartment in the trendy Gaslamp Quarter of San Diego, where he lived alone for the remainder of his life. This fifth and final ex-wife became ill with cancer again fairly soon after their divorce, and he commented to me with his smirking half-laugh that he had told her she could call him "if 911 failed." She died soon thereafter. He had no contact with her family and did not go to the funeral. I remember feeling disgusted at his apathy, aghast—and sickeningly reassured: I at least was spared his disapproval, although I was keenly aware that his capacity for unrelenting rejection was ever-present, to a gut-wrenching fault.

Albert had girlfriends after that fifth wife, but his final, obvious fixation during his last several months, as he was dying of Parkinson's, was with his 30-year-old care provider. She was bone thin and looked about 13 years old, but she was gentle, indulgent, and accommodating with him. He told her how special she was, how she performed even simple chores like no one else ever before. As he loudly called others' attention to her many incredible attributes, crowing about how beautiful her hair was, for example, she visibly glowed. I could see the familiar glint in her eyes. She informed me passionately that she was going on her own to visit him in the hospital, even though the service that employed her forbade her to do so, and she knew it might cost her the job, which she clearly needed. I urged her not to jeopardize her employment. Their plan was for him to move into her apartment building so that she could attend to him around the clock; however, it became evident that he would not survive. She deeply grieved his passing, his last sweetheart, whose love and devotion he was able to invoke even at 84 years old. Trembling with Parkinson's, he could still produce his captivating synthesis of charming repartee and seductive flattery, notwithstanding the episodes of dementia that rocked his final two weeks.

Family History

Albert's early origins murmur the precursors of his personality development. He essentially felt deprived of affection from both of his parents, for different reasons, and he had a troubled relationship with both of them. His father was passive and mild-mannered, and Albert never quite connected with him. His mother, in contrast, was five feet two inches of pure spunk: dramatic and strong-willed. According to Albert, she tyrannized and verbally abused his father. Albert never felt that he received what he needed from her. Consequently, he avoided her and forever replayed that unmet need with many females, including me.

In retrospect, his relationship with his mother may have been at the root of his own wounded feminine aspect—his inability to relate naturally to his own feelings or to genuinely empathize with others. Some similarities in their personalities were evident, including quick wit and the capacity for harsh judgment. Perhaps he identified with his mother at an unconscious level, although consciously he tried to escape her, even geographically. He left his family home in New York permanently when he joined the military. As a young adult he relocated as far away as the continent would allow, to the opposite coast, where he remained.

Albert experienced his mother as overbearing, as what Jungians would call the *devouring mother*. Despite his insistence otherwise, I suspect that he felt he had disappointed her. One way in which that fear of inadequacy manifested was in his adamant resistance to acknowledging his own expectations of others, to avoid risking a similar letdown, which he found intolerable. Instead, his attitude was that interference was the closest thing to a cardinal sin. He appeared to be passionately committed to utmost independence of thought and action. However, without compassion to temper his fervor and lend it meaning and value, it could become self-focused inflation, in which his actions disregarded others' feelings under the guise of some higher calling. In retrospect, the shadow side of this rigid "independence" bordered on the kind of callousness, lack of empathy, and absence of remorse that are trademark characteristics of psychopathy.

Albert was adept at engaging people, but he also rendered scathing judgment of those he felt were not operating in accordance with his unconventional but precise standards. His mother's intolerance of him and his own subsequent intolerance of himself were projected most readily onto those closest to him. Such a mother complex, absent the softening factors of love, forgiveness, and grace, made him a formidable person in relationship with any intimate partner, let alone a child.

As part of my doctoral program years ago, I had an assignment that involved obtaining biographical information on my family of origin, and it was only then that I found out any details about Albert's parents or early life. Despite considerable missing pieces, such as relatives who seemed to disappear without explanation, he eventually gave me a fair sense of his origins in this regard. He then gave me a lecture on how Jung had "proven" that external experience had nothing to do with individuation, rendering the whole enterprise of my project meaning-less, and canceled the family brunch we had planned for the following weekend, because suddenly it "didn't fit in with his plans." Still, in between the barbs and bouts of defensiveness, he provided some bits of his personal family history I had never heard before. Contrary to my expectations, he seemed happy to be interviewed. After the project was completed, including an album of his family photos, I displayed it at our home during one Thanksgiving celebration back when he used to join us, and his irrepressible delight and interest are forever emblazoned in my memory. It was the only time I recall his ever reacting to something I had written or accomplished without any criticism whatsoever.

Paternal Ancestors

This biographical information is presented with the caveat that most of it was provided by Albert, which would inevitably reflect his unique perceptions. As such, one must bear in mind the source. Alternative versions exist. For the purposes of this writing, however, I think his own personal understanding of the truth is more relevant to our consider-ation, since that reality informed his personality.

My father's paternal grandfather was born and lived in Austria. Apparently he had a first wife, my grandfather's biological mother, but at some point she vanished, at least from retrievable memory. My great-grandfather and his first wife conceived two sons, my grandfa-ther and his younger brother. Then he had a second wife, my father's step-grandmother. They were all Jewish. The boys came to America when my grandfather was about 12 years old; my father believed they came alone.

My father's maternal grandfather lived in Russia. They were also Jewish. Somehow, he "disappeared," sometime between when his wife and five daughters left Russia and when they arrived in America. One story was that he met another woman on the boat, with whom he absconded, but another explanation was that he departed from the family back in Russia. All five of his daughters, including my grandmother, named a son after their absent father. He became a revered legend of sorts, even though my grandmother did not see him after age 2, when she traveled with her sisters and mother to the United States. They all settled in New York. I wondered in retrospect if the legend of Albert's grandfather impacted him as a model for his own behavior in some regard, in that his mother and her sisters all made a hero of him, and his most memorable act, at least in my father's telling, was that he had disappeared—somehow.

Albert's mother had polio when she was a child, and as a result one leg remained shorter than the other, but it never appeared to slow her down at all; on the contrary, the disability may have made her tougher and more persistent. I did not see her often, but I clearly remember her chasing me to the bus stop when I was around 11 years old, while my mother and I were on a rare visit; she was aggressively trying to jam money in my pocket. My mother always avoided charity and reacted by yelling, "Run, run!" at me. I was significantly taller than my grandmother even then and in robust health, but she moved with surprising alacrity, caught me, and succeeded in her determined effort to be generous, with my mother left protesting in the distant background.

My grandmother was the last of the five sisters to marry, although she was the middle child. She had a deep love affair with a man just before she met my grandfather, but her beloved died of tuberculosis. As Albert described it, she then became a "ward" of her sisters, living with the eldest, so the family essentially "married her off" to my grandfather.

I do not know what happened to their mother, but my grandmother and her four sisters were part of a huge extended family network I only heard about. I was aware they had a "family newsletter," and one relative had engineered a comprehensive family tree, upon which my name and the names of my children are included. My father's attitude regarding all of this ancestry was dismissive, whereas I have always been interested. When I was in my early 40s and before he died, my father's older brother hosted an extended family reunion where I met some of my paternal relatives for the first time.

Albert's attitude toward his ethnic heritage was complicated, although I am sure he would deny as much; he minimized any affiliation, period. My impression is that in some private, fundamental way, being Jewish influenced his life experience, in his inimitable style. Certainly, the religious aspect meant nothing to him, and his attitude about the cultural implications of his roots was not obvious, other than via his disparaging comments emphasizing his independence from his early origins. However, despite his disapproval of stereotypes, his speech was spontaneously interspersed with an automatic, informal expression of his Jewishness, such as classifying others as *yids* or *shiksas*, which suggested an understated familiarity and identification—like a relationship he both loved a little and avoided admitting, a shy affection, at best a conflicted one. Of his five wives, notably, none was Jewish, and his only consistent reaction to traditions of any kind was to avoid being predictable.

Like so many other aspects of my father's life, his relationship with his extended family was full of contradictions. He seemed determined to be somehow in it but not of it, and he developed a reputation for being a cavalier, intriguing, offbeat, but lovable character. Most of these relatives did not know him well or see him often—if at all—so their impressions were largely based on the many stories about his behavior. Although he did not visit often, throughout his adult life Albert traveled back East for various family occasions, always maintaining contact, although minimal.

His older brother and sister-in-law moved to a retirement facility in San Diego near where Albert lived just before that brother died; and when his brother became terminally ill, Albert demonstrated an unprecedented commitment to him, visiting him daily and providing voluntary hospice care. After his brother's death, Albert continued to provide hospice services for elderly patients, volunteering through his own managed care medical provider.

My paternal grandmother was tiny, peppery, and expressive, with a terrific sense of humor and a harsh temper I heard about but never witnessed. She always treated me with special tenderness, even though I was outside their immediate constellation: My parents divorced when I was 2 years old, I was not Jewish, my mother and I lived far away, and my father was the black sheep of the family. From what my grandmother did and did not say, I also had the impression that despite the obvious conflicts between her and my father, in some indirect way he was her favorite—or maybe she just felt guilty about him. He did not maintain much contact with his mother throughout his adult life, reinforced by his settling permanently in California, 3,000 miles from his childhood home on the East Coast, where she remained.

I never met my grandfather. He was reportedly passive and friendly, although never demonstrative or affectionate with my father. Albert said he recalled his father hugging him one time. Other children loved his father, however. When he came to childhood baseball games ostensibly to see Albert play, he would pay more attention to the other children than to his own son. He seemed to prefer them, to the extent that it was difficult to tell whom he was there to watch. Still, Albert said he made efforts to connect with his father and felt protective of him; he remembered feeling hurt and defensive when his uncle called his father a "hulk."

Albert described his father as a "very simple guy with no distinguishable mental alertness. He loved baseball and opera." My father recalled a scene when he was a toddler and overheard his parents engaged in a serious fight; they were downstairs yelling that this argument was the end of their marriage. Then only 4 years old but apparently impervious enough to the drama to intercede on his own behalf, Albert walked downstairs into the middle of the fray and threw himself at his father, hugging him, and saying, "Daddy, if you're not going to come back, take me with you." The outcome: They all just continued living together as though nothing had transpired.

According to my father, his parents had many arguments and violent fights, primarily perpetrated by my grandmother. She also physically disciplined both my father and his older brother, but never the youngest child, my father's sister. Albert said he remembered only one time when his father fought back with his wife; most of the time he was "just defending himself." Albert came home from high school that singular day, and his mother was simply sitting still, which was very unusual for her. He asked her what was wrong, and she told him that his father had pushed her down the stairs. At least in the telling of this story to me so many decades later, Albert evinced no particular emotional reaction to this disturbing disclosure, other than interest.

Albert had no memories of his mother ever treating him tenderly. He told me he recalled her holding him on her lap and putting his arms around her on one occasion. His older brother was ill frequently, and both he and their younger sister received privileges, such as music lessons and summer camp, that Albert did not. I asked him the reason, and he said he had no idea. Albert began running away from home frequently when he was a young child. He said he did not know why, he just would. He would run to his parents' close friends' home, or to visit his aunts, whom he liked. He thought they were all "more loving" than his parents.

Albert's father died at age 59, of a heart attack and cancer, four years before I was born. His mother died 36 years after her husband, at age 90. She was mentally alert until her death and was reading three newspapers a day at the time, which my father recounted with some obvious pride. She never remarried, although she had boyfriends as long as I can remember. My father clearly enjoyed telling a story about one of his infrequent visits to see her as an adult, when she baked a creative pie, half his favorite flavor and half her boyfriend's. She owned her own neatly kept home, where I visited her several times over the years, and she worked. I remember that she owned her own antique store at one point and assisted in an attorney's office in her later years. My grandmother's sense of humor was noteworthy. Once many years ago, Albert and his fourth wife were trying to persuade her to fly to California for a visit. After just the right pause, and with the perfect tone for her dry, comedic delivery, she responded: "How 'bout just my ashes?"

Albert said he figured out that he was neglected during his growing-up years only after listening to what everyone said at the family reunion my uncle held in 1994, when Albert was 70 years old. If accurately reported, his delayed perception is significant, suggesting the kind of emotional disconnection I am referring to as a form of psychopathy, only in this case in response to himself rather than to others. Of course, it remains unknown whether he was even telling the truth or just being entertaining, the latter of which was both possible and characteristic of him. Either way, even as a child, he appeared to have responded to the most significant people and events in his life with some detachment—a whispered clue about the thread of inner psychopathy woven into his complicated soul.

Reflections in the Aftermath

My memories of Albert include coexisting contradictions not unlike the complexity of his character when he was alive. Now my feelings are mixed: peace and hopelessness. The dream of somehow earning his love and approval, which was always deep within me, is now over, not because I chose it to be, but because he no longer exists. He quashed my hope in one final act of irrevocable abandonment. The grieving process has been an arduous journey. I had an image the other day of sliding slowly down a gravel mountain with my feet braced against the descent; subsequent to his death I lost a toehold and was now slipping inevitably and without brakes, approaching my own ending with a finality I had never felt before.

The death of a close parent with whom you grew up can feel like losing a witness to your very being; an invaluable container for your memories and details of personal history is suddenly gone, along with a sense of familiar identification. My father's death was like being forced to surrender something left permanently unfinished, the chance for a life and identity I never had but always wanted.

After Albert's passing, the reality of my perceptions about him was tested by some of the responses from my estranged and angry siblings and the trail of ex-wives and girlfriends he had left behind over the previous six decades, most of whom did not appear inclined to forgive, for reasons that were understandable. Part of me yearned otherwise, wished that their resolve to hold him forever accountable would melt into an easy peace. Resolving to hold the person who hurts us liable offers safety; however, at least when it came to my father, I could locate no such determination. Perhaps I needed to love him more than I needed to feel safe. A heart less guarded may be flexible to a fault. Whether compassion or weakness, this leniency has been to my detriment at times, exposing me to pain I might otherwise have avoided. Nonetheless, the tendency prevails. Others wisely avoid risking that vulnerability by being more cautious, withholding love not earned. I always loved my father unconditionally—at least my idea of him.

I did not see Albert from the age of 5 until I was 19 years old, so during that period I was left to integrate my fantasy of his ideal image without the challenge or benefits of a real relationship. He lived in my imagination, a composite of my mother's stories and old photographs. With the scant information I had, I invented a character that became quietly rooted in my soul. Because I did not really know or live with him, I could alter my conception of his personality and behavior to suit my emotional needs, and my loyalty was inherent. In some ways, this may have been a blessedly insulated way to undergo the significant developmental milestones of those growing-up years; my mother held that opinion. In other important ways, his absence affected everything about my life and relationships, and I missed him unfathomably at some level too deep to touch, despite my accomplishments. From our reunification when I was 19 until his death 36 years later, we remained connected. Now I still carry the inner image of him, but grounded in—and tempered by—my actual experience with him over the years.

Albert's passing created a confluence of real and idealized memories that serve a purpose along the path of my own individuation while offering a challenge and an opportunity to illuminate and integrate the many introjects he contributed to my personality. This awareness feels like peeling back layers, the random sensation that what I am experiencing in a given moment reflects the presence of his energy. For example, during those first months after he died, I attended a Jungian lecture and noticed the sharp, judgmental nature of my own inner commentary in response to the speaker. I recognized the peculiar tone of a complex, a set of intense, intertwined thoughts and feelings, so familiar it was elusive—and reeking of my father's harshness. Differentiating it was like trying to catch a glimpse of a shadow blocked by its owner.

Despite the frustration I feel about his lack of expressed insight at the end of his life, I also realize that this discomfort is more about my own need for closure than his, and like so many of his other actions, I see another aspect that is opposite. He knew his death was approaching and it was so much bigger than he was, his only way to retain some sense of precious control was to take charge of how he surrendered to it: fully accepting it alone. A seriousness and singularity of purpose dominated his final years; he made dying his last creative act.

Albert's denial of his obvious medical condition was annoying. His resolute determination to hold fast to his "independence," manage his own care, and figuratively walk off into the woods and die "naturally," without interfering with his body's own process of demise, was aggravating and unrealistic. It was also considerably inconvenient for others, especially at the finale, when the police responded to more than one emergency call because he was yelling out of his balcony window at all hours, ranting at the hallucinations in his studio. Nonetheless, he decided to end his life when he perceived it to be over, rather than prolonging it in a compromised form with medication or intervention. He maintained his characteristic personal style as best he could under gravely compromised conditions—which suggests a unique integrity. Although it may have been less a selfless gesture than a final stroke of determination to do things his way and be true to himself—against all odds and in spite of how it might affect others—the result was the same, and his death was as simple as he could make it. He may have had no estate, but he also left behind no debts, no matters to resolve, and no mess to clean up. His affairs were organized, right down to the disposal of his remains: he carried a University of California, San Diego Medical Center donor card in his wallet for years.

Albert was typically so critical of whatever I produced in work or school that for self-protection, I learned to avoid telling or showing him anything. Initially I had a copy of my doctoral dissertation bound for him, but then reconsidered and never gave it to him; as it was, he ridiculed the school I attended and the title of my degree. When I received a recognition plaque at work, I decided to tell him about it in brief rather than show it to him, so that his predictably dismissive response would be less likely to hurt me. However, the last birthday card my father ever sent me was affectionate, light, and supportive, signed "Love, Dad" and completely out of character: a large pink card with a very large yellow cartoon bear bearing the message, "Daughter, didn't want to embarrass you by bragging about you to other people, so this year, not a word to anyone . . . REALLY . . . It's just between us . . . HOWEVER, here's a modest LITTLE poster for you to take to work!" Here an arrow with directions to OPEN, and the card unfolds to about three feet square, with enormous purple lettering declaring

"HAPPY BIRTHDAY to a WONDERFUL DAUGHTER and a TERRIFIC HUMAN BEING!" I was delighted and moved—with just the barest tinge of suspicion.

Months before he began his rapid decline, he asked for my thoughts regarding what he should do about any inheritance. I suggested he might want to use this time as an opportunity to redress in some small, symbolic gesture the bridges he had burned, the hearts he had broken, the wives and children abandoned in the past. He said no.

My father did not have an estate and left what little he had to me. I managed his affairs for the last five months he was alive. We transitioned his accounts to include me, completed the paperwork granting me power of attorney for medical decisions, and talked about related matters. None of the ex-wives, girlfriends, or my four half-siblings was involved with him through those final months. In retrospect, given his facility for engaging others when he felt like it, I suspect he was intentionally limiting his associations during this phase when his mind and body began to fail him, as though saving his reputation for some nameless audience.

The reasonable reactions of many once-significant others following his death, from ambivalence to resounding silence, serve as painful reminders to me of the depth of damage he did to those relationships—something he never acknowledged. In his final weeks, Albert made no testimonial statement of regret or remorse and expressed no profound insights, other than to adhere adamantly to his resolve to die a "natural" death. He did stop in his tracks with his walker one day while I visited him in his studio apartment, about two weeks before he died, pausing as though to deliver a sermon on the meaning of life. He pronounced he had figured it out, now that he was in this phase where he cared about things less and less: the problem was, he announced, he had never had a conscience! In a flash of newfound insight, he concluded he had spent his life so ego-driven and absorbed in his work, there was insufficient energy left for caring about others in the way he recognized was typical. I quickly grabbed pen and paper and waited with bated breath for the related insight that would surely follow, eagerly anticipating some statement about the impact of his self-focus upon those who had suffered as a result. However, instead he said that it really did not make any difference!

He had come upon the final truth: he was a natural believer in solipsism. He told me to look it up, which naturally I did later, although I already knew what I would find. It is a term from philosophy: the theory that only the self exists or can be proven to exist, with a secondary definition of extreme preoccupation with and indulgence of one's own feelings, desires, etc.: "egoistic self-absorption," clearly akin to narcissism. The implicit meaning of his communication was clear, beyond the words. He had found a final strategy to rationalize and intellectualize the pockets of emptiness in his soul and avoid meaningful interchange, understanding, or relatedness.

There were at least two occasions during the last weeks before Albert died when I felt his love providing some closure and peace for me, but also maintaining the uncanny dual reality that was our relationship into perpetuity. One incident occurred when I was at his studio on one of the many days when I went there to visit, do a load or two of his laundry, run errands, shop for groceries, or just share a meal, as it became less feasible for him to go anywhere. As mentioned, we completed the medical directive form, granting me the authority to make choices for him if he became incapacitated, which we both anticipated. This involved discussing his preferences about the details of his dying, such as life support options and burial. The subject was excruciating for me, but I realized the practical necessity, so I doggedly persisted in asking him the questions and documenting his answers. About midway through the process, I began crying, and by the end was sobbing uncontrollably. I finally blurted out, "I don't want you to die!" Instead of making some sarcastic comment, which would have been typical, he held out his arms from where he was seated, gave me a tender hug, gently patted my head on his shoulder, and told me, "It's all right, honey, at this rate we could go on like this another five years." Of course within seconds, he added with his half-laugh, "You done yet?"

The next moment like that was when my husband and I brought his caregiver to visit him at the board-and-care home where he stayed briefly, before he deliberately stopped eating and drinking and was placed at the final hospice. We all knew on some level that this was not just a visit; it was a goodbye. Even his cavalier humor was wavering, although intact. As we were leaving, I kissed and hugged him and placed my head on his chest, and he began to cry, stroking my hair, patting my shoulders, and telling me, "It's OK, it's all right"—doubly impactful because we knew he was also reassuring himself.

For Albert, telling his young caregiver farewell during that last visit with him may have been the hardest of all, because she was his very last lady-love—and he knew it. She was equally moved and choked back tears as she left, telling him, "See you later." He was clearly tearful as well but still managed to mutter a characteristic snicker and a quick retort: "Later—when's that?"

His rare softness came at random moments and was gone so swiftly; it always caught me by surprise. I was barely able to feel it before it was withdrawn, and it was never consistent or reliable. I suppose my own softer side was affected in some way by the transient nature of his affection. I learned to view his acts of kindness with cautious reverence and his insensitive treatment with the empathetic tolerance of an insider, as a way of feeling closer to him. This dynamic influenced the origins of my own psychopathic aspect even before we had any real relationship. I suffered at least two kinds of pain in connection with my father: the ongoing, subterranean ache of his complete absence during my growing-up years, and the deep, sharp sting of recognizing his callousness toward others, including my mother and me, which on some level I knew was abhorrent and could not really be rationalized. To shield my heart from the sorrow that was my first, true intuitive feeling response,

I created my own version of pseudoinsensitivity. The extent to which I identified with him came at a price—although the process of my own excavation has also been healing and instructive.

Albert never had the conversation with me one might expect on his deathbed, particularly given his personal history. The only scene resembling such a theme occurred in the hospital just prior to his very brief placement in the board-and-care home at the end, from which he was sent to hospice. It was a gruesome, noisy, cramped hospital room where he lay pale and weak with a thin sheet hanging from the ceiling separating his bed from that of his roommate: an elderly male suffering from dementia who shouted, screamed, physically attacked the nurses, and grabbed fiercely at the curtain to leer and rant at us. With his usual dry humor in a rare moment free of his own delusions, my father conspiratorially drew me near, grinning widely, and in a hoarse whisper, gesturing at the vibrating curtain, said he thought we really should have a long talk, "only not here." Within days, of course, his condition worsened, and within the week he was gone, forever unavailable for comment.

My adoptive half-sister came around for his last three days in hospice, when he was already unconscious and dying. He had "fired" her as his caregiver about two years before and had avoided subsequent contact, despite her having volunteered to help care for him when he was first diagnosed with Parkinson's, at which point he extolled her virtues. When she called me unexpectedly the day he went into hospice, I told her his circumstances, figuring she had a right to know. She had not spoken with him for prolonged periods for understandable reasons, but she came to his bedside at that point. There was no opportunity to resume communication. She was left to create her own sense of closure and her own version of a parting vigil as he slept. He never regained consciousness, although we both wanted to believe he knew we were there. We met at his hospice room where he lay unconscious and emaciated, each breath hoarse and labored.

Albert had made a request of his young female caregiver to get him Beckett's tragicomedy *Waiting for Godot.*[4] As we were cleaning out his apartment for the last time, she handed it to me. I found the play as annoying as ever but decided to read it aloud to him at his hospice bedside: a last request of sorts. It seemed fitting that Albert should deliberately exit the stage of his life with an existential drama about meaninglessness and a God that never appears droning in the background. He entered the hospice facility on a Tuesday. I visited that Wednesday and Thursday, reading aloud half the play each day as he snored his death rattle. He passed away early Friday morning. When the inevitable phone call came, it was first a relief.

This would all be simpler to process if the only aspect of Albert was the callous, thoughtless cad. In truth, he was also genuinely beguiling, bright, talented, creative, and capable of saying just the right thing at the right time. He was not either/or—he was all of these disparate aspects. The only thing predictable about him was that he was a mass of contradictions. He demonstrated the capacity to remain in a stable marriage for 27 years, raising those two children to adulthood. In a conversation I had with my stepmother the day before he died, she described how when their two adoptive children were young, he was a devoted and energetic father, taking them to the park and delighting them with his warm, playful attention. After he died, at the small luncheon my husband and I threw in his honor, his lifelong friend, another architect who had known him well when they worked together many decades prior, gave a heartfelt, glowing homage to Albert that reflected his perception of him as a loving family man with a rebellious streak.

Albert was consistently clever about displaying his refinement, taste, and intelligence. The aspect of him that carried psychopathic energy was his relational callousness. His brutality was emotional.

---

4   Samuel Beckett, Waiting for Godot (New York: Grove Press, 1982/1954).

He was nonpaternal—but never violent. Certainly, he also personified dimensions of genuine talent, charm, and creativity. He made a
contribution to the world through his work. He parented at least two of
his five children. As my father, he was neither patriarch nor provider.
His inner psychopathy does not appear to have been integrated, even
at the end of his life; his defenses remained intact. He intellectualized
his emotional brutality and self-focus, expressed no final insights, and
dismissed the repercussions of his treatment toward once-loved others
over his lifetime.

Reviewing the experience of Albert as my father puts me in touch
with his monumental donation to my psychic inheritance. Loving
such a father contributed vastly to my expectations and perceptions
about men and intimate relationships—and certainly influenced my
ability to accept the opposites within myself and others. To cope, I
made loving him more important than his response to me, at least
unconsciously attempting to minimize my vulnerability, protect myself,
and undermine the power of his rejection and criticism. The downside
of such a strategy is that it carries the potential danger of a parallel
psychopathic process that appears completely different but is really
another one-sided way of avoiding intimacy and genuine relationship.
There was also an upside of coping as I did with Albert's vast range
of opposites: doing so informed my capacity to tolerate ambiguity and
inconsistency, enabling me to respond to the humanity in individuals
who display callousness or even more heinous qualities.

What my father meant to me has become part of my inner identity: a familiar animus figure, to use a Jungian term, my internalized
masculine aspect. My dreams and fantasies are forever riddled with
criminals and charming charlatans, elusive and unavailable lovers, or
on darker days, more decrepit, disabled, or depraved male figures with
worse problems yet. It is no mystery why I am comfortable working
with criminal behavior and sexual disturbance, pathology, child abuse,
and forensic psychology. Although I have managed to operate relatively

unscathed in terms of my academic and professional performance, my experience of Albert impacted my psychic development.

I first heard my father referred to as *a psychopath* by my stepmothers and two of my half-siblings. Initially, I felt shocked and defensive, but I had to acknowledge that my father *was* missing something important in his soul, something that kept him, apparently, from connecting with genuine empathy, from sharing others' joys or sorrows. However, he was not violent. He did not appear cruel or emotionally callous, although his periodic, abrupt abandonment of intimate relationships throughout his life certainly suggested those qualities. On the contrary, his clever charm, magnetic wit, intelligence, and random acts of kindness engaged others. He could be warm and demonstrative. He was successful in his education and career overall, served in the military, and had no criminal record. Whatever he lacked was deep within him.

When I heard my stepmothers and half-siblings refer to Albert as a psychopath, I shuddered and felt protective of him, instantly composing a mental argument to defend him against this false, extreme accusation. Because I identified with him, I felt under attack along with him, like a secret agent among enemy forces. They apparently assumed that I was more kindred to them than like him, at least sharing their attitude about him even though we had not seen each other for decades, but in truth I felt fiercely and irrationally loyal to him. I was not really from their tribe, did not share their assumptions about him, although I had suffered some similar treatment. Some of my reasoning held up as I later reviewed my inner responses to their comments about Albert. He was not *a psychopath* in the classic sense—he did not meet most of the criteria on the psychological tools that measure the characteristic. But I also understood what they were referring to: his ability to suddenly disconnect from the most intimate and meaningful relationships in his life, to abandon his wives and children, to disappoint those with whom he had established his closest ties. He hurt a lot of people deeply— evidently without remorse.

Albert had a lifelong intermittent pattern of this kind of behavior without a backward glance or an explanation. How much awareness or intentionality there was involved, if he deliberately manipulated others . . . whether malice of forethought was part of the equation—all will remain unsolvable questions. He was much too well defended to allow such information about himself to be known to others, although I felt there were some leaks toward the end of his life. His cocky manner and dismissive attitude if questioned suggested that he thought his conduct was not only justified but superior to that of ordinary mortals, even if understandable only to him, or maybe even enhanced in worth because it reflected his unique, private set of values.

Although they were not psychological professionals, my relatives' reactions showed that their associations with the term *psychopath* had more to do with inner qualities than criminal behavior, which is consistent with my perspective. What their observations lacked was the acknowledgment that such characteristics occur on a continuum. For them, this characteristic was a defining condemnation rendering Albert's positive qualities of no interest or relevance. I must acknowledge that *part* of my enthusiasm for my conceptualization of a continuum of psychopathy that applies to us all reflects a yearning to make logical sense of the harsh reality of Albert's abandonment and to align myself with him—which I am now free to do in an unprecedented way since he died—to feel I somehow belong to and with him, that we had some special commonality, a genuine thread of deep connection.

I cannot know what motivated his callous conduct, but what I experienced with and about him suggests to me that when he felt *expected* to be responsible to someone, some inner alarm sounded, and the terror of being absorbed was more compelling than his capacity for loving compassion. At some deeper level, at some earliest time in his life, he may have felt acutely impotent; perhaps it was that his efforts to please inevitably disappointed his mother, at least in his perception, so it became his nature not to try. Any attempt on his part to accommodate a significant other, to give of himself in that fundamental way, carried for him the impalpable risk of not being sufficiently appreciated, the measure of which became a bar so high by his own design, it became impossible to attain anyway—so he would simply walk away from it, not try.

That being said, clearly one cannot live with someone for 27 years, as Albert did with his fourth wife, without some ability to accommodate. Nonetheless, another noteworthy dimension of his apparent ability to accommodate her and their marriage was the very fact that he *was* able to act the part for that long—and still walk off abruptly and forever without feeling his wife's pain and confusion. I suspect that one reason she was safe for him for such a prolonged duration was because she was not intrusive or demanding of his soul; she was an introverted, devoted intellectual type (I liked her—a lot—but also recognized that she was not needy of him or perhaps even available in that intimate way he would have found cloying). As such, she did not tap into his fear; she was mainly hugely amused and impressed by him—as were many women—but she was able to hold his interest the longest. She did not appear to demand that he be responsive/responsible to her at some deep level, which ironically may help to explain both the fact they lasted so long and the reason that he was able to leave the way he did, without her having any idea why. I suppose part of what we do to survive in a relationship with such a person as Albert is to think that, surely, he will be different with us, that we have the formula. Fortunately, many women would never even comprehend that perspective.

Albert was almost religious in his commitment to not being accountable to anyone. Terror of being absorbed, or more fundamentally, of disappointing any significant other he may have attempted to please, apparently prevented my father from accommodating any expectations and overrode any inclination he might have had to allow loving compassion to prevail.

I recognize that my need to understand my father's behavior, which I am exploring by questioning our presumptions about psychopathy, also reflects a need to validate myself. Something in me wanted to save him from himself, or more perhaps more accurately, to save him for me; he clearly did not see himself as needing to be saved. I could not justify or rationalize his hurtful behavior, but it felt important to me to try to understand it, and to view it in the context of his other positive qualities, which I knew to be equally real.

Perhaps in spite of us both, eros appeared in the end: healing love between us was evident in the final chapter of our shared lives. I will never know if that twist of fate helped him face death with hope, but it helped me—even after he was gone, I felt the healing energy of eros at work on us both in some regard.

Processing my father's essence within me now, in the aftermath of his death, generated a painful realization about his psychopathy—and my own. This reflection has stimulated and affirmed my thoughts about the trait as a human characteristic on a continuum, further inspired by the convergence of this realization with my forensic intro-duction to the concept in practice and my recognition of related ideas in my Jungian studies.

CHAPTER 5

Psychopathy and Jung's Central Concepts

P sychopathy is usually discussed as a personality disorder character-ized by a conspicuous disregard for the rights and needs of others. As I described earlier, much of what I learned initially about psychopathy was from a forensic perspective, involving judgments defined in the courtroom. Of all the psychiatric diagnoses, psychopathy viewed from this standpoint is the most legalistic, which seemed potentially at odds with my Jungian orientation. The very nature of judgment—at least in that forensic milieu—typically entails devaluing other aspects of the individual, as opposed to accepting and integrating shadow areas, which is the central point of Jungian work.

In my studies of Jungian psychology, I have come to understand the *shadow* or *shadow aspect* as referring to unconscious parts of the personality that the conscious ego denies or does not recognize as its own. These are contents we are not directly in touch with, either invol-untarily or because we want to avoid them, usually because they do not fit with our self-image or persona: the way we think we are, or want to be, perceived. Because we tend to reject or remain ignorant of the least desirable aspects of our personality, the shadow is often construed as negative. However, positive aspects can also remain hidden in the shadow. Although we are inevitably influenced by collective values, determining which personality qualities are either acceptable or unwanted is an individual matter; accordingly, so is the content of each person's shadow. Whatever the specific content, the less aware I am of my shadow areas, the more likely I am to make judgments based on rigid categories rather than genuine reflection, especially if what I am reacting to in others is an aspect of myself that I find intolerable.

The Shadow Archetype

Understanding and working with the shadow archetype is hugely important to moving toward the wholeness that is the goal, so to speak, of individuation. Jung's concept of the shadow as "the thing a person has no wish to be"[1] and "the sum of all those unpleasant qualities we like to hide"[2] fits our typical associations with psychopathy. One area of overlap between the shadow and psychopathy is the capacity for aggression. In the following text, Guggenbühl-Craig discusses some important distinctions between Jung's concept of the shadow and what is proposed here about psychopathy—and why that difference matters.

> The shadow is a complex matter comprised of different elements. Because it is a complex, it has as its basis an archetypal core, a potential for behavior with which we have probably been born, which might be designated the murderer or suicidal element, that which is in and of itself destructive. . . . Jungian psychologists assume that human nature includes an archetype which is primarily destructive. . . . It would be easy to conclude that the shadow with its destructive core and aggressive component is of central importance in the understanding of psychopathy, especially when we regard psychopaths as individuals who commit shocking and aggressive acts. However, remember that we

---

1   C. G. Jung, *The Practice of Psychotherapy. Vol. 16. The Collected Works of C. G. Jung*, 2d ed. (Princeton, NJ: Princeton University Press, 1966), 262.
2   C.G. Jung, *Two Essays on Analytical Psychology. Vol. 7. The Collected Works of C. G. Jung*, 2d ed. (Princeton, NJ: Princeton University Press, 1966), 66*n*.

have distinguished between aggression—or the instinct of self-assertion—and the shadow element of psychic destructiveness. . . . Even that archetypal core of the shadow, what we have called the ultimately destructive elements of murder and suicide, does not really have that much to do with the actual problem of psychopathy. That core we all have and worry about. . . . While the murderous and suicidal aspects may seem uncanny or even inhuman to us, they are crucial for our lives because they are linked to the psyche's creative potential . . . truly creative individuals also possess destructive sides. . . . One is tempted to conclude that a strong archetypal shadow . . . results in a high degree of creativity *when combined with an equally powerful sense of eros.* . . . What the murderer would destroy, eros would renew, and out of the admixture of the two—destruction and renewal—comes something creative, comes the Creative. Though a pronounced Archetypal Shadow is not characteristic of or determining for psychopaths, *a shadow without eros, which can wreak considerable havoc, is.*[3] (emphasis added)

This distinction between the shadow and psychopathy primarily concerns the presence or absence of eros, which is consistent with the idea that the possibility of healing psychopathy within depends upon love. As I am defining it here, psychopathy refers to that bleak zone in the psyche inherently devoid of love; if transformed by eros, it becomes something else altogether.

It seems easier—and less threatening—to detect psychopathy in others than within oneself. Particularly when I care about people, evidence of their gaps—of their moral failings—may appear strikingly obvious, unreasonable, and certainly reparable. However, my subjective observations (and any helpful suggestions) are irrelevant to

---

3   Guggenbühl-Craig, *Emptied Soul*, 136–139.

their healing, which requires personal motivation in response to the inner demands of each individual's psyche. Individual reparation at such a deep level is further stymied by the often necessary defenses we humans instinctively develop over a lifetime to guard us from the painful awareness of our unwanted inner contents.

Differentiating Definitions

We all have a shadow—that is, we all have aspects that are unconscious. Some of these aspects may overlap with what we are terming psychopathy, in that the shadow often includes characteristics we associate with heartlessness and want to avoid: those most painful areas, such as personality features we judge undesirable or acts of which we are ashamed and wish we could change. Dr. Jekyll and Mr. Hyde are classic literary embodiments of this persona–shadow dichotomy.

However, appearances can be deceiving, as the proverb goes. This is especially true with respect to our inner opposites and our shadow aspects, since the unwanted contents of our characters are as uniquely individual as we are. Everyone has a shadow, but one significant way this shadow component differs from psychopathy within is that the shadow is simply *unconscious* contents, not necessarily negative aspects or psychic gaps. In Jungian psychology, the terms shadow or shadow aspect may refer to the entirety of the personal unconscious—that is, everything of which a person is not fully conscious—or more selectively, to an unconscious aspect of the personality which the conscious ego does not recognize in itself. The parallels between psychopathy and the shadow aspects of personality or opposites within us seem obvious, since both generally describe unwanted inner material. However, *shadow* refers to the *presence* of a universal archetype to which we are all subject. *Psychopathy* refers to an *absence*—emptiness in an area of an individual's psyche, personality, or character.

Because we tend to reject or remain unconscious of the least desirable aspects of our personalities, the shadow is largely negative for most of us; psychopathy would overlap that wider category, representing psychic lacunae, absent eros, that inevitably manifest in detrimental ways. There are positive aspects that may also remain hidden in the shadow, particularly in people with low self-esteem.[4] It is an important distinction to reiterate that the Jungian term *shadow*, referring to all that lies outside the light of consciousness, can be positive or negative, which differentiates it from psychopathy. Our values about what constitutes *positive* and *negative* content are relative.

We all live in a shared collective culture at some level, yet our ego identification and our perceptions about how community values pertain to us individually vary enormously. Therefore, our struggles to reconcile splits between our persona—the face or self-image we show the world—and our shadow contents are likely to manifest differently. In other words, there are inevitable conflicts between how we think we should be seen or how we want to be seen and how we are actually perceived or truly are. However we experience our personal struggles in this regard, we are naturally inclined to emphasize and display whatever we consider our more socially acceptable qualities, although our preferences reflect our individual values and cultural identification.

For example, a hard-core convict's ego identification might be the opposite of what we consider desirable by politically correct, collective standards, although it does reflect the popular and adaptive values of his cultural milieu. His version of notoriety and status with his family and friends may be based upon his lifelong record of arrests, convictions, and incarcerations—being rebellious, wild, dangerous, or tough—although he may privately wish he had done something different with his life. He may genuinely regret having been such an unavailable husband and father—which he would stringently avoid telling any person in authority. If he begins to notice or reveal his hidden *good citizen* or *good father* aspect at all, he may quickly sabotage himself by illegal behavior or use others to remind him of his familiar

---

4   Polly Eisendrath and Terence Dawson, *The Cambridge Companion to Jung* (New York: Cambridge University Press, 1997), 319.

outlaw reputation. For example, he may display exaggerated remorse for his past and make overstated promises to his long-suffering wife, thereby setting her up to discount his sincerity and remind him of who he is ("You'll never change—I know you, you're born bad!"), so that his criminal persona is all the more insulated and reinforced. Therapy sometimes provides the only outlet for such an individual to identify and accept his prosocial shadow! In other words, the criminal might have a shadow that would characterize an upright family man, just as the upright family man might have outlaw shadow contents.

Jung called unconscious inferior personality traits the shadow, "the thing a person has no wish to be,"[5] including but not limited to "the sum of all those unpleasant qualities we like to hide."[6] I perceive the shadow as an inner realm filled with content but shrouded in darkness and the weight of negative judgment. Psychopathy, as described here, is qualitatively the opposite: It is an *absence* of content, an *absence* of judgment, a void, a gap, a lacuna.

Splinter Psyche

Psychopathy within also seems to fit Jung's description of an inferior "splinter psyche," a sliver of dreaded emptiness held in shadow. I can envision the inner psychopath as a symbol spontaneously produced by my psyche. I understand the splinter psyche to be a *complex*, a knot of unresolved content in the fabric of the personality, or in the case of psychopathy, a hole. Jung asserted that "complexes behave like independent beings . . . fundamentally there is no difference in principle between a fragmentary personality and a complex. . . . They reveal their character as *splinter psyches*."[7] Describing the inner psychopath as a splinter psyche is consistent with the idea of psychopathy on a continuum, in that it represents a more common, subtle phenomenon

---

5   Jung, *Practice of Psychotherapy*, 262.
6   Jung, *Two Essays*, 66*n*.
7   Jung, *Two Essays*, 121.

than the definitive term *psychopath* implies. Although such an aspect may be part of most of us, it usually does not dominate our functioning and, in fact, may not ever be apparent. Thus described, the inner psychopath is usually a shadow aspect of personality, in that it is unconscious and generally not an aspect one would choose to reveal or flaunt, but the shadow is a far broader category. The shadow has many varied manifestations, not all of them unpleasant; not all of them are psychopathic or devoid of love. One of the most fascinating dimensions of shadow material is this versatility—that it is primarily defined by *whatever* we remain unconscious of, rather than the value we assign to specific contents. Working with criminals has heightened my awareness that we certainly do not all share the same ideas about what is valuable or what should remain hidden.

In addition to Jung's profound concepts of *shadow* and an *inferior* or *splinter psyche,* his sage ideas about *anima* and *animus,* the two contrasexual archetypal aspects in the unconscious, are of rich significance to a Jungian perspective on psychopathy.

Psychopathy and the Inner Masculine and Feminine Aspects of Personality

My forensic therapy cases as well as my private therapy work continued to inspire my curiosity about the meaning of psychopathy, my burgeoning sense of my own gaps, and the ways in which they corresponded to my father's psychopathy and our relationship. I imagined that the potential for healing inner psychopathy required understanding it, integrating it, and somehow finding love in the equation: a reconciliation of opposite inner contents. I found some Jungian concepts especially helpful in understanding this notion, including Jung's ideas about the contrasexual aspects of personality in males and females: the anima and animus.

Psychopathy can be perceived as a *masculine* process in Jungian terms, because it is generally revealed as a discriminating, defining function that somehow directs actions in the world. This is in contrast with a *feminine* process (creative, diffuse, and more about simply *being* than *doing*), with the important side note that we all contain both masculine and feminine aspects. Psychopathy is represented differently in each sex, in terms of an inner process—one that can be evident in both sexes, to be sure, but in different ways.

Jung's concepts of *anima* and *animus*, the two contrasexual archetypal aspects in the unconscious, helped me to envision and understand how inner psychopathy might appear in both sexes. As Jungian analyst John Sanford states in *Invisible Partners*, "The most important contribution Jung makes in his concepts of the anima and animus is to give us an idea of the polarity that exists within each of us."[8]

Jung's Concepts of Anima and Animus

Jung identified the anima as being the unconscious archetypal feminine component in men and the animus as the unconscious archetypal masculine component in women. I have always best understood the *anima* as a man's relationship to his feelings and his access to the fertile unconscious, through which he can tap his creativity, and the *animus* as a function in women that focuses and directs actions, allowing them to achieve goals in the world. Both sexes express these elements primarily through relationship with each other.

Post-Jungian writers have reformulated the concepts of anima and animus as they apply to consciousness and gender, suggesting that every person has both an anima and an animus. There are at least two generally accepted contemporary interpretations of the anima and animus. The first argues that anima and animus archetypes exist in the psyches of both genders.[9] The second posits that the contrasexual is the

---

8   John A. Sanford, *The Invisible Partners: How the Male and Female in Each of Us Affects Our Relationships* (New York: Paulist Press, 1980), 112.

9   James Hillman, "Anima II." *Spring*, Volume 20 (1974): 113–146; see also Hillman's *Anima: An Anatomy of a Personified Notion* (Woodstock, CT: Spring Publications), 1985.

least developed "other" (that which is different within us), whether or not the individual is male or female.[10]

Jung's original way of defining these terms provides the primary frame of reference for the purposes of this writing. Summed up briefly, this is the standpoint that there are essential masculine and feminine principles unrelated to social and cultural norms, sexual orientations, or lifestyles. For this discussion, the fundamentally relevant concept is that how psychopathy manifests and is displayed by males and females may differ in terms of psyche, personality, and behavior.

The more a man is in touch with his own feminine element, the more he can handle his feelings and the less he needs his girlfriend, wife, or partner to carry all that feeling material for both of them. The healthier the masculine energy in a woman, the better equipped she is to succeed in the outer world—to focus, organize, and express her creative ideas tangibly. Usually, the animus of girls is activated and shaped by their father, when the father is part of the household. If the father was absent, as in my case, a girl's animus might be activated and shaped by her perceived image of him or by her mother's animus. For example, my mother had a reasonably well-developed animus herself, somehow, which contributed to some healthy aspects of my masculine function; my mother taught me, as best she could, how to succeed in the world.

Jung focused more on the male's anima and wrote less about the female's animus (his longtime student and then colleague, Marie-Louise von Franz, undertook a thorough exploration of the animus).[11] The anima tends to appear as a relatively singular female personality, but she manifests in different stages. Jung believed anima development has four distinct levels, captured by the names of archetypal female

---

10 Andrew Samuels, *Jung and the Post-Jungians* (New York: Routledge & Kegan Paul, 1985); Ann Belford Ulanov and Barry Ulanov, *Transforming Sexuality: The Archetypal World of Anima and Animus* (Boston: Shambhala, 1994).

11 Marie-Louise von Franz, *Archetypal Dimensions of the Psyche* (Boston: Shambhala, 1999).

symbols: *Eve, Helen, Mary,* and *Sophia.* The names speak volumes through our automatic associations. *Eve* represents instinct and sexuality, *Helen* personifies beauty and the soul, the *Virgin Mary* suggests the possibility of relationship with God, and *Sophia* embodies the principle of relationship to the highest wisdom.[12]

The process of anima development in a male manifests as an increased receptivity to feelings, which in turn enables broader intuitive processes, creativity, imagination, spirituality, and psychic sensitivity. Akin to the presence or absence of eros, *receptivity to feelings*—or its absence—is central to inner psychopathy as defined here. My father's behavior clearly illustrated this dynamic in the apparent absence of any receptivity to feelings—a psychopathic gap.

Jungian analyst Toni Wolff, Jung's close collaborator, made a study of personality types in women somewhat parallel to Jung's depiction of the anima levels. She termed her four types *maternal, hetaira, amazon,* and *mediumistic.*[13] Jungian Irene Claremont de Castillejo provides a beautiful description of these four feminine personality types in *Knowing Woman.*[14] In brief, the maternal or motherly type is caretaking, and sees the man foremost as father to her children. The hetaira is nearly opposite; she is a man's companion, unlikely to have or prioritize children, and essentially bases her identity on male approval. The amazon is a warrior: independent, self-contained, and focused on her own achievement, although she may have male partners and children. The mediumistic woman's primary role is that of mediator, in some ways comparable to a shaman. I visualize the physical appearances of these feminine personality types to help me understand and remember them. In modern form, the mother might be a large-breasted sweetheart; the hetaira might be a boyish-looking seductress who appears barely

---

12 Ibid, p. 68.
13 Toni Wolff, *Structural Forms of the Feminine Psyche* (Zürich: Students Association, C. G. Jung Institute, 1956).
14 Irene Claremont de Castillo, *Knowing Woman: A Feminine Psychology* (Boston: Shambhala, 1973).

adolescent but exudes a histrionic, flattering energy; the amazon might be Xena the warrior princess; and the mediator would be a powerful sorceress, perhaps Angelina Jolie.

These are broad-stroke personality types by which women can be classified. Jung described his anima levels; Wolff and Claremont de Castillejo described four broad personality types or categories of actual women. These four characterological types can also be seen as anima images in men.

Men tend to gravitate to a particular anima image consistent with their level of psychic development, although I have never met a man whose anima appeared neatly, consistently confined to one category.

To illustrate how these archetypal images might manifest in an individual, I envision my father's predominant anima as a mother type whose unconditional love he was never able to feel, whose approval he sought forever but could never safely experience. Histrionics and amazons would have scared him, and he had no admitted spiritual dimension. He found refuge in well-educated, intellectual women who radiated a maternal-style glee in response to his shenanigans—mother figures whose signature quality was responding to him with unadulterated adulation. He captivated these women, which delighted him, especially when they laughed at his jokes or blushed when he was deliberately outrageous. He gravitated to females who were caretaking of him and cautiously effusive in their acknowledgment of his charm and intellect. He sneered at overt displays of emotion, so his most successful partners tended to be doting but not excessively so. At least in some respects, his anima image also had definite hetaira energy: He encouraged—even demanded—that his partners base their identities on his approval, and he wanted to maintain center stage. Although three of his five wives bore him children, he did not share his wives' enduring devotion to them.

Jung viewed the animus as being more complex than the anima, postulating that women have a host of animus images, whereas the male anima consists of only one dominant image. Unlike a man's anima, the animus, Jung believed, may consist of a conjunction of multiple (male) personalities.[15] Jung conceived of four parallel levels of animus development in a female. This quartet can be roughly depicted as the athlete, the hero, the scholar, and the sage, reflecting the personification of (1) physical power, (2) the romantic figure who possesses initiative and takes action, (3) intellect, and (4) meaning and spiritual profundity.

To further illustrate how these archetypal images might manifest in an individual, as a teen and young adult, I identified with my athlete animus by seeking relationships with male athletes, perhaps hoping that this external representation of physical prowess would offer me the protection and mastery I needed and lacked. My hero animus was unconscious for a long time, and when he emerged, represented in a relationship, I had difficulty recognizing him; he did not appear as I had pictured him, which was rare anyway. As for the scholar animus, my father was an intellectual, and his real-life presence created an inner template that was grandiose and impossible to locate, either within me or in a relationship. My sage animus made occasional—although deeply impactful—appearances, evident when my own innate wisdom was activated through a relationship or experience.

Beyond this quartet of archetypal animus images—the athlete, the hero, the scholar, and the sage—I envision one of my animus aspects as the inner psychopath, mirroring my father's intellectual austerity and abandonment, but by turning it inward rather than acting it out. Usually, this was a self-contained dynamic that resulted primarily in my own suffering as I, in effect, abandoned myself, tolerating situations that ended up hurting me. At other times, my inability to consciously integrate my thoughts and feelings and respond authentically in connection with a partner caused others pain as well, but there was no callousness in my experience of those incidents—if anything, I was

---

15 Jung, *Man and His Symbols*, 194.

tortured by them. My father may have been able to dismiss or rationalize the pain he caused others; I am the opposite. Even the thought of perpetrating another's pain is agonizing to me; I have no choice but to acknowledge and accept responsibility for hurting others, if I do. I suspect my father figured that he was fundamentally *not* responsible for anyone else's suffering—a blanket alibi he generalized to a grandiose philosophy about life and the nature of humanity. Although my inner psychopathy did not manifest as deliberate conduct toward others, I occasionally experienced it as a numbness or puzzling disconnection between my feelings, intellect, and will in the context of relationships with men.

A man's relationship with his anima, or the female anima figures in his life, is akin to his relationship with his own feelings. One way to understand psychopathy is in terms of a disconnection from the feminine aspect within: the anima. For a man, as his anima is the path of connection with the self or soul, his anima is his source of relationship on every level. The soul is seen as an essentially feminine aspect of human existence, carrying the ability to bridge unconscious and conscious experience: the gateway to the transcendent function, bringing unconscious material to light.

A male might experience psychopathy through his anima, his inner feminine, when he is emotionally disconnected or tortured by his true feelings. If his psychopathy is inner-directed, he might be self-rejecting, withdrawn, or addiction prone. When a man's psychopathic character aspect is outer-directed, it often shows up as a shadow projection; his inner weakness manifests by projecting inferiority onto others, presenting a barrier to genuine or satisfying emotional experience. This psychopathic character quality is likely to be expressed through insensitivity to others, especially females, manifesting in various kinds of abuse or neglect toward partners— relationships in which a man is narcissistic and chauvinistic, needing constant reassurance that he is in control of his partner to protect himself from experiencing the emptiness of his actual lack of control and absence of emotional connection.

Generally speaking, a woman's connection to the unconscious, the wellspring of her feelings, is innate, spontaneous. Her psychopathy within may appear as a gap or lacuna, a disruption of this natural connection; her own feminine aspect may be wounded and inaccessible. Or she may have problems with her animus, her inner masculine aspect, so her inner psychopathy may affect her functioning in the world.

A female's psychopathy as expressed through her animus, her masculine function that directs her actions in the world, may be projected outward such that she chooses men who take advantage of her and violate her in one way or another. An abusive male partner may enact her psychopathic animus. She may be consistently involved in relationships in which she is victimized or at least dominated and directed. If unaware of this complex or process, she may find herself unconsciously drawn toward involvement with psychopaths—an arrangement destined to be frustrating, unsatisfactory, and even dangerous. Or she may enter relationships with individuals who constellate and trigger her own acting out of psychopathic qualities, giving her apparent justification to be heartless, cruel, or insensitive. Consequently, she may become a perpetrator against men, victimizing them through emotional manipulation, seduction, or violence. This pattern reflects her inability to develop those qualities associated with positive masculine energy in the world, which she needs to guide her and help her to find meaning and direction for her natural creative inclinations—a lack that can cause her to make important life choices that are self-defeating or worse.

Masculine and feminine energies work together. Both are indispensable in different ways. Masculine energy is associated with consciousness, definition, and direction, providing form and expression to unconscious material, to the feminine. Michelangelo's statement comes to mind: "Every block of stone has a statue inside it and it is the task of the sculptor to discover it."[16] Following that analogy, the feminine is the stone, and the masculine is the sculptor who finds the image of the statue within the stone. Claremont de Castillejo provides my favorite depiction of this dynamic in *Knowing Woman*: an illustration of a woman holding a candle with beams that light up a canvas in the corner of a dark room. The candle and its beams represent the male energy needed to illuminate the treasures she holds in diffuse awareness but cannot see without that guidance and focus.[17]

We naturally seek to actualize both masculine and feminine aspects within us. When that actualization process is impeded or inadequate, for whatever reason, we suffer as individuals and in relationships. One way to describe such a gap in our functioning is in terms of *inner psychopathy*. Life generally offers us opportunities to notice and heal these gaps, if only we learn to recognize those opportunities and gather the courage to consciously invite change—or at least accept it, even when it arrives unsolicited.

---

16 Michelangelo, *BrainyQuote.com*. Retrieved August 18, 2014, from http://www.brainy-quote.com/quotes/quotes/m/michelange386296.html.
17 Claremont de Castillo, *Knowing Woman*, 84, 85.

CHAPTER 6

Psychopathy as an Archetypal Concept

The magnitude of psychopathy extends beyond a random personality trait to a dimension of human existence that is archetypal in scope. Psychopathy belongs to the constellation of Jungian concepts fundamental to understanding wholeness, including persona, ego, self, and shadow archetypes. For example, the distancing dynamic inherent in psychopathy, whereby an individual is unavailable for genuine relationship at a deep level and cannot really be known by others, might be described in Jungian terms as an overidentification with the persona, the first topic of this chapter.

Overidentification with the Persona

Originally the word *persona* meant a mask worn by actors to indicate the role they played. This definition suggests a protective covering and possibly an asset when mixing with other people—and only a feigned individuality.

In Jung's words, "The persona is that which in reality one is not, but which oneself as well as others think one is."[1]

---

1   C. G. Jung, "Concerning Rebirth." In *The Archetypes and the Collective Unconscious. Vol. 9i. The Collected Works of C. G. Jung*, 2d ed. (Princeton, NJ: Princeton University Press, 1990/1959), par. 221.

The persona is the mask reflecting the values and preferences of the ego, while unwanted characteristics or shadow aspects are typically projected onto others—especially one's most significant other(s). As Jung (1970) states: "Any man who becomes one with his persona can cheerfully let all disturbances manifest themselves through his wife without her noticing it, though she pays for her self-sacrifice with . . . neurosis."[2] Such an arrangement in close relationships suggests a form of abandonment of the self, obscured by the appearance of a partnership, different from true intimacy. This dynamic is common and might even be viewed as archetypal.

Archetypes are prototypical patterns of behavior that we perceive via universal symbols representing unconscious psychic contents—instinctive patterns or ways of behaving. Guggenbühl-Craig described archetypes as "an inborn pattern of behavior in a classical, typically human situation."[3] Because psychopathy is an archetypal concept, the psychopath as an archetype is not bound to any particular population, group, or culture, but represents a timeless aspect of human character and existence. Individuals who manifest overt or extreme psychopathy can be considered identified with that archetype.

Someone with a psychopathic, disconnected approach to living might not have the experience of passionate conviction about anything, other than ideas or goals based upon external responses and superficial reinforcements. Such a character is likely to spout a barrage of projections disguised as personal opinions and reactions, which can have the quality of mimicking a personality without any real substance. An example of this often hidden dynamic and its potential hazards occurs when high-functioning, ostensibly successful people seek treatment during a midlife crisis, maybe even following a shocking suicide attempt, reporting that despite all of their impressive accomplishments,

---

2   Jung, *Two Essays*, 194.
3   Guggenbühl-Craig, *Emptied Soul*, 7.

they have a vague sense of meaninglessness, the world lacks color, their lives feel flat, and their relationships are boring.[4] This symptomatology might be understood as an aspect of such an individual's experience carrying a *complex*, a knot of unconscious feelings and beliefs that has a powerful influence on perceptions and behaviors—in this case, an *archetypal psychopathic* representation in the psyche.

Although there is a mass of content in the feelings and beliefs that constitute a complex—not a gap, per se—we might *experience* such an unconscious pod of psychopathy as inner numbness or emptiness. When we are in the grip of a complex, we may be unaware of why we act the way we do. The psychopathic archetype might manifest by our losing track of (or disregarding) who we are at the core.

Jung's concepts of the ego, persona, self, and certainly the shadow archetype are tremendously important in understanding the archetypal drive toward wholeness. One way I visualize the interplay of these is to think in terms of a road trip: If the car represents my life journey, my ego is the driver, my persona is the face I show the policeman who stops me for speeding, and the self/soul/psyche is the whole map. The shadow might be the backseat driver I barely glimpse in the rear-view mirror, but who nonetheless continually directs—or undermines—my navigation. Jung's writing on this topic was prolific and eloquent. One condensed snippet gives a minuscule peek at his colossal vision:

> By ego I understand a complex of ideas which constitutes the centre of my field of consciousness and appears to possess a high degree of continuity and identity. Hence I also speak of an *ego-complex* . . . a psychic element is conscious to me only in so far as it is related to my ego-complex. But inasmuch as the ego is only the centre of my field of consciousness, it is not identical with the totality of my psyche, being merely one complex among other complexes. . . . The ego is only the

---

4   Guggenbühl-Craig, *Emptied Soul*, 126.

subject of my consciousness, while the self is the subject of my total psyche, which also includes the unconscious.[5]

For Jung, the individual ego complex exists not only relative to other complexes within the psyche but draws its stability and growth from a larger, more complete sense of human *wholeness* that is archetypal in base and scope.

Wholeness, the Self, and Individuation

Guggenbühl-Craig's description of psychopathy as a gap in the psyche, as "lacunae—empty places—where each and every one of us is lacking in something,"[6] conjures an image of inner blank spaces, of being unwhole in some regard. If wholeness were understood as a state in which the conscious and unconscious domains of a person work together in harmony, being unwhole would suggest a poor working relationship between the two—an inner communication breakdown. Although "wholeness" seems to be only an abstract, neutral idea, it has rich objective meaning at the level of the psyche, where it is symbolized in spontaneous or autonomous forms, such as the quaternity or mandala symbols to which Jung often referred and which he painted often (see *The Red Book*).[7] These symbols appear not only in the dreams of modern people who have never heard of them but have been ever-present throughout time and across world cultures. Their significance as symbols of unity and totality is amply confirmed by history as well as by empirical psychology.[8] Wholeness, as I use the term here, pertains to Jung's idea of it in terms of individuation, where the goal is a vital connection with the self, inner opposites included. I began to explore the connection between this perception

---

5   C. G. Jung, *Psychological Types. Vol. 6. The Collected Works of C. G. Jung*, 2d ed. (Princeton, NJ: Princeton University Press, 1976/1971), 425.
6   Guggenbühl-Craig, *Emptied Soul*, 79.
7   C. G. Jung, *The Red Book: Liber Novus* (New York: The Philemon Foundation & W. W. Norton & Co., 2009).
8   Jung, *Aion*, 31.

of being unwhole and my dawning understanding of psychopathy as a parallel concept.

I perceive psychopathy as a unique symptom indicating the disconnection of a soul from its source, a kind of psychic breach that results in unrecognized suffering, leaving that aspect of the individual's personality unmoored. Eros—love in the sense of psychic relatedness—involves the spontaneous, deep-rooted urge to connect and thus holds the potential for healing psychopathy. This eros yearning might also be described as the innate desire for wholeness, yielding the satisfaction of relating with others on a deeply feeling level. The absence of that innate desire is psychopathic, like an inner gap.

Jung called the archetype of wholeness the *self* and noted that it functions as a supraordinate, organizing principle of psychic individuality.[9] The self in Jungian theory signifies the coherent, whole, unified conscious and unconscious domains of a person—the totality of the psyche. Jung wrote:

> As an empirical concept, the self designates the whole range of psychic phenomena in [us] . . . the unity of the personality as a whole . . . only in part conscious . . . a transcendental concept, for it presupposes the existence of unconscious factors on empirical grounds and thus characterizes an entity that can be described only in part but, for the other part, remains at present unknowable and illimitable.[10]

In Jungian theory, the self is the primary archetype, larger than life as we know it. The idea of the self bridges our unique, time-bound personal essence with our inborn connection to eternity. According to Jung, an overarching purpose of human existence is individuation, which in his view is the process of integrating the various aspects of

---

9   Robert H. Hopke, *A Guided Tour of The Collected Works of C. G. Jung* (Boston: Shambhala), 96.
10   Jung, *Aion*, 460.

one's personality and becoming a fully differentiated individual.[11] This endeavor is an ongoing one that represents the work of a lifetime, whether or not one consciously accepts the proposition.[12]

Individuation might be described as the goal of the self, about which one can discover clues through an array of symbols. Impersonal symbols for the self in dreams or images include circles, mandalas, crystals, and stones. Personal symbols include a royal couple, a divine child, or other manifestations of divinity. Great spiritual teachers, such as Buddha, Christ, Krishna, and Mohammed, are also symbols of the self that represent a wealth of meanings: wholeness, unification, the reconciliation of polarities, and dynamic equilibrium—the goals of the individuation process.[13]

Our personas, the values and preferences of the ego, require our attention and are vital to thriving in the world, and yet overly identifying with the persona, while ignoring or failing to perceive the nudgings and callings of the larger self, amounts to an inner abandonment that is a form of psychopathy. Most of us lived from our personas at least through our young-adult years, even if we were not morally weak (as defined by society, culture, religion, or the courtroom) or in danger of hurting anyone other than ourselves for the lack of deep inner connection. Nonetheless, many of us engaged in conduct that we learned, over time, did not satisfy us, and even caused us suffering at a soul level, the suffering of an unseen self whose urgings were eclipsed by persona needs. Growing out of the persona identification is also a normal developmental phase, so being ruled by it in those early years is not necessarily an indicator of a character weakness but a natural part of development. Such a phase is not uncommon or pathological as much as adaptive, and yet the feelings of inadequacy

---

11 Jung, *Aion*, 448.
12 Joseph L. Henderson, "Ancient Myths and Modern Man." In *Man and His Symbols*, ed. C. G. Jung (London: Pan Books), 120.
13 Edward Edinger, *The Aion Lectures* (Toronto: Inner City Books, 1996).

that are often associated with that mercifully temporary transitional period—if we are fortunate—may be understood as a kind of inferiority complex within.

Fears of Inadequacy and the Psychopathic Process

Jung (1968) described the underlying essence of an inferiority complex in the form of a tormenting inner aspect, a dimension of the personality that may catch our attention as a clinical symptom, but it is also something in "each of us" that shows up as

> . . . exaggerated claims. . . . irritable self-assertiveness. . . . We know from experience that such a symptom is due to unadmitted feelings of inferiority, i.e., to a real failing of which one is usually unconscious. In each of us there is a pitiless judge who makes us feel guilty even if we are not conscious of having done anything wrong. Although we do not know what it is, it is as though it were known somewhere.[14]

This inner critical propensity suggests a psychopathic process, a missing link deep within the psyche that leaves us feeling vaguely incomplete and unworthy. Jung's reference to the pitiless judge in "each of us" infers that the dynamic represents a universal, fundamentally human characteristic that is present in us all—in degrees. This fundamentally human characteristic suggests a collective unconscious motif of guilt and worry about being found inadequate by blaming ourselves and our perceived failures. This unconscious sense of inadequacy may be experienced in a diffused, vague way or in a pervasive manner.

I can usually find logic to rationalize this kind of uncomfortable feeling in myself, so that it seems finite, knowable, and most importantly, reasonable. I attribute my sense of unworthiness to deficits,

---

14 C. G. Jung, *Alchemical Studies. Vol. 13. The Collected Works of C. G. Jung*, 2d ed. (Princeton, NJ: Princeton University Press, 1942), 128.

misfortunes, errors in judgment or conduct, and ways I believe I fall short—but if pressed, I must admit that this unworthiness actually hails from a moonscape nether region in my psyche, far removed from the day-to-day reality of my circumstances and behavior. I then develop compensations and defenses to further insulate me. The powerful, destructive self-attributions of the inner critic may take the form of unspoken—or even unconscious—conditional clauses to justify a sense of being unwhole, without identifying the gap deep within that needs healing: *If only I* (. . . had been born into a different family, gone to a different school, married/not married, had a smaller nose, bigger breasts, more money, ad infinitum), *then I would be worthy and valid*. The self-attributions of the inner critic may be perceived and expressed relatively directly, or manifest indirectly through an inflated sense of self-worth, grandiosity to mask the fragile ego, as in narcissism. With regard to Albert, for example, there was no obvious evidence that he ever suffered from a conscious feeling of inferiority. On the contrary, his psychopathic gaps included an inability to perceive his own flaws and subjectivities. Healing this inner lacking—akin to what I am proposing constitutes a form of psychopathy—first necessitates illuminating it.

Psychopathy as an indicator of a psychic inferiority complex may manifest in psychopathic conduct or in disturbed relationships with others, but as Jung (1966) states, whatever the manifestation . . .

> the sense of moral inferiority always indicates that the missing element is something which, to judge by this feeling about it, really ought not to be missing, or which could be made conscious if only one took sufficient trouble. The moral inferiority does not come from a collision with the generally accepted . . . arbitrary moral law, but from the conflict with one's own self which, for reasons of psychic equilibrium, demands that the deficit be redressed. When-ever a sense of moral inferiority appears, it indicates not

only a need to assimilate an unconscious component, but also the possibility of such assimilation."[15]

Seeking the self—inviting archetypal wholeness into our experience, fundamental to our individuation—inevitably involves recognizing and accepting the very different aspects of our existence, including our darkest corners where love is absent: our psychopathy within. Our common struggle to contain the opposite aspects of human existence within and between us suggests a shared birthright far beyond the scope of our individual experiences: the presence of a greater universal order to which we all belong. This perspective is related to Jung's profound ideas about *synchronicity* and the *collective unconscious*.

Synchronicity

Synchronicity applies to all aspects of our existence as a principle of connection whereby all things, within us and in the world, are related and somehow relevant to a greater whole, like a vast, invisible, multidimensional web. This principle can free us to view even the most difficult of our experiences through a broad lens, suggesting the potential to find some kind of order and meaning in life circum- stances—even aspects of ourselves—that we would much rather avoid, an observation that is valuable as it relates to understanding psychop- athy. The concept of synchronicity describes a governing dynamic that underlies the whole of human experience and history, including social, emotional, psychological, and spiritual dimensions. Simply put, concurrent events may first appear to be coincidental but later turn out to be acausally related. Jung believed that this acausal connection suggested the manifestation of meaningful parallel events or circum- stances, reflecting this governing dynamic.

Events linked by synchronicity are connected via similarity and meaning, rather than by obvious linear sources of causality.

---

15 Jung, *Alchemical Studies*, 273.

Synchronicity permeates our life matrix and everything in it—art, science, and a sort of atypical theology, veering toward quantum physics. As an *acausal connecting principle*, synchronicity steps outside the Western scientific notion of locally based cause-and-effect relationships, per Newtonian physics, and goes beyond the bounds of time and space.

Synchronistic events are *simultaneous occurrences that are meaningfully related*, with an inherent logic that is not literal, chronological, or causal in nature. For example, thinking of a friend with whom you have lost contact for several years and then receiving an unexpected phone call from that friend moments later is a synchronistic experience. Synchronistic events offer us perceptions that may be useful in our psychological and spiritual growth and may reveal to us, through intuitive knowledge, how our lives have meaning and sources of interconnection we could never fathom from a purely rational level—or at least make life more interesting.[16]

Here is another example: A friend of mine was scheduled for exploratory surgery due to unexplained fluid around one lung and a definite mass showing on a CT scan. The medical professionals around her at this time all thought that the mass was a cancerous growth. A few days prior to the surgery, my friend received an email from another friend of hers, who was then in England, saying that, after pondering what the mass could be that was not cancer, came up with "an aspirated seed" (she knew that my friend ate seeds and nuts as a source of protein). The very night before the surgery, my friend was distracting herself with the television show *Grey's Anatomy*, which she had been watching for a month, starting with Season 1. By this time, she had seen countless subplots of medical issues. That night, of all nights, one of the subplots involved a man with fluid around the lung and a mass, whose surgery revealed an aspirated seed, literally!

---

16 Jean Shinoda Bolen, *The Tao of Psychology: Synchronicity and the Self*, 2d ed. (New York: HarperCollins, 2004), 7.

In preop the next morning, my friend lightheartedly told the surgeon to "stay on the lookout for an aspirated seed." He laughed, indulgently. Following the surgery, the surgeon emerged to report that indeed it appeared to be "an aspirated food particle of some kind," which was confirmed one week later by the pathology report.

The concept of synchronicity denotes an abstract, intangible relationship between minds and ideas, yet when it is experienced as my friend did, in the above example, it is anything but intangible. Synchronistic events reveal an underlying pattern, a conceptual framework or matrix that includes any of the systems that display the synchronicity. This larger framework is fundamental to the definition of synchronicity as originally conceived by Jung. Although this idea is tremendously complex, it has a much simpler, common-sense analogy—reflected in homespun adages such as "Things have a way of working out" or "Things happen for a reason."

Synchronicity is the term Jung chose to denote *meaningful coincidence*, what he called "temporally coincident occurrences of acausal events." Jung variously described synchronicity as an "acausal connecting principle," a "meaningful coincidence," and an "acausal parallelism." He introduced the concept in the 1920s but only gave a full statement of it nearly 30 years later, in 1951, at his last Eranos Foundation lecture, and in a 1952 paper—"Synchronizität als ein Prinzip akausaler Zusammenhänge" ("Synchronicity: An Acausal Connecting Principle"), published in a volume with a related study by the Nobel laureate physicist Wolfgang Pauli. Pauli bridged the gap between science and theology: he was an Austrian theoretical physicist and one of the pioneers of quantum physics—who was also referred to as a mystic!

According to Jung, life is not a series of random events but rather an expression of a deeper order, which he and Pauli referred to as *Unus Mundus* (Latin, one world). This perspective led them to the insights that each individual is both embedded in an orderly framework and the focus of it. This realization was more than an intellectual exercise for Jung; it also contained elements of a kind of spiritual awakening for him. Synchronicity shares characteristics of what might be referred to in theological terms as *divine intervention* or *grace*. Jung also believed that synchronicity served a similar role to dreams in an individual's life, with the purpose of shifting one's egocentric conscious thinking to greater wholeness.[17] The concept of greater wholeness is relevant to our exploration of psychopathy: Awareness of synchronicity can help us perceive our inner gaps, and those of others, with grace and perspective. The larger perspective that synchronicity provides can act as a container, a *temenos*, for our discoveries.

Evidence of synchronicity at work may be subtle and symbolic. In his book *Synchronicity* (1952), Jung tells the following classic story of a synchronistic event, which has become a template for what he meant by the term:

> A young woman I was treating had, at a critical moment, a dream in which she was given a golden scarab. While she was telling me this dream, I sat with my back to the closed window. Suddenly I heard a noise behind me, like a gentle tapping. I turned round and saw a flying insect knocking against the window-pane from the outside. I opened the window and caught the creature in the air as it flew in. It was the nearest analogy to a golden scarab one finds in our latitudes, a scarabaeid beetle, the common rose-chafer (*Cetonia aurata*), which, contrary to its usual habits had evidently felt the urge to get into a dark room at this particular moment. I must admit that nothing like it ever happened to me before or since.[18]

---

17 C. G. Jung, *The Structure and Dynamics of the Psyche. Vol. 16. The Collected Works of C. G. Jung*, 2d ed. (Princeton, NJ: Princeton University Press, 1981/1960), 421–504.
18 C. G. Jung, *Structure*, 438.

One of Jung's favorite quotes on the concept comes from *Through the Looking-Glass* by Lewis Carroll and exemplifies how understanding synchronicity involves questioning our ordinary assumptions about chronology and logic. Understanding psychopathy from a new perspective also requires questioning comfortable assumptions about who we are inside (gaps included) and about our lives, as they unfold in the apparently unreasonable way they often do. The White Queen's dialogue with Alice delightfully epitomizes this potentially liberating perspective, with the comment, "It's a poor sort of memory that only works backwards."[19]

> "The rule is, jam to-morrow and jam yesterday—but never jam to-day."
>
> "It MUST come sometimes to 'jam to-day,'" Alice objected.
>
> "No, it can't," said the Queen. "It's jam every OTHER day: to-day isn't any OTHER day, you know."
>
> "I don't understand you,'" said Alice. "It's dreadfully confusing!"
>
> "That's the effect of living backwards," the Queen said kindly: "it always makes one a little giddy at first—"
>
> "Living backwards!" Alice repeated in great astonishment. "I never heard of such a thing!"
>
> "—but there's one great advantage in it, that one's memory works both ways."
>
> "I'm sure MINE only works one way!" Alice remarked. "I can't remember things before they happen."

---

19 Lecture notes, Jung Foundation, New York City, 1980s. Available online at wikipedia. org/wiki/synchronicity.

"It's a poor sort of memory that only works backwards,"
the Queen remarked.[20]

Loosening our expectations regarding chronological time,
meaning, value, perception, significant others, and the circumstances
of our lives, although disconcerting, enables us to step back and marvel
at our personal journeys with less attachment to our plans and preconceived notions about outcomes. Most of us have asked ourselves "Why
me?" regarding life events and realities, or even "Why am I like that?"
about our own conduct on occasion. It is easy to feel betrayed by life.
Guilt, pressure, and self-blame interfere with our ability to face life
with courage and objectivity: the idea of meaningful coincidence can
help to liberate us by offering a broader perspective to make sense of
our lives—anyway.

Our inner psychopathy and our experiences of such aspects in
significant others—those psychic gaps absent eros—are an essential
part of the totality of our lives. For example, would I have been the way
I am, had the life I have, if not for Albert—the whole of him? Change
one thread in the tapestry, and the whole design is altered. My experience of Albert as my father, in combination with my personality, set
me up in a special way to expect, tolerate, and navigate a world that is
inconsistent and unfair. Like so many things, this has been both a curse
and a blessing. Jung's concept of synchronicity helps me to accept and
even treasure the precious, mysterious weaving of my unique history,
instrumental in helping me to find some needed meaning and purpose
therein—gaps, gifts, and all: to recognize that life is not a series of
random events but rather an expression of a deeper order.

The idea of synchronicity empowers me to accept and to put
into perspective the mysterious script of my life story, with all of its
colorful characters, plot twists, and unexpected resolutions. The
concept of synchronicity, of meaningful co-occurrence, can unlock

---

20 Lewis Carroll, *Through the Looking-Glass* (Kingsport, TN: Kingsport Press, 1946), 217, 218.

understanding—even of our bitterest realities—and can help make sense of the psychopathy within and around us, when our pressing needs for reason, control, and fairness are unmet. Synchronicity cannot be engineered, only discovered, so it challenges our ideas about logic and predictable outcomes. As an example, I once visited a training program in which I was interested and was surprised when I saw a painting on a flyer in the library that remarkably resembled a wise and beloved friend who had been a powerful influence in my life, until he died. I readily interpreted this sighting as a sign that I was in the right place and applied to the program. When my application was rejected, I felt devastated, hollow, and misled. Years later, however, I realized that my contact with the program had indirectly led me down a path that served my individuation, after all—although not in the form or time frame I had expected. Recognizing synchronicity takes flexibility and patience, neither of which came naturally to me, but eventually I was able to perceive the synchronicity of this whole experience, which filled me with restorative hope, although the healing process required relinquishing my preconceived ideas about what I thought I wanted and deserved.

The concept of meaningful coincidence provides a frame for understanding and offers healing hope, when one's innate need for order and logical consequences is frustrated. Synchronicity is also a principle that Jung felt gave conclusive evidence for his key concepts of the archetypes and the collective unconscious. Human nature embodies some timeless essence that is intimate and yet impersonal, alive in our souls always, even without conscious invitation. Therein we are all beyond judgment—equal and ignorant. Jung's signature concept of the *collective unconscious* epitomizes this unifying theme:

> In addition to our immediate consciousness, which is of a thoroughly personal nature and which we believe to be the only empirical psyche . . . there exists a second psychic system of a collective, universal, and impersonal nature which is

identical in all individuals. This collective unconscious does not develop individually but is inherited.[21]

Even my father, who perceived most kinds of belonging—certainly anything remotely theological—as an intrusive threat akin to the *devouring mother*, acknowledged this idea of a greater universal order (*his* idea of God) at the end of his life, although he was careful to specify that this realization was on his own terms, as it pertained uniquely to him. The idea of such a great universal web to which we all belong seemed to me analogous to Jung's concept of the collective unconscious, which, under the circumstances, I perceived as a bridge that might help salvage the gaps in Albert's psyche, his psychopathy, through a sort of impersonal but loving connection—as close as he was likely to get to acknowledging a sense of spirituality or faith in something greater than himself—a kind of psychic adhesive. I took some satisfaction in this grudging admission that Albert was connected to the rest of humanity, whether he liked it or not, perhaps also because this affirmed that, by extension, so was I.

Reminders and clues about this synchronistic, unconscious dimension of our existence, fortunately, are available to us all unsolicited, immediately accessible, and priceless, in the world of our own dreams and in the myths and fairy tales from cultures around the world. Jung's awareness of this *expansive universe of equanimity* seems fundamental to his life's work. No wonder his contributions survive him into perpetuity, continuing to deeply impact such a broad range of individuals worldwide, his ideas proliferating anew. When I was at the Küsnacht C. G. Jung Institute, there was a huge poster-sized photo of him hanging on the wall in one of the training rooms, and some student had planted a large pink kiss-mark on his cheek—which might have been considered flippant (Swiss-style graffiti), but actually captured some essence of his magnetic energy in that special place. This man, his philosophical

---

21 C. G. Jung, *The Archetypes and the Collective Unconscious. Vol. 9i. The Collected Works of C. G. Jung*, 2d ed. (Princeton, NJ: Princeton University Press, 1990/1959), 43.

brilliance, his prophetic writing, and his broad-scale eros continue to inspire the lives of so many disparate souls everywhere with his immortal ideas, venerated by self-proclaimed or officially certified "Jungians" along with a host of other random seekers. Canadian writer Robertson Davies provides a telling poetic description of Jung as "that old fantastical duke of dark corners."[22]

Certainly, our inner psychopathy resides in one of those dark corners.

---

22 Robertson Davies, *The Deptford Trilogy* (New York: Penguin Books, 1990), 176.

CHAPTER 7

Psychopathy as Lacunae: My Inner Psychopathy

Throughout history, humankind has struggled to define and understand human diversity: the contrasts within us and the reasons individuals and groups differ from each other. Psychiatric circles in the 19th and 20th centuries conceptualized human nature as an interactive accumulation of various abilities and capabilities, which might be developed to greater or lesser degrees, provided one was born with them; particular characteristics or abilities might, in effect, be missing from birth. Guggenbühl-Craig described this phenomenon in terms of his psychopathic gap theory: "These absent . . . traits were . . . labeled lacunae, 'unoccupied rooms in the house of the psyche.'. . . Following this analogy . . . those areas which were uninhabited or uninhabitable, the deserts, barren areas, or lacunae would represent psychopathies."[1]

This problem of lacunae—something inherently missing in an individual—seems to reflect a kind of disconnection with the soul, an absence of inner continuity, or simply a primitive relationship with one's unconscious processes. An extreme example of an individual suffering in this way might be someone who leads a superficial existence, experiencing life almost exclusively in terms of the external object world—as

---

1   Guggenbühl-Craig, *Emptied Soul*, op. cit., p. 77.

though the person has no self. This problem may be evident to degrees, in any number of ways, not only in terms of a full-blown personality disorder or an obviously cutoff approach to life, but also by abandoning the self in more subtle ways, by the most fundamental form of betrayal: unavailability to one's deepest being, one's innermost truth. This is one way to understand inner psychopathy: as turning a blind eye to the self. Modern popular psychology refers to a related dynamic as *living a lie* in terms of our chosen career, significant relationships, or even the values and priorities that have guided our lives: an unconscious conflict that poses a struggle between growth and destructiveness within us. Struggles notwithstanding, we humans are innately predisposed to grow, to heal, to seek wholeness. While a certain amount of self-deception may be necessary for self-protection, "Fooling yourself can have devastating consequences, especially in the domains of money, career, sexual identity, and relationships,"[2] as a recent article in *Psychology Today* stated.

The abandoned self is the product of a disconnection between ego consciousness and psyche or soul, and the consequences of this disconnection can be expressed through acts of commission or omission: various forms of injury or sabotage that may include lack of compassion for others or self-inflicted abuse. Tormented psychological or emotional processes typically become projected outward as well, appearing as the torturing of others—psychologically, emotionally, or even physically. Such overt behaviors fit our typical understanding of psychopathy, which may also be present in ways that are far subtler and internalized.

Guggenbühl-Craig's conception of psychopathy as *lacunae*, gaps in the self that lack eros or love, resonates deeply for me, so again I provide an example of my own experience here as illustration. His description opened a door to a part of my psyche, onto a whole world of understanding: rich, nourishing, and anchoring. The image that captures Guggenbühl-Craig's notion of psychopathy for me is that of

---

2   McGowan, Kat. "Living a Lie." *Psychology Today* 46/Issue 1 (2013), pp. 78–84.

an unexpected rabbit hole, into which one catapults in the middle of a flat, ungraded green lawn. That image of falling into a rabbit hole fit my sense of psychopathy within, conveying my own experience of being so very functional in most ways, and then running across areas within myself, unseen by others, that felt completely out of character, and left me feeling mysteriously numb or out of touch. I usually experienced these sudden rabbit holes in interpersonal relationships with men. I easily grasped the shape and content of our interaction, could readily accommodate what was wanted to please the other person, but had to stretch to locate the deeper personal meaning and implications of my behavior or his, and when I did so, there was often an intellectual quality to my understanding, as though disconnected from feeling.

Personal stories, though illustrative, cannot be assumed to be universally representative or applicable. Such literal generalization is not realistic, nor is it universally human to want to tunnel the dark, empty gaps within to work toward healing. As I was developing my ideas about an expanded definition of psychopathy, all I really knew with conviction was that it was fundamentally important—not even a choice—for me. I had no solid evidence for a broader-based theory, despite longing to rationalize one. I had to admit that my father never seemed similarly motivated, never seemed to consciously struggle with unrest in his soul: That unrest was mine.

My Inner Psychopathy

I identify my inner psychopathy by the psychic wounds I suffered as a result of my father's abandonment and his emotional unavailability even when I had contact with him. I was aware of his callousness in his other significant relationships, including with my mother, half-siblings, and stepmothers, which put me in a double bind: I knew such behavior was wrong, but I yearned to align with him somehow, to create a connection, at least in my mind. To feel close to him I convinced myself that I understood and accepted behavior I actually perceived as undeniably hurtful. I identified with him—at a cost to my own integrity and wholeness of character.

By the time I was in elementary school, I already knew Albert had deserted three marriages, two of them with children involved, including me. Although I had no obvious barometer of the meaning and implications of Albert's behavioral history other than my own inner reaction, a veiled heartache, I did have environmental cues that were collective rather than personal. My mother's commentary on Albert was extremely rare and intellectualized, typically focused upon how he would have been difficult for a child to grow up with anyway (which was probably true). Her underlying message was that he was dispensable, and thus we were better off without him. Still and anyway, somewhere in my hidden heart, I really needed my father.

This was the era of the TV family sitcoms, featuring the middle American father archetypes of the early 1960s in series such as *Father Knows Best, Leave It to Beaver, Ozzie and Harriet,* and *The Patty Duke Show,* presenting a cultural ideal that made a tremendously strong impression on me that was all the more enticing given the utter unattainability of this perfect fantasy, even for those whose lifestyles much more closely approximated the image than did mine. It was obvious to me that if these role models were appealingly "normal," they were also radically different from what I knew of my father—polar opposite, in fact—so the values disparity between that life and mine was dramatic. I needed to somehow reconcile these polar opposites.

My father's abandonment of his wives and children most of all made me sad. If there was anger, I could not access it consciously. Conceiving of my father as simply heartless and myself as a helpless victim was too painful. I had to protect him in order to protect myself. There had to be more to the story. Besides, he was also charming, brilliant, and talented. So much of him was a mystery. I had to withhold judgment. Thus there was no way for me to hold Albert accountable for his behavior. Blaming him would not bring him closer. Demonizing him felt worse than trying to accept and understand the whole of him, as best I could imagine it by piecing together what I knew and had heard.

The choice to try and contain this dichotomy was innate, because I loved my father irrationally and unconditionally. Although the constancy of my devotion to Albert, unearned by him, was a testimony to the healing power of love, it also inevitably affected my expectations about men and relationships: I responded to men with a combination of indiscriminate glorification and distrust, coupled with the tendency to disregard obvious character problems and my own true judgment about them. This mixed bag of responses netted a capacity to love so selflessly that I could—and did, on occasion—get lost somewhere in the process. Given my personality, I also became prone to tolerating a broad spectrum of humanity, a tendency that has proven both misleading and helpful. The challenge to accept and integrate the opposites within myself and others thus became instrumental to my life's work from an early age. The loveless void of my father's absence was the origin of my own inner psychopathy—although that darkness also held the potential for healing within me and in my work with others.

A personal example of my experience with this problem of lacunae, gaps in the self that lack eros or love, was a relationship I had when I was 22 years old. I became involved with a college football player and found out months into our affair that he had been lying to me about his residence and was actually living (some of the time) with another girlfriend and their baby. When I realized the situation, my first, true reaction—stinging sadness and outrage—was so fleeting I could barely feel it before it became inaccessible. Instead, I was rapidly flooded with determination to demonstrate that I could handle this upsetting news; I would stand by him tenaciously, prove my loyalty unswerving. Without consciously intending to, I managed to distract us both by comforting and reassuring him, instead of acknowledging or exposing my vulnerability, disappointment, and pain—or my justifiable anger. He was surprised and delighted, and only months later, after he moved in with me and then carelessly broke my refrigerator, did the relationship end. At that point, my Swedish practicality could no longer be squelched; I firmly demanded that he pay for the damaged appliance to be repaired. He was taken aback by the sudden emergence of a normal reaction to his maltreatment and acted outraged, but complied, though never to return.

I felt as though I had my life back, strangely relieved, like awakening from a lucid dream. In the aftermath, as I reflected upon what had transpired, I found myself confused that I had allowed this somewhat torturous relationship to endure over a prolonged period without my usual level of reason and assertiveness—where had those aspects of my personality gone? I could readily access my hurt about the loss of this physically attractive partner. However, there was an intangible numbness, like a gap in my usual consciousness, about having tolerated this intolerable situation for so long; at least intellectually I was unavoidably aware of how problematic the relationship had been all along. At a feeling level I suffered an equally atypical inner response, as though somewhat desensitized to the ongoing maltreatment I had experienced. I felt sadness, but in retrospect, although I perceived logically that some justifiable outrage was warranted, in that regard, I felt nothing.

When I accommodated a partner whose behavior or treatment I found unacceptable, it was because I could not bring myself to respond truthfully, as though my intellect was adrift somewhere, separated from my feelings—or at least my passion—and my will was disarmed. I was vaguely conscious of a deep-seated terror that if I allowed either of us to know my true negative feelings, they would threaten the loss of an invaluable love. Perhaps at an even more unconscious level I also worried that disclosing how I really felt might actually succeed in bringing me closer to this partner, whom I innately distrusted, even disliked in some aspects. Nonetheless, I was inextricably hooked on the conscious priority of unconditionally preserving our relationship (just as I unconditionally loved my father!), although doing so compromised my sense of integrity. I regretted this cost, but in a weird, paralyzed way I felt impotent to choose otherwise and protect myself, as though something deep within me had gone missing. This kind of paralyzed and seemingly submissive behavior was markedly different from my solid functioning in other areas, and known only to me. Such an experience was like temporarily losing myself in a partnership I was never really available for, because I was out of touch with myself—deep in the rabbit hole of my own lacunae, my inner psychopathy.

This was the only area where I struggled to be conscious of my own intuition, which otherwise came naturally. I know now that this blind spot had everything to do with my experience of my father. Deep in my psyche I had internalized his abandonment of me, where I replayed that story of emptiness and all the compensations I developed to cope, as I *continued to abandon myself* when my life experiences triggered associations with my original loss of Albert. Recognizing this application of Guggenbühl-Craig's definition of psychopathy to my inner process was both liberating and unsettling, and reinforced my curiosity to learn more about the possible broader meaning of the term. My own experience illuminated a telling nuance of this expanded definition: *psychopathy as a phenomenon that manifested within, where no one else was hurt by it*; unlike my father, in my case, the primary victim of my disconnected behavior—my inner psychopathy—was myself.

CHAPTER 8

Guggenbühl-Craig's Symptoms of Psychopathy

Guggenbühl-Craig's insights about the character traits, symptoms, and implications of psychopathy as psychic *lacunae* are luminary, along with his recognition of the potential for healing it through love/eros, which brings depth and meaning to our attempts to live with conscience. He describes the relevance of these ideas about psychopathy for humanity, within the context of analysis and universally, far beyond the parameters of a therapeutic setting.

> No analysis is finished until we clearly recognize our empty or at least half-empty spaces—our inner deserts. And this applies to the endeavors to know oneself, because most of the search to recognize and see oneself and others, to become conscious, happens with people who have never heard of analysis.[1]

My studies of psychopathy, my forensic experiences, and my formative father experiences have coalesced into ideas about the topic that resonate with Guggenbühl-Craig's. This resonance is the basis for my focus upon his ideas here, although some of his terminology and specific references, admittedly, no longer correlate with our modern

---

1   Guggenbühl-Craig, *Emptied Soul*, xi.

culture. Fundamentally germane and relevant, however, is Guggenbühl-Craig's message that we all have lacunae: empty or inconsistent places in our psychic composition. He pioneered the concept of a broadly applicable definition of psychopathic character traits, rather than qualifying these aspects in terms of the all-or-nothing presence or absence of diagnostic criteria. He described five primary symptoms of psychopathy, although they are neither generic nor absolute: inability to love, deficient morality, absence of psychic development, depression, and fear.[2]

Inability to Love

First among these symptoms of psychopathy is the inability to love, the lack of true attachment—although the *performance* may be fully present. This inability is not to be confused with a deficit in the feeling function, which in Jungian terms is one of the four ways by which one perceives and evaluates the environment: through thinking, feeling, intuition, and sensation. We can experience the world with any of these functions (typically, one is primary), independent of the presence or absence of *eros*, love. Furthermore, love can be expressed through any of the functions. Feeling is often mistaken for love, which overlooks the fact that relationships involve more than emotional responsivity. Feelings are a broad, deep experience of value orientations and convictions, often forming the basis for judging people or situations. Frequently, we limit our understanding and experience of love to interpersonal relations and then confuse love with feelings.

Love also binds the elements of the intrapsychic world. As a force, love affects the connection between elements in our psyches, between our complexes, as Jung described our deep, unresolved, stuck issues in the development of self and relationship. Such developmental problems with love, or a lack thereof, at the psychic level may be evidenced in

---

2   Guggenbühl-Craig, *Emptied Soul.*

dreams, through dream characters that represent actual problematic relationships in the individual's life or through archetypes: innate behavioral patterns in the psyche. The lack of love, or the relative inability to love, in psychopaths, often manifests in relationship difficulties; rather than love, there may be manipulation or superficial stimulation. An individual with pronounced psychopathy may be distracted by personal appetites at the expense of pursuits that fulfill true desire and destiny. Jung said that when love retreats, power advances—and power is of signal importance in individuals acting upon psychopathic tendencies. Where love is absent, manipulation, control, and domination—strategies to gain power—are apt to take over.[3]

Deficient Morality

A second primary symptom of psychopathy is a missing or deficient sense of morality, a lack of moral foundation.[4] Defining morality, and therefore grasping the implications of its absence, can be elusive because the concept is ultimately a subjective construct with numerous cultural and religious permutations. The Judeo-Christian framework is a basic foundation for this collective culture's morality, and it is the larger pool from whence Freud derived his views. Morality based upon Freud's model is connected to the *super-ego*, itself the result of internalizing parental images that form the precursors of conscience. Jungian psychology regards morality from differing points of view. Guggenbühl-Craig provides the perspective that each archetype has a morality of its own, so an individual's behavior would depend on the operant archetype in his or her personality and life situation. For example, Aphrodite, the lover, would operate from different guiding principles than Hermes, the merchant and mediator.[5]

---

3   Guggenbühl-Craig, *Emptied Soul*, 92.
4   Guggenbühl-Craig, *Emptied Soul*.
5   Guggenbühl-Craig, *Emptied Soul*, 96.

Guggenbühl-Craig describes another Jungian perspective regarding morality as the expression of a divine spark in each of us. This type of morality, in its profound sense, emphasizes and prioritizes whatever contributes to individuation, the process of self-realization.[6] The Jungian ideal of individuation is deeply rooted in the alchemical imagery of the transformation of lead into gold and involves becoming conscious of and integrating the shadow traits (i.e., the lead) of character as development proceeds to maturity (i.e., the gold). This process unfolds not through elimination but through illumination (i.e., insight, consciousness).

In a related perspective to these ideas about morality, psychiatrist and Jungian analyst John Beebe suggests that *integrity* can be understood as the self's willingness to be responsible and accountable for its impact on others, as "a connection with ourselves that permits an ethical connection to everything else in the universe."[7] This willingness and accountability is what individuates in deep psychotherapeutic work on the self, meaning the psyche or soul.[8] Beebe describes the concept of integrity as a psychological notion, in which one's own pockets of shame and anxiety can actually be gifts of guidance. In an interview discussing his book, *Integrity in Depth*, Beebe stated:

> My real goal in this book was to discuss integrity, as nearly as I can tell, for the first time in such an extended presentation as a psychological concept rather than just a moral concept. We have always been taught that integrity is standing up for what you believe, and keeping your agreements, and being principled in your behavior. What I say in this book is that integrity is essentially a willing sensitivity to the needs of the whole, and it's not enough just to defend one's particular part, but that one has to take into account the whole. . . . When you

6   Guggenbühl-Craig, *Emptied Soul*, 96–97.
7   John Beebe, *Integrity in Depth* (New York: Fromm Psychology, 1992), 32.
8   Ibid, 19.

take responsibility for the functioning of all of these [aspects] within yourself, and admit that they are all part of you rather than splitting them into those that you like, and those that you don't like, and disowning the fact that you are always acting and behaving, and that there is a whole world for which you have to take your rightful share of responsibility. That seems to me really what integrity is.[9]

Integrity, defined this way, is guided by the process of becoming whole, which involves accepting the opposites within and between us, rather than by an imposed morality. As Jung reputedly stated, "I'd rather be whole than good."[10] And a moment for Emerson: "Nothing is at last sacred but the integrity of your own mind. Absolve you to yourself, and you shall have the suffrage of the world."

The development of integrity enables an individual to embrace and contain personal limitations of character that *belong to the human condition*: a form of broad, genuine acceptance, with a touch of eros. This view of morality may pose problems, since acts injurious to oneself or others could be rationalized in the name of the divine individuation process. Any definition of morality inevitably contains contradictions and loopholes. The key principle here appears to be not *self*, but *eros*, caring, the ability to love altogether. Love anchors us, making us responsible to the best in ourselves and in each other. Unless our behavior is guided by love, attempts to live in accordance with a superimposed morality are likely to be unsatisfactory or at least rigid and superficial. The *ego* has more to do with our common understanding of morality than the *self*, for the definition of self involves a higher and wider level of consciousness, beyond the inevitable confines of our collective social order.

---

9   John Beebe interview, "A Jungian Analyst Talks about Psychological Types: John Beebe" (Midland, Oregon: Inner Growth Books and Videos), www.innerexplorations.com/catpsy/a.htm.

10   Richard Smoley, *Forbidden Faith: The Secret History of Gnosticism* (New York: HarperCollins, 2006), 122.

The shadow aspect of a psychopath will naturally express itself as the opposite and may manifest as an extreme, compensatory persona that *appears* to be highly moral: the religious zealot, for example. On the contrary, an individual who appears to be functioning as an obvious psychopath may have shadow areas of intact morality or the capacity to develop them. The individual who functions as a model citizen may have as a shadow aspect the criminal, the child molester, or the murderer. The career criminal who lives seemingly without ethics may have the kindhearted family man as a shadow aspect. This shadow side may show up in dreams or in unexpected lapses in typical behavior or communication. Psychopaths are characteristically glib and charming, and are often certainly capable of speaking about morality, as well as defending, teaching, or even fiercely advocating for it. The difference between this display and the real thing, however, is that the psychopath is able to do so while attaching little or no significance to it personally. Needless to say, this type of hypocrisy is not confined to clinical or criminal populations.

Individuals approaching the psychopathic extreme are not totally devoid of morality, perforce, but they often sense a weakness in themselves, an awareness that something is missing in their experience of life, which can be privately frightening to them. They may suspect that their capacity to give and receive love is not all that it could or should be.[11] To adapt, they often begin to compensate for these deficiencies by becoming morally rigid. Since compensated psychopaths of this order cannot depend on eros—on love—their egos work out a moral system that appears impenetrable across situations. The result, paradoxically, is usually an airtight appearance of heightened morality and obedience with an emphasis upon the ego's role, but the "moral" behavior is lacking in substance and devoid of love.

---

11 Guggenbühl-Craig, *Emptied Soul*, 130.

Compensated psychopaths are likely to be both convincing and sinister, since the appearance of rigid conscientiousness prevails flawlessly, irrespective of the task at hand and disconnected from conscience. An example of this profile would be a man with a strong sense of duty in the complete absence of eros: Adolf Eichmann, the German Nazi official whose duty it was to direct the extermination of Europe's Jewish population.[12] A more current example would be American swindler Bernie Madoff, who pleaded guilty in 2009 to 11 federal felonies, having defrauded thousands of investors of billions of dollars. He was also—and most visibly—a family man and a noted philanthropist, who supported many worthy causes, donated to charities, and "generously" supported cultural, educational, and religious organizations.

Many individuals with pronounced psychopathy adapt readily in daily life, functioning effectively enough as spouses, professionals, and in other roles, but they play these roles without any real personal involvement. A psychopathic father, for example, may molest his daughter, not because he is particularly attracted to her, but just because his wife is gone and his daughter is available. Similar kinds of emotionally detached behavior have been observed in those suffering from brain damage due to chronic alcohol abuse. One way to describe this phenomenon of emotional detachment is in terms of an absent eros. Specifically, the lack of morality in psychopaths can be attributed to a lack of eros. Psychopaths can comprehend morality intellectually and can even imitate it convincingly, but morality has no genuine meaning for them because it does not include eros. Only love can bring authenticity and substance to our attempts to live with conscience.

Whether or not we believe humans to be innately good, some kind of prevailing positive energy moves us toward the perpetuation of life: *lux ex tenebrarum,* light out of darkness. After all, the human race continues to survive somehow, generation after generation, despite all

---

12 Guggenbühl-Craig, *Emptied Soul,* 132.

of its foibles. This inevitability thus far, anyway, is often contingent upon the triumph of attributes such as truth, honesty, and caring for others over deceit, victimization, or maltreatment. A similar idea is contained in Shakespeare's pithy phrase "the truth will out"—a universal, timeless concept. Specifically, in Shakespeare's *The Merchant of Venice,* Launcelot proclaims: " . . . truth will come to light; murder cannot be hid long; a man's son may, but at the length truth will out."

Laurens van der Post, Jung's eloquent friend and colleague, illustrated this concept in his description of a tribal people in the interior of Africa who believed that there was "no secret so small that nature sooner or later would not extract it." Van der Post tells of a member of this tribe who committed a murder unobserved in a dark wood, only to have a small bird track him all the way home, despite his futile attempts to kill it, loudly announcing his crime until finally all in the village heard the news he had tried so desperately to conceal.[13] Van der Post draws parallels between the symbolic message of this phenomenon and how the murder in Shakespeare's *Macbeth* comes to light, the truth mysteriously broadcast in the inanimate surroundings of this very different setting, but similarly, in a way that cannot be explained rationally: "Stones have been known to move and trees to speak."[14] This kind of sovereign conscience is not volitionally moral; it manifests the miracle of *earth wisdom,* fundamental to human existence and survival. Such a prevailing, life-affirming energy seems akin to the spirit of eros, an unconditional guiding love that holds the potential to heal our psychopathy, or at least alert us to its presence, whether or not we seek that guidance or choose to heed it.

More modern examples of this dynamic might be clandestine affairs or surreptitious office crimes that are revealed or wreak havoc with the participants in unpredictable or "coincidental" ways, resulting in an odd kind of random justice. The married woman having a secret

---

13 Laurens van der Post, *Jung and the Story of Our Time* (New York: Vintage Books, 1975), 117.
14 Ibid., 118.

affair has an unplanned pregnancy, or the office manager who has been stealing from the business writes a check to herself and forges the boss' signature, as she has many times before, but unwittingly drops it in the parking lot right by his car, where he spots it. Another manifestation of this phenomenon is the development of physical infirmities that somehow parallel a psychic process: somatic symptoms such as a sudden onset of laryngitis, for example, right before a scheduled long-distance telephone conference to seal an illegal deal, or before a public speaking engagement one would rather avoid but feels obligated to deliver.

It would be easier to draw predictable conclusions about right, wrong, and fair if true morality were as concrete and definitive as our laws are, but instead it is fluid and relative. Sometimes *bad* things happen to *good* people, sometimes good people do bad things, and vice versa. History and literature are replete with familiar examples—consider Robin Hood. An individual with pronounced psychopathy is unable to comprehend true morality from any inner locus because the person lacks the eros that would provide a connection to that source of guidance from within.

Absence of Psychic Development

A third primary symptom of psychopathy is the absence of any psychic development. For diagnostic purposes, this is practical and recognizable; as a symptom, it is troubling. This characteristic may be expressed by stagnation. We may note the torpor in an acquaintance who, over years, does not seem to change; in working with a patient who has no sense of inner process; or in a marriage where nothing develops over time, no intimacy, only repetition and role playing. Rather than a deepening integration and maturity, the psychopath exhibits a pseudodevelopment manifested by adaptation to external situations usually involving a facile implementation of different roles.

This absence of genuine development may also express itself in dreams; the psychopath's dreams may contain little or no change in content over years, as though the soul, or psyche, were static. Nothing changes with psychopaths; at best they grow tired, and problem behaviors may diminish, not due to insight or awareness but to a gradual lessening of libido. Psychopaths experience a stuck quality within, a lack of connection with the self, and in relationships with others over time.[15]

The lack of psychic growth and development, like a lack of morality, can be understood as resulting from a weak or absent sense of eros. An individual who is not drawn to something in life with genuine commitment and enthusiasm may lack a means to inspire any inner connection to an active psychic process. Related to the lack of development in psychopaths is their fear of typical initiation rituals in our culture: those rites symbolizing the transition from one life phase to another. For example, the psychopath may avoid marriage or dismiss it as meaningless, unable to deal with the transition from single to married life, even if unaware of the implications of the change on any deeper level. Incapable of experiencing psychological development, the psychopathic individual may regard any ritual that formalizes such development with fear and rejection.[16]

Depression

The fourth of Guggenbühl-Craig's primary symptoms of psychopathy is background depression—although this contention is controversial, since the *inability* to grieve or experience true sadness has been identified in much of the existing forensic and popular literature as characteristic of psychopathy and even central to it. This disparity in perspectives may also reflect significant differences between the populations examined by modern criminal forensic researchers such as Hare (representing the *inability* theory) and Guggenbühl-Craig—in addition to a multitude of other contrasts. Guggenbühl-Craig's work is, of course, decades old

---

15 Guggenbühl-Craig, *Emptied Soul*, 105–106.
16 Ibid., 108–109.

and derived from a very small, homogeneous Swiss population. My intent here is not to juxtapose Hare's methodological and widespread work with Guggenbühl-Craig's theorizing. As discussed in Chapter 2, although modern forensic psychiatrist William Martens emphasizes the psychopath's hidden emotional suffering and vulnerability, his perspective is not representative of the field of psychology these days, whereas Hare's theory about the psychopath as callously indifferent and emotionally apathetic, is.[17]

Bearing in mind the preceding, consider Guggenbühl-Craig's description of the psychopath's underlying depression: "Psychopaths are isolated. . . . Their sense of eros . . . is impaired. Somehow they feel that they lack a quality that moves and guides other human beings, which accounts for their understandably chronic sadness as well as their chronic mistrustfulness."[18] Such an individual feels isolated, unwhole in some regard, and unable to experience relatedness to others—fertile ground for chronic feelings of sadness, mistrust, and emptiness: an underlying depression, as such, characteristic of psychopathy. Guggen-bühl-Craig posits:

> This background depression . . . frequently results in suicides of a nature which appear inexplicable to an outside observer . . . The individual's life just seems to be taking on some semblance of order when with no warning, suicide occurs. *Where Eros is absent, where there is no growth, no psychological devel-opment, there is no meaning and no reason for living.*[19] (emphasis added)

The life of the psychopath may appear orderly and successful, with no signs of criminal behavior. Such well-adapted psychopaths may commit what Guggenbühl-Craig describes as *social suicide*. They

---

17 Martens, "Hidden Suffering."
18 Guggenbuhl Craig, Emptied Soul, p. 111.
19 Ibid., 113.

may become high achievers only to sabotage or "destroy every-thing they have achieved through a thoughtless act or provocative behavior."[20] For example, one of my therapy clients was a wealthy businessman with no criminal record whose life took a breathtaking tailspin when he was arrested for stealing mail—for reasons even he did not understand. He made an unsuccessful suicide attempt and was subsequently sent to federal prison. Years later he entered treatment, where he began developing some awareness of his inner opposites and rebuilding his life, although there remain aspects of his lifelong achievements he cannot recoup. Among a myriad of other adjustments, he must now redefine success in order to cope with the radical consequences of his self-sabotaging behavior.

These examples are not provided to suggest that all suicidal depression is psychopathic, or that whenever individuals inexplicably sabotage their lives in other ways, psychopathy is necessarily the reason—although it may be a factor. Nor are all psychopathic indi-viduals depressed; certainly those on the extreme end of the scale are unlikely to care enough to be. However, the emotional isolation, lack of genuine feeling connection to others, and inability to find meaning in life associated with psychopathy are also characteristic of chronic depression. The premise of this writing—the idea of a gradated defi-nition of psychopathy—means that the presence of psychopathy does not necessarily lead to a complete absence of feelings or to ubiquitous callousness and emotional isolation. Guggenbühl-Craig's hypothesis about depression as a characteristic of psychopathy can be best under-stood and useful in light of this alternative definition.

Fear

A fifth primary symptom of psychopathy, according to Guggen-bühl-Craig, is chronic background fear. At some level, a psychopath

---

20 Ibid., 113.

does not trust the world. Unfamiliar with the eros within, this individual is subsequently unable to identify eros in others, except abstractly. Even behavior that is clearly eros-directed, such as expressions of genuine love or generosity, may seem suspect or meaningless to the psychopath—who is likely to assume that others must have an ulterior motive for acts of kindness or grace, since behavior directed by this kind of love is beyond the scope of such an individual's personal experience. This fear is different from neurotic anxiety. In situations of actual danger, the psychopath is likely to experience less fear than the average person. The characteristic psychopathic form of fear Guggenbühl-Craig describes is generalized, subtle, and pervasive—thinly veiled with a guarded exterior.

Secondary Symptoms

In addition to these five primary symptoms, Guggenbühl-Craig describes several secondary symptoms, "those which, though not found in every psychopath, characterize the various types of the disorder."[21] These secondary symptoms include:

1. An absence of guilt feelings.

2. An absence of any real depth of understanding or emotional insight, despite possibly having high intelligence.

3. The ability to evoke pity, which psychopaths may use to manipulate for sexual gain, in a histrionic manner, engaging others to save them.

4. Charm, often with the appearance of bewitching others.

5. Asocial or criminal behavior.

6. Boredom or deep apathy.

---

21 Ibid., 117

7. Social climbing, often as a compensation (i.e., because psychopaths cannot relate through love, they relate through power).

At variance with our central theme of a gradated definition of psychopathy, these characteristic symptoms are listed above in a manner that may sound as though they pertain only to those whom we consider to *be* psychopaths, in whom psychopathy is primary or pronounced. However, it is the premise of this writing that not all psychopaths exhibit all of these symptoms, and many individuals who do not even approach diagnostic criteria for psychopathy exhibit some of them, or may have these qualities at an unconscious level, contained within their shadow, for example. Consistent with Guggenbühl-Craig's perception of psychopathy as an *aspect of personality* common to the human condition, to varying degrees, the symptoms of psychopathy noted above may also be understood accordingly: on a continuum.

CHAPTER 9

Psychopathy and Eros

Guggenbühl-Craig described psychopathy as the absence of eros and wrote about the problems that arise from psychopathy when living without love's guidance.[1] He stated: "To experience eros is to be rooted. Eros binds to the specific and the particular, to family, to social class, culture, people, language, and nation. Lacking eros one has no connection, one levitates above the world, one has no roots."[2] Guggenbühl-Craig further described this lack of rootedness—of emotional depth or integrity—as due to a disconnection from the archetype of love, and noted that it not only results in shallow, thoughtless behavior, but also explains the subsequent lack of remorse in favor of a smooth exterior, akin to the callousness we typically equate with psychopathy. As Guggenbühl-Craig explained:

> The presence of eros makes life difficult for people. . . . Eros
> means caring, and if someone cares for whatever or whoever
> it may be, worries, nervousness, and even neurotic tensions
> can be the result. Loving persons are seldom cool and relaxed,
> but people suffering from a deficient eros are unconcerned
> and so do not worry; often they are very relaxed and easy-

---

1   Guggenbühl-Craig, *Emptied Soul*, viii–ix.
2   Ibid., 127.

going. . . . Relationships . . . [are] things of the moment. . . .
Their motto seems to be, "out of sight, out of mind."[3]

Such individuals seduce others into caring for them rather than
actually experiencing any deeper, relational process within. Allowing
themselves to genuinely relate with another and be impacted by
that connection, if conceivable at all, would be experienced as an
unwanted, threatening development. When these disturbed individuals find a loving person to carry their rejected feeling function,
they only succeed in objectifying themselves. They cannot really be
known; there is no genuine interchange. This dire-sounding outcome
represents an extreme example of a psychopathic personality type.

The concept of eros, as used here, is love defined in the sense of
psychic relatedness: that is, the essential drive for genuine interaction with
others; the spontaneous, deep-rooted urge to connect; and the innate
desire for wholeness that enables one to experience the satisfaction
of relating with others on a deeply feeling level. Eros encompasses a
broader, richer range of meaning than our overused term, *love*.

Jung considers eros to be a feminine principle, the counterpart
to logos, a masculine principle of rationality: "Woman's psychology
is founded on the principle of *Eros*, the great binder and loosener,
whereas from ancient times the ruling principle ascribed to man is
Logos. The concept of *Eros* could be expressed in modern terms as
psychic relatedness, and that of *Logos* as objective interest."[4] Jung
suggests that eros is ultimately the desire for wholeness. Although eros
may take the form of passionate love, with which we tend to associate
it, it is more essentially a desire for interconnection and interaction.

Love helps us to live in a genuine way and to develop a sense of
responsibility and attachment. Psychopathic or sociopathic individuals,
as described by Cleckley et al. (1988) and others, appear unable to

---

3   Ibid., viii–ix, 41.
4   C. G. Jung, *Aspects of the Feminine* (Princeton, NJ: Princeton University Press, 1982), 65.

distinguish adequately between their own superficial mimicking of compassionate intentions, remorse, and love, and the genuine responses of a "normal" person. According to that model, this oblivion allows them to deliberately cheat others while being fully conscious of their own lies, and yet experience no real regret. Such individuals are often capable of compartmentalizing different aspects of their lives or relationships to an extent that enables them to behave in contradictory ways without experiencing inner conflict. Thus apparently blocked from eros at deep levels, the psychopath is able to pursue the fulfillment of personal needs at whatever cost—without the filter of moral sensitivity or compassion. As a consequence, weak impulses and fleeting gratifications may produce impulsive, damaging behavior.

Problems arising from an absence of eros are surely not uniformly pathological, as suggested by an understanding of psychopathy as a characterological trait on a continuum. Being human generally entails confronting challenges involving love and morality. Considering the less extreme manifestations of obvious psychopathy means that the concept and its definition apply to many more of us than those relatively few at the far end of the spectrum. I have known any number of individuals who have lied, compartmentalized aspects of their lives, or behaved in contradictory ways, but whom I would not consider—and who certainly do not consider themselves—to belong to a special pathological category. Rather, I would say that these individuals struggled with morality at certain times in their lives, even as they manifested strengths in many other areas.

Turning to examples from personal experience to illustrate this struggle, young men and women I knew in college were seduced by temporary partners with shallow motives, who manipulated them into brief sexual encounters under the guise of "love." Such behavior was callous, self-focused, and probably reflected fears about true intimacy, but it was also situational and developmental rather than reflective of intrinsic pathology. A few of them went on to behave accordingly for much longer, which *does* suggest pathology—but most did not.

My relationship with my father offers another example of eros problems. Did Albert belong to that special pathological category, the psychopathic group chronically lacking eros? Jung's description of love as eros does correspond to my understanding of the missing dimension in Albert and in our relationship. We loved each other, but there was never a sense of deep-rooted relatedness. In addition to feeling the unreliability, the inconsistency of his love for me personally (although it was like warm sunshine when he made it available), the impression I have from his life story, as much as I know it, is that he did seem to have an impaired capacity for loving connection. I have no way of knowing the extent to which he deliberately lied, cheated, or hurt others and ignored these actions without regret or inner conflict, or if his callousness was relatively unconscious. I see some parallels between Albert and this special pathological category but remain troubled by an all-or-nothing verdict. Part of my resistance to this definitive categorization is that in addition to his obvious characterological problems, I am convinced of the many significant ways in which he did *not* fit the profile of a psychopath—as his daughter, this latter reality is particularly important. A less personal reason for my resistance to the notion of a special group lacking eros—beyond whether Albert qualified for it—is that it diametrically opposes the continuum concept of psychopathy.

Instead of pertaining to only a finite classification of noxious individuals we can avoid if we are lucky, the broader interpretation of *psychopathy* yields more universally relevant meaning—with implications for increasing our understanding of the problem and beyond that, the potential for healing it. How might we assimilate this unconscious component of moral inferiority? How might we heal inner psychopathy? The premise that psychopathy is the absence of eros also suggests that the missing archetype holds the potential for restoration. Accordingly, once psychopathy within is illuminated by awareness, there is the possibility of transformation through eros: the potential for healing through love. At the extreme end of the continuum, however, psychopathy may not be amenable to such transformation under any circumstances: It would stand to reason that the potential for healing would be as gradated as the severity of the problem.

The Impact of Inner Psychopathy upon Love Relationships

Our inner psychopathy is related to problems with love, with eros, that can cause disconnection from our feelings, leaving a sense of inadequacy. In addition to causing a withdrawal from relationships, inner psychopathy may generate an exaggerated response to *being in love*: an overvaluation of the experience.

Reflecting on my own experience, the absence of a father constellated a tension of opposites within me. My own need to rationalize the inconsistency between his actual behavior and my idealized image of him also meant that within, I somehow paired attraction and superiority with thoughtlessness and unreliability. Albert was never abusive, unless abandonment constitutes abuse, but he was also never available and offered no support or validation while I was growing up, from the age of 2 years old, when my parents divorced. At the same time, I knew enough about him to fabricate an exaggerated and appealing image to internalize: that of the charming, intelligent, talented playboy, inconsistent and irresponsible toward others but in a superior class that superseded all mundane expectations about responsibility or consistency. I believed that his own unique variety of genius could operate beyond the bounds of any presupposed morality, and that he could talk his way around anything or anyone.

My own inner psychopathy, as I understand it, inevitably mirrors the psychic wounds I suffered as a result of my father's abandonment and his emotional unavailability even when I did have contact with him. I was also aware of his incredible callousness toward other significant people in his life, including my mother, half-siblings, and stepmothers. As I have noted previously, desperate to feel close to him, I periodically abandoned my own truest instincts to align with him, determined to understand and accept behavior I actually perceived as terribly hurtful. I identified with him—not without some sacrifice.

My relationship with my father inevitably affected the development of my own inner masculine aspect, or animus. Since I had no contact with him between the ages of 5 and 19, I lacked enough real information about him to respond to anything beyond the character I imagined him to be and mostly felt his absence. Although I had no reason to believe he thought ill of me, I knew he had left my mother and me when I was 2 years old, about which I had had no choice or influence. In retrospect, I grew up feeling that he was apparently unaffected by my existence. I rarely experienced this void; it dwelled somewhere just below conscious awareness, like a vapor requiring an equally unconscious, ever-present effort to ignore. In reflection, this "homeostasis" of sorts probably benefited me by contributing to my tenacity and the ability to withstand pain or persevere when faced with adversity. Such a coping strategy helped to make me a competent survivor in the world, representing positive animus energy. At the same time, this capacity also held a darker opposite, creating a strategy of voluntary numbness to my own true feelings, potentially compromising my ability to accurately identify and respond to my feelings with sensitivity and compassion: my own inner psychopathy, where eros did not enter.

One way an individual might compensate for a lack of trust, integrity, and patience—*good father* qualities—is by working too hard at relationships, essentially doing it all. Such industrious types may appear nurturing and generous—and actually may be—but trying to play both roles in a relationship inevitably compromises the possibility of true partnership between the two in the long run.

A former patient of mine was the perfect wife with this complex. She had selected a husband who fit her preconceived image of her ideal mate, busied herself creating a picturesque home, maintained a high-powered career, attended scrupulously to her appearance, consistently greeted her spouse with a smile, and feigned interest in sex whenever he wanted it even if she did not. In short, she steadfastly kept the marriage stable and her husband happy, while hiding her feelings. He enjoyed the fruits of her labor but did not really know her on any deep level, although they lived together for years. Her efforts were ostensibly loving, to the best of her ability, but they were also fear-based: distracting him, avoiding intimacy, and insulating herself from threats to the superficial stability of the marriage. Over time, the very arrangement she herself had created morphed into resentment and even rage. As she began to reveal her genuine thoughts, feelings, and interests to her husband—almost as though they were leaking out of her unbidden—he felt confused and misled, and the marriage collapsed. Had they both been willing and able to risk closeness in this next phase, the relationship might have survived and they both might have grown. In this case, however, their mutual disappointment and anger prevailed, and they found they were not really attracted to each other once the truth of their distinctive personalities became evident.

I remember a scene when I was in my early 20s, watching as my father thumbed through a box full of old photos of his various conquests. He looked up and pronounced: "Loving is knowing" and "You can love anybody," pontificating about his collection of serial relationships. Mesmerized by his cocky delivery, I memorized the two statements as pearls of his universal wisdom. It did not occur to me to question his logic, not to mention his cockiness, and recognize the mixed messages in these statements until years later. Although he may have been reflecting accurately enough upon his perceptions of his own experience, his versions of "knowing" and "loving" were both problematic. You can "love anybody" if what you relate to in a partner is your own projection, particularly if the partner cooperates with your demands, but once partners in a couple become differentiated enough to emerge with their own unique characteristics, the relationship becomes more grounded and real, if it survives. At that point, *knowing* may not equate with *loving* at all, but trigger the opposite response. When the two individuals actually do get to know each other, difficulties and potential ruptures may be even more likely than love, particularly if there was no deeper connection drawing them together initially, or if they prefer their projections to the truth.

Relationship choices driven by mindless emotion, shallow contrivance, and instincts tend to be fantastical creations based on projection. The potential to activate healthy intuition and thinking is undermined by undifferentiated feelings. It is no surprise that individuals with this energy often attract others who can join them in mutual projections, creating a *folie à deux*. Marriages are sometimes founded in this way; both partners in such a match may awaken later as from a dream, wondering how they ever ended up with each other. The gaps in psyche, our inner psychopathy, our lack of connection with eros can result in a raw neediness that is vulnerable to pseudosolutions. The capacity for genuine relatedness may be tenuous and fragile. To create and maintain a deep relationship requires bravery and perseverance, all the more challenging without a frame of reference founded in genuine personal experience.

Throughout our early lives, many of us struggle to gain a feeling of validity, regardless of real achievements at school or in the family. For an adult female with unresolved father issues, relationships with men often elicit the most undeveloped aspect of her personality in ways that may even astound the individual herself, because opinions and behavior in that area may be so incongruous with the rest of her functioning. The process of developing a sense of self-worth in relationships with men can parallel a woman's long-term individuation process, if it occurs at all. The quest for relationships may involve a dark, unconscious effort to be truly seen, leading the woman to plunge desperately in one wrong direction or another. Driven by fantasies of an idealized partnership and excessively preoccupied with physical appearance and sexual attraction, she is less attentive to true character qualities or practical realities, including the presence or absence of deeper commonalities—when, ironically, those are the very prerequisites to the kind of closeness for which she yearns and fantasizes.

Lack of eros might be understood as a weak or missing inner moral foundation, suggesting problems with the feeling function or with one's inner feminine aspect, often connected to a negative mother experience of some kind. This problem area may manifest as a self-focused empathic failure, allowing the person to behave in ways that hurt or harm others, without sufficient impact on the injurer to deter such actions. Stealing and infidelity are two examples. Most often these problems coexist with other positive characteristics that disguise or distract from the dichotomy within. Whereas a false persona can provide a necessary coping strategy for survival, it can also conceal an unconscious life that becomes increasingly inaccessible and potentially dangerous.

Problems just below the surface of consciousness tend to claim our attention eventually at some point, whether through our own self-sabotaging conduct, somatic symptoms, or disturbing dreams. Avoiding our inner struggles may stymie the individuation process and undermine our potential for wholeness—often experienced as anxiety or a vague sense of unease. I have never deliberately avoided my inner struggles, and on the contrary have been consistently devoted to facing them whenever conscious of them, but my inner psychopathy—the areas of my psyche lacking eros—still influenced my early relationships with men, despite my preemptive efforts. Out of character, I sometimes tolerated intolerable behavior or doggedly made and then held onto bad choices, as though to prove a misguided point, at the expense of my own comfort and integrity.

My vantage point over decades, particularly as a therapist, has led me to realize that this kind of functional disparity often reflects the nature of the relationship with the father—or lack thereof—both real and symbolic. The underlying unconscious assumption of this relatively common—and socially reinforced—mindset is that no desirable man could possibly love the woman for herself, apart from her physical attributes or how she accommodates him, so she presents a smiling face no matter what she is actually feeling. Fear of abandonment leaves her afraid to do otherwise. Such a defense mechanism has obvious ramifications in terms of developing true intimacy or trust.

A parallel dynamic exists for males with similarly unresolved issues, as they struggle for confidence in their own masculine potential and for closeness and trust in relationships with partners. As such, points made in this chapter regarding females can be understood as applicable and relevant to males as well, particularly bearing in mind the contrasexual aspects of both genders.

How one develops genuine confidence and a belief in one's own validity—certainly in love relationships—may reflect the relationship one has with one's father, regardless of gender. The father wound can become a kind of psychopathic gap within, making real intimacy threatening and creating a frustrating dichotomy. An individual carrying such a wound often yearns intensely for, and experiences, a heightened need to be in a loving relationship to feel whole, while innately—and contrarily—resisting true closeness and attachment for fear of being hurt and abandoned.

From a Jungian perspective, problems with love, with eros, and feelings of inadequacy in men are primarily described as associated with the mother and the anima, which is greatly influenced by the mother. My work with male inmates and therapy clients, however, has convinced me of the importance of these men's fathers in determining their core values, life choices, relationships, and feelings of self-worth. Lacking a good-enough father can affect one's belief in one's self-worth in relation to the outer world and one's capacity to love deeply and consistently. Two of my male patients, both abandoned by their fathers as young children, illustrate this problem in different ways.

One patient was fixated on young teenage girls and struggled arduously with intimacy in his marriage to a same-age female. As a result of his insecurity and fears of inadequacy, he could not allow himself to be truly known in relationships with other adults at all—he was much too vulnerable for that—so he found immature images, and all they represented to him, irresistible. His primary sexual attraction was to underage girls; the idea of genuinely relating with his wife frightened him, although he valued her almost wistfully. He cautiously avoided communication of any depth with her, deliberately behaved in ways to distract them both—and eventually was arrested and convicted for illegal sexual conduct with a minor, which finalized the disconnection from his wife, in addition to permanently crippling his functioning in the world.

A second example is a male patient who described experiencing a pervasive sense of inner dullness, despite ongoing enterprises and many sexual relationships. Even in the aftermath of terminating his third marriage, he was left simply feeling flat and empty rather than suffering a conscious crisis or even being particularly relieved. He proudly described himself as shallow and his life as superficial and compartmentalized—which also enabled him to cheat on his partners without remorse and commit minor crimes, despite a smooth exterior. His descriptions of his loneliness and his efforts to initiate new activities and connections after his marriage ended had a numb, mechanical quality to them—suggestive of a lack of eros, inner psychopathy.

Adolf Guggenbühl-Craig wrote that those who cannot love want power.[5] The energy of the psychopath archetype—either within a male as part of his masculine identity, or within a female as an aspect of her animus—is the presence of potentially destructive, instinctual power, often presenting as aggression without consciousness or conscience. It may manifest in the contest for control, ownership, or sexual conquest—

---

5   Guggenbühl-Craig, *Emptied Soul*, 92.

another notch in the belt. Most of us know at least one couple where one of the partners described managing to *catch* the other—a perceived victory usually based upon physical appearance, power, money, or combinations of all three. Even in the context of an enduring relationship, this attitude involves objectification of the partner as caught prey.

The natural urge to connect in relationship is among the most powerful expressions of our humanity. Inner psychopathy—gaps in the psyche lacking eros—may result in continuous frustration, despite zealous efforts to meet this need, to have an *in love* experience that will somehow magically lead to the perfect ultimate conquest or an ideal marriage.

Overly Valuing "In Love"

This intense need to feel *in love* may draw a variety of temporary "containers," often partners with compatible, parallel projections. The passion, however, may be fleeting, ephemeral, and easily displaced from one person to the next because it is essentially superficial—even impersonal—despite fervent efforts to actualize the dream relationship. Although the exhilaration of the resulting encounters may feel real, intense, and magnetic in the moment, such connections usually lack depth, groundedness, and maturity: qualities associated with the responsible male or a positive animus. For the individual caught in such a complex, however, being in love is a compelling, forever unresolved need based on an idealized, projected sexual image rather than attraction to a separate, living, breathing other.

The kind of *in love* that has a driven quality may be generated by a variety of psychic wounds, including a psychopathic gap in the soul. Although it often appears otherwise initially, and sometimes longer, this amplified *in love* experience is not really a genuine response to a desirable separate entity as much as projected need, rendering it oddly impersonal despite the display of other-directed intensity. In other words, the beloved *appears* to be passionately adored—or is "fooled" into thinking this—but the perpetrator may be neither conscious nor deliberate, and may well be under the same spell. The object of such desire is not really recognized as a unique, separate individual, despite glowing commentary, except in terms of the pursuing admirer's projections and fantasies. This is usually unknown to the ensnared, who is likely to be pleasantly distracted, even overwhelmed, by the surge of ardent adoration. My father spread that kind of fairy dust as a lifestyle.

This kind of *in love* may have the quality of a delusion but is really more like voluntary enchantment, an experiential opposite of *participation mystique*: no mysterious undifferentiated connection to others at all, but a problem experiencing the genuine gestalt of relationships or perceiving others' responses accurately. The psychopathic lover may not be consciously trying to fool or manipulate a partner. Because the capacity for relatedness is impaired, that energy is focused inward: introverted and narcissistic. Disruption of plans by the intrusion of reality is likely to leave the psychopathic lover feeling disappointed, frustrated, confused, or bewildered by a vague sense of inadequacy or injustice. The partner who is successfully deluded by the psychopathic lover may feel understandably hurt, surprised, and misled. This is usually the phase when the affair falls apart, mutual projections are withdrawn, and even the memory, in retrospect, may have a quality of unreality to both parties. The fickle suitor may seem relatively unaffected in any conscious way, finding some rationalization for the relationship failure to protect a fragile ego, usually blaming a negative outcome on the once-beloved—and then proceeding quickly to the next fantasy conquest.

To illustrate how this dynamic might evolve and manifest, I return to my father's case. I suspect the roots of his resistance to intimacy and commitment had less to do with a fear of abandonment by his partners than a terror of emasculation and inadequacy, the kind of threatened soul-loss rendered by what Jungians would call the *devouring mother*. His mother never smothered him, but he witnessed what he perceived to be her blistering tirades against his father. He had no way to be close to her or to get his needs for approval and unconditional love met by her, and still hold onto his precious sense of identity and independence. There was apparently a lack of eros in Albert's relationship with his mother that might be understood as contributing to a weak or missing inner moral foundation in him. As described previously, problems with the feeling function are often connected to a negative mother experience of some kind. This dynamic apparently influenced Albert's subsequent relationships with women throughout his life.

Such an eros problem may manifest as an emotional style rather than actual physical actions or infidelity. This possibility helps to explain why my father was able to maintain an apparently stable marriage for 27 years despite his rather obvious gaps. His life appeared driven by his own self-focused version of *in love* as long as I knew him, with various targets he selected to mirror his charm and satisfy his need for reassurance. He easily engaged women by making them feel singularly special—when his focus was really on how *they* perceived *him*.

The spotlight was on me when I first reunited with him at age 19, after 14 years of no contact whatsoever. His attention was intensely riveted on me, in a manner that was first delightful, then unsettling. He was effusive in his adulation of my apparently incredible attributes, particularly what he noted to be our miraculous similarities, such as the similarity of my hands (in a feminine version) to his hands. At one point during my first visit, in front of the stepmother I had just met in their living room, he grabbed my hands, gazed into my eyes, and gushed feverishly, "It's like being in love!" I was confused, surprised, and disgusted—but also uncomfortably flattered.

When Albert died at 84, his body and finally his mind riddled with Parkinson's disease, he was still addicted to the intoxicating rush of that magical *in love* spark. This was illustrated in his somehow managing to captivate one last female, his young caregiver, who became truly devoted to him well beyond the call of duty. She was even willing to jeopardize her job for him and eager to move him into her apartment complex, just so that she could be there for him full-time. I remember the first time I saw her—in some way I already knew the whole story from the look in her eyes—before I discovered who she was. I was standing with my father on the sidewalk in front of his complex, having finally navigated the painstaking journey down the stairs with him unsteadily grasping his walker. I noticed a young female stranger approaching us with a facial expression absolutely radiating such tenderness and adoration that I greeted her, still unsure what was going on; my father then introduced her, and I realized she was from the agency I had contacted to help care for him. She was clearly already mesmerized.

Albert's last love adventure maintained his enduring pattern. At this final stage of his life, it mattered less than ever what his motivations were, although he appeared to have seduced her with his characteristic charm, despite the worsening severity of his physical and mental limitations as his illness progressed. He found a way to meet his ultimate need, to be "loved" passionately by an adoring female, and somehow managed to ensnare her above and beyond the scope of her job description. I never knew if it actually became sexual. I was impressed by his irrepressible tenacity, while feeling the usual pang of annoyance and betrayal at his self-focused machinations. He found an almost desperate joy in this last paramour, especially delighting in her obvious appreciation and devotion to him. In her, he found one final recipient/object to impress with his clever flattery, a last female audience to giggle and gasp at his personal stories and outrageous, adamant opinions.

Puer Aeternus and Puella Aeterna

Such a lifelong pattern as my father displayed with females can be viewed as a shallow overvaluing of the *in love* experience that is based on magical thinking. One way to describe this dynamic in psychological terms might be as a narcissistic self-focus with a fragile ego masked by grandiosity, also consistent with the Jungian concept of the *puer aeternus* (Latin for *eternal boy*). The Jungian concepts of the *puer aeternus* and *puella aeterna* (*eternal girl*) describe archetypal patterns representing eternal youth, forever *in love*—easily capable of engaging attraction, but not of sustaining mature loving connections.

Such individuals may lure partners with what feels like a flood of eternal sunshine but turns out to be only a roving flashlight beam: intimacy without constancy. The classic *puer* character is often charming and glib—qualities associated with psychopathy. The effervescent manner that bespeaks unreliability is also appealing, engaging, and often seductive. One prison inmate I interviewed comes to mind as a perfect example. He was middle-aged, with neatly groomed white hair and bright blue eyes. He hailed from a large, devoutly religious extended family, which he made sure to emphasize. He even brought an 8-by-10 family photo to the interview. His sexual crime had occurred years ago, but it had been violent and bizarre. His appearance was quite counter to the impression I got from reviewing his weird criminal history; he looked and behaved as though he belonged at a golf resort having a leisurely lunch rather than chatting with me across a dingy table in a prison. He had never established stability in his work, relationships, or living circumstances, and had a lifelong trail of random arrests and convictions, many drug-related—and he really was charming! When I asked him a routine question about whether he had ever been deeply in love before, without pausing, he leaned forward, looked straight into my eyes, and responded with twinkling eyes and a warm grin: "Every time!"

I remember one occasion when my father was attending a business conference in the county where I lived. He called me to meet him at the hotel, and when I did, he took me to his room where he promptly presented maps; he wanted me to help him locate the home address of an attractive female radio talk show psychologist who apparently lived in the area. He was absolutely convinced that if only we went there so that she could meet him in person, she would be instantly transfixed by his irresistible charm and inevitably become his next girlfriend—in real life! I managed to distract him somehow.

Marie-Louise von Franz wrote the seminal Jungian book on this topic, *The Problem of the Puer Aeternus*, decades ago.[6] She concluded from her experience with such characters that they choose flight as a revolt against maternal earthiness. Presenting a marvelous visual image to illustrate the dynamic, she described the *puer* males as flying upward, ever ascending, out of fear of the magnets some women hide in the ground in the hope of luring light-headed men down to the ground of marriages, jobs, and long-range commitment.[7] The young ascenders, who may continue the pattern long past chronological youth, often find themselves achieving spirit, but at the expense of a fully developed life or their own grounding in masculine adulthood. According to von Franz's description, "the young *puer aeternus* men are by no means negative; they love spirit and embody much of the spiritual energy of the nation. . . . So the grandiose ascender is a complicated person."[8]

A parallel *puer* process can be identified in females, with animus energy that is similarly flighty and avoidant, and also eternally adolescent. As noted above, the Latin term for the female counterpart to the *puer* concept is *puella aeterna*. One might also speak of a *puer* animus when describing the masculine side of the female psyche, or a *puella* anima when speaking of a man's inner feminine component. The *puella* is a relevant archetype in today's youth-oriented, image-driven world. Although Jung focused on the archetype of the *puer*, post-modern Jungian analysts such as Clarissa Pinkola Estés and Linda Leonard have written extensively on the subject of the concept's female counterpart. Our modern media deliver a barrage of images and messages reinforcing the collective imperative to achieve physical perfection and

6   Marie-Louise von Franz, *The Problem of the Puer Aeternus* (Toronto: Inner City Books, 2000/1970).

7   Ibid.

8   Robert Bly, *Iron John* (New York: Vintage Books, 1990), 58–59.

to stay young forever. Our cultural value of what constitutes beauty suggests a new cast of feminine archetypes, albeit with historical equivalents, including the Barbie doll, the emaciated supermodel, and the seductive, barely adolescent waif. Despite inevitable exceptions, the generic ideal female is represented as a kind of ageless superficial goddess. This mentality is promoted and reinforced by innumerable commercial interests. Reflecting this pervasive pressure, the suicide rate for obese adolescent girls is among the highest for any specific group in America.[9]

A society obsessed with outward appearances unconsciously attempts to fill the resulting inner void—a form of collective cultural psychopathy—with artificial images. Such a dynamic comes at a great cost to the psychological and physical well-being of both sexes, deeply impacting their attitudes about themselves and others, relative to the popular, often unattainable qualities and characteristics that they consider ultimately attractive and essential.

In a related process relevant to understanding the emergence of a puer, Robert Bly describes how males may grow up feeling devalued or inadequate: If a man has been compromised early in life by someone in a position of trust, maybe even a family member, the experience can leave him resentful and defensive, with a need to get even or to escape.[10] Possible scenarios include males with parents who were unavailable, seductive, or abusive. Such an individual may adopt a persona as a shield against trauma, and take on various affectations of being unavailable. The result is a doomed cycle of always looking for love in all the wrong places, as the saying goes, mainly because this version of narcissistic self-focus does not notice the kind of reciprocity fundamental to true partnership. Instead, although such an individual is often a heartbreaker to those who become ensnared, he also suffers

---

9   "The Puella: Eating Disorders." Designed, built, written, and maintained by Kent Carr, 2003: www.thearchetypalconnection.com.

10 Bly, *Iron John*.

an ultimate neediness, akin to inner psychopathy—a void in the psyche absent eros.

When a woman has lacked a good-enough father and was never cared for or provided for consistently as a child by a responsible male parent, she is likely to develop trust issues, and her ability to attach to a male partner is usually affected in some way. If she dares to enter intimate relationships with men at all, her focus may easily move from one love interest to the next. Such behavior suggests the *puella aeterna*; another way to describe the origins of this dynamic in Jungian terms is as a *negative father complex*. Manipulation and deception are likely traits of both men and women caught in such a dynamic. Despite positive efforts and intentions, their relationships are often shallow; their problems with intimacy, commitment, and ambivalent feelings about safety abound—the seed having been planted long ago by their formative parental experiences of abandonment, abuse, or mixed messages.

We tend to attract partners whose personal evolution and woundedness somehow correspond to our own. Lovers' wounds or gaps in the psyche, their aspects of inner psychopathy, seem to find each other along with those characteristics of which they are conscious.

Transcendent Love

The nature of a couple's inner psychopathy is an incredibly potent influence on mutual attraction. A woman's male aspect, or animus, inevitably has a relationship with her partner's anima, or female aspect.[11] This invisible connection may be experienced as the intuition that attracts the two to each other. How they express their mutual attraction matters tremendously, since that potentially transcendent magnetic energy can yield a wide range of consequences affecting them both. Powerful attraction can be acted out concretely or it can generate healing through creativity, guided by love.

---

11   Sanford, *Invisible Partners*.

In *Alchemical Psychology*, Jungian psychologist and author Thom Cavalli wrote: "At the center of the heart is a consciousness that knows no distinctions between inner and outer, above and below. At the heart of the matter, alchemy is about coming to the realization that we already possess the philosopher's stone and its name is love."[12] Cavalli described three kinds of love and their corresponding sexual aspects: first, animal connection, meaning essentially an instinctual level lacking in eros or relationship; then lovemaking, a deeper, consensual connection; lastly, eroticism, which, in the Jungian view, includes the merged mind–body–spirit dimension. This third kind of love is represented in its ideal form by the Jungian concept of the *coniunctio*, in which two become one, forming sacred wholeness and entering the realm of the self or psyche, which integrates all.[13]

There are certainly individuals who are consciously interested in pursuing a deepening connection with their partners; even those who were not initially inclined toward a deep relational experience sometimes learn to be if they end up in dynamic, consensual relationships. Still, Cavalli's first kind of love probably best characterizes the most prevalent form of sex-love connection in our popular modern American culture. Seeking a partner based upon physical appearance is often augmented with additional expectations regarding status, power, and money, which are all essentially temporary and superficial. This kind of love may be self-focused, primarily fueled by sexual attraction or ambition rather than deeper awareness or connection, and as such, not fundamentally designed to be lasting or exclusive. Such unions may be built upon rigid requirements, and inevitable problems result as life unfolds. The relationship may erupt in dramatic conflicts. In other cases a feeling of creeping dullness prevails. The partners may manage a monogamy that feels like monotony to them both, especially over time.

---

12 Thom F. Cavalli, *Alchemical Psychology* (New York: Tarcher/Putnam, 2002), 313.
13 Personal conversation with Thom Cavalli, May 21, 2009.

Fidelity due only to painful willpower—the deliberate curbing of pressing urges to behave otherwise—rather than fidelity born of a soul-deep commitment, creates a marriage that survives in name only. The marriage is an empty vessel, without eros. These are the partners who no longer gaze at each other, whose eyes stray hungrily, seeking to hold onto the shape and form of their youthful physical appearance and habits against the natural pull of time. Without symbol or substance to sustain them, they stay married primarily because of habit, fear, or shared material investments, while drowning their sorrows in a variety of distractions: hidden or imagined affairs, cosmetic surgery, drugs and alcohol—or television/iPads/tweeting/twerking.

Of course, love is neither logical nor chronological, and relationships rarely fall neatly into categories of any kind. Many couples have moments of deep connection interspersed with drama and dullness. Most young people enjoy a period of time when being carefree about their lives and partnerships is simply fun. To label that kind of freewheeling experimentation as lacking in empathy or eros is unfair, even though this youthful lifestyle may indeed contain elements of lawlessness, lack of consideration for others, and random sexual behavior. It is when this phase gets out of balance or becomes a permanent, stuck lifestyle that it may reflect psychopathy. There is no rigid, generic formula to predict or measure when normal life-cycle patterns of behavior end and psychopathic ones begin, although we try hard to find collective rules to follow and guide us, through religion, laws, or other external constructs.

The disparity between how we lived during those experimental years and what we expect of ourselves as more stable adults may plague us later in life if past actions and experiences are not integrated with maturity, humor, and perspective. Fond memories may be dampened with regrets if one is left mourning and clinging to a life phase that has irrevocably ended. Such a state can be another symptom of the *puer aeternus/puella aeterna* archetypes: the longed-for eternal youth that seeks to soar above gravity, avoiding the reality of aging. Or guilt may wake us in the night, as we endlessly rehash perceived past sins or mistakes we can neither forget nor change, unable to move on and accept personal history in the full context of the self, to live an authentic life.

Healthy masculine identification is instrumental for both men and women to function well and live authentic lives, both individually and in relationships. Women with positive animus characteristics are better integrated in both their inner and outer worlds. Women stuck grappling with a negative animus or inner psychopath archetype project those unhealthy aspects onto males in the outside world, which results in a variety of calamities: doomed serial relationships, unrealistic expectations that sabotage intimacy, or shutting down emotionally and avoiding connection altogether. Men often have a parallel story, but it may appear different because our social and cultural expectations of males and females are dissimilar. Even in today's modern culture, men are more likely to be supported in their superficial sexual conquests of women and less likely to be condemned for avoiding commitment than women.

For both sexes, the impulse to consummate an erotic connection typically feels overpowering, and yet holding that tension, which may be necessary for a variety of reasons, may produce creative growth and potential healing through eros. During one of my magical summer sessions at Küsnacht, I heard Jungian analyst and author John Haule describe how resisting the urge to merge sexually or romantically with a desired other can "open up the archetypal imagination" to express passion in expansive, creative ways.[14] In simplistic terms, although the urge to merge sexually is innate and powerful, the archetypal dimension to our human character offers the possibility of satisfying alternative resolutions. Dr. Haule described this phenomenon by referring to archetypes as "behavior patterns driven by instincts with an innate

---

14 John Ryan Haule, "Lectures: Eros and Human Relationship." Based upon notes from his lectures within the C. G. Jung Institute Zürich Summer Intensive Study Program, July 2010.

sense of direction," thus reflecting a correlation between biological and emotional drives.[15] The nature of archetypes can be understood as similar to animals in nature, but related to all common universal human experience. The archetype gives aim to instinctual behavior. Marie-Louise von Franz effectively describes the distinction and inter-action between instincts and archetypes and talks about "delaying the angel" to find out what is behind a particular sexual urge, especially if the timing or target is unlikely or confusing. Under such circumstances:

> You want to become conscious of what is behind the urge, namely the strange connection between instinct and arche-type. . . . Jung in his writings sometimes refers to instinct as if it were the same thing as the archetype and sometimes as if it were different. What he means is that the archetype, if we look at it as opposite to instinct, would be an inherited and instinctive way of having emotions, ideas, and repre-sentations with symbols, and instinct would be the inherited way of acting physically, a certain kind of physical action. Naturally, the two are connected.[16]

Delaying the angel, holding the tension of romantic or sexual love, has a power all its own, potentially constellating a *transcendent function* that may produce a nonrational solution. Jung refers to the transcendent function as the mediating force between opposite contents within the psyche, arising out of intense and concentrated conflicts within the individual. Extreme, painful paradoxes can lead us to a new perspective where we must transcend the ego so that our perception of reality is no longer split into two opposing forces. Jung posits that holding the tension of these opposites is essential to bridging the gap between ego-consciousness and the unconscious. If the tension between the opposites can be held long enough without succumbing to the urge to identify with one side or the other, the

15 Ibid.
16 Marie-Louise von Franz, *Alchemy* (Toronto: Inner City Books, 1980), 59.

third, completely unexpected image—one that unites the two in a creative new way—comes into view.[17]

As we engage in our own self-fulfilling processes of individuation, it becomes more likely that we can take such sexual feelings to this higher—or at least abstract—form of expression, with or without making any conscious decision to do so, perhaps using unrequited love as a creative inspiration rather than needing to act it out concretely in ways that can prove destructive or disappointing. Haule described a patient who fell deeply in love with him, feelings he did not reciprocate. After more than a year of analysis together, she told him that thanks to his rejection, she had been able to actualize creative projects of her own that were fulfilling and unexpected; she realized that she had transmuted her frustrated passion into alternative forms of expression that stimulated her own growth in lasting ways.[18]

As eros infuses our attitudes about ourselves, the kinds of relationships we draw and manage to sustain and the ways we choose to express attraction can change accordingly in a mutually beneficial manner. Our natural inclination to seek relationships, to partner, is a saving grace in more than one respect; without that drive, of course, humankind would cease to exist. The quality and depth of our connections and our motivations for forming them reflect and influence our inner state of being, including our gaps in psyche. The magic of love is a veritable wellspring that can affect us in unforeseen ways. We are all, in some way, searching for eros—the sense of art and wonder representing that dimension of our human experience holding the promise of emancipation. Eros is the magic potion, the fountain of youth, the sorcerer's stone: love that holds no bounds. Eros holds transformative potential, crucial and mysterious—healing energy that can potentially flood the lacunae of our inner psychopathy with the light of hope. Activating that healing energy can occur through various means, including therapy.

---

17 C. G. Jung, *The Transcendent Function. Vol. 8. The Collected Works of C. G. Jung.* 2d ed. (Princeton, NJ: Princeton University Press, 1960).
18 Haule, "Eros and Human Relationship."

CHAPTER 10

Psychopathy and Therapy

I began to notice how the continuum of psychopathy appeared in my therapy cases, both forensic and private. My clinical observations reminded me again of Guggenbühl-Craig's ideas, where he referred to psychopathy as a "form of psychic invalidism" in which "something in the psyche is crippled or missing."[1] Encountering these strange pockets of emptiness and vulnerability—weak or missing components in otherwise intact personalities—was like discovering a wormhole on the underside of a perfect apple.

It follows that when psychopathy within remains hidden, unconscious, or avoided, it is more likely to do harm to us and others in ways we may not anticipate or recognize and therefore cannot control. My experience of Jung's work, which has been tremendously healing in my life, has involved learning to identify and love those aspects of the psyche that are wounded, empty, or destructive, believing that to do so creates the possibility of growth and wholeness—a belief I have seen corroborated. This value affects my personal process, my relationships, and my functioning in the world, including how I practice therapy.

Projecting shadow contents is as ubiquitous as the air we breathe. I have seen many examples of this dynamic in my private therapy practice, mirroring what goes on in the world at large every day: Clients

---

1 Guggenbühl-Craig, *Emptied Soul*, 40, 47.

project undesirable contents outward to avoid recognition of unwanted inner aspects of personality or functioning. Most therapy patients are fairly adept at identifying others in their lives who have made them feel rejected, abandoned, or devalued. Though painful, this is usually preferable to finding the source and potential solution for these difficulties within themselves.

As an example, I think of one young woman who tearfully described how her parents had targeted and abused her, and how she later found herself involved in one relationship after another that led her to experience the same sharp pain. She expressed some insight about the early origins of this repetitive pattern. She sounded as though she had been trying resolutely to win affection and stability but somehow, mysteriously and unfairly, never received what she deserved, despite her efforts. This failure was no mystery to me, because she usually picked partners and friends who perfectly corroborated her self-defeating expectations. She experienced the slow evaporation of each new attachment with her stomach in knots.

She described a scene where she was terrified of saying what she really felt to her boyfriend for fear it would drive him away, even though it was agonizing for her to sit on the couch next to him staring at the TV, suffering in self-imposed silence. Her rational mind occasionally emerged with the awareness that this unresponsive partner was not a good prospect for her anyway, even if he were to make himself available. Then it immediately rattled her to understand that she really did not need him and was unsure whether she even liked him, and that her efforts to win his love would be unfulfilling even if she succeeded: He was not the solution to her pain. Her fleeting clarity was just that, and she was quickly swept away in her swirl of memories, projections, and past associations—logic lost. As though on autopilot, she reminded herself that he was fundamental to her existence, that it was entirely her responsibility to make the right moves to keep him, and that it would be *her* devastating failure if he left her.

She was unable to perceive how these dire messages about her inadequacy, which began so long ago, were no longer really outside herself—she could hold onto her safe projections, given the types of people she chose to engage, who ably reinforced her old learned convictions. She wrote self-absorbed, miserable poetry on *Facebook* about being alone, falsely accused, and misunderstood. She found her pain tolerable as long as she could pinpoint the source of her problems as external to her. Being the victim and feeling sorry for herself was familiar territory. However, the inner demon she would not face actually generated her darkest depression and triggered her most desperate thoughts, not this particular rejecting boyfriend or her mean relatives. The harsh, unforgiving judge *within her* was her true nemesis.

She perceived herself as innately flawed and felt guilt-ridden for errors she could neither forgive nor forget. She had committed crimes, hurt others, and broken the law. She had been thoughtless, immature, and consumed by her own needs at the expense of her integrity. I experienced those characteristics and behaviors as reflecting the psychopathy within her, the dark regions in her soul devoid of love: feelings, attitudes, behaviors, and circumstances she yearned to reverse. On the other hand, she was also able to respond to others with genuine kindness and compassion. She was forgiving, gentle, loving, and upbeat, but she could not consciously identify with those positive parts of herself. In her case, these more desirable qualities were *her shadow aspects*, the unacknowledged features of her personality. All of these dimensions existed within her, but she could not embrace her duality, so she disconnected—into the lacuna of her inner psychopathy.

As her therapist, I saw the beauty of opposites in her and thought about the transformative potential of holding that tension in awareness, though not knowing how this delicate process would play out with her. This tension was fertile ground for Jung's *transcendent function*, as described in the previous chapter: the emergence of a symbol that might help her to transcend the struggle in a new, creative way—a spontaneous, mysterious, deeply personal gift from the wisdom of the psyche.[2] I could only hope that my consciousness of this potential would inform our therapeutic interaction, although her receptivity and responses were predictably *un*predictable. Sadly, this young woman fervently believed the painful messages that constituted her earliest impressions and took them to heart. Those messages were a defense to avoid her own inner psychopathy. Facing her own gaps was so much more abhorrent than attributing her shortcomings and sorrows to external triggers; she perceived herself to be the victim of her relationships and circumstances. She blamed her pervasive feeling of rejection on others, which was uncomfortable but familiar and finite. Thus she was able to avoid the intangible reality of the profound archetypal emptiness within her, which she experienced through a core feeling that loving herself was too hard.

For my forensic therapy clients referred to me by the court, probation, or parole, readjusting to life in the community after having been incarcerated also means trying to connect with and integrate radically different aspects of their personalities. They often struggle to understand their own criminal behavior in the context of their previous successes or those dimensions of their lives that had always been fully functional, which they now want to emphasize but feel painfully disconnected from. This process inevitably involves some confrontation with their inner opposites, as they also cope with the unavoidably harsh reality of their external circumstances. Being caught and punished for breaking the law sometimes represents a shocking, sudden fall from grace, leaving the individual surprised, confused, and reeling in the aftermath.

Like the rest of us, the healthy parts of these individuals' lives and personalities were in sharp contrast to their inner psychopathy. However, unlike the rest of us, their psychopathic gaps were strikingly obvious because they committed crimes and suffered serious legal

---

2   Jung, *The Transcendent Function.*

problems, which now affected every dimension of their existence. In many cases, getting in touch with their innate integrity—which they may have previously avoided and obliterated with drugs or other distractions—led to severe self-condemnation of their own misconduct that was even harsher and more painful than dealing with the courts or incarceration. Making sense of their seemingly disjointed life experiences and finding the meaning therein is a torturous but potentially enlightening process, always grist for the mill in our work together.

One male patient of mine in his early 50s presented with a menacing exterior he had perfected over a lifetime of entrenched criminality and drug abuse, but his steadfast work to integrate his inner psychopathy in treatment belied his gruff appearance. The first time he appeared in my office waiting room, slouched in a chair with his dark sunglasses on, one of my colleagues took me aside and expressed concerns about my safety. During the course of therapy, it became clear that for the first time in his life this man was surviving well in the community, maintaining a steady job using skills he had sustained for decades despite his history of frequent incarcerations, sharing his residence with his ill mother for whom he was caretaking, and abstaining from all drugs. He had paid rapt attention to the judge's parting message to him at his last trial, which was that ultimately, he had to "fix himself"—a phrase he frequently repeated to me in treatment. He spent his prison sentence developing a sense of personal organization and doing a lot of reflection. He presented initially as someone who was less likely to demonstrate insight than to try stealing my car, but his appearance was deceiving.

During his growing-up years, this man's parents were unavailable and neglected him. His family was dysfunctional and chaotic, and he never felt deeply valued or unconditionally loved. As a young adult, he unwittingly sought partners who were rejecting and whom he disappointed, no matter what he did—similar to the way his parents had responded to him. This was the maltreatment he expected and at some level felt he deserved; these critical, forever dissatisfied women had a special lure for him. He was determined to keep trying to save them or win them over, neither of which was likely anyway, and then even further sabotaged his own efforts by avoiding any remote possibility of true closeness with infidelity and drug abuse.

In midlife he discovered some stability with a clear, drug-free head and began to identify and question some of his underlying assumptions—and to love newfound dimensions of his own personality. As he felt better about himself, he realized that he really wanted a caring, mutual connection with others, and he resolved to wait until he could have that kind of partnership instead of returning to his old behavior patterns. The positive change was evident when he independently made a difficult decision to set limits with an attractive, seductive, available woman he knew was trying to manipulate him and take advantage of his generosity. His emerging patience was generated by eros within him, yielding a new sense of self-worth and hope for the future.

Many of my forensic therapy patients who are transitioning back to life in the community after committing crimes and being incarcerated are faced with a serious dilemma about the truth of their personalities that affects their mental health and their potential for positive adjustment. If they are attempting to build a new life—what probation and parole jargon refers to as a "prosocial" lifestyle—they often feel that they need to be a *completely different person* from the old self that got into trouble. This is, of course, impossible and unrealistic, but the alternative—admitting and somehow consciously integrating their inner psychopathy and making different decisions—requires accepting parts of themselves they now yearn to avoid altogether. Such a Spartan process calls for an inner dialogue that can feel intolerable. A similar challenge occurs with individuals and couples whose inner psychopathy is much less obvious. They might need to admit unwanted thoughts, feelings, or behaviors of which they feel ashamed in order to make conscious choices *not* to act on them, rather than simply ignoring or denying them.

CHAPTER 11

Psychopathy and the Therapy Process: Diagnostic Issues

We have met the enemy and he is us.
> —Cartoonist Walt Kelly's *Pogo*

One can only face in others

What one can face in oneself.
> —James Baldwin

Be the change that you want to see in the world.
> —Mahatma Gandhi

Viewing psychopathy as a gradated human characteristic potentially enriches the practice of psychotherapy. Mental health practitioners' familiarity with their own inner psychopathy can be a vital enhancement to the process of clinical assessment and certainly to the overall therapeutic process. It is fundamentally useful for therapists dealing with psychopathy to question how to best understand these aspects of the human condition. The quality and extent of the therapist's own awareness inevitably influences treatment outcomes; thus the prevailing consensus within the profession about the importance of "doing your own (inner) work" across widely varying theoretical schools of psychology. This premise suggests that for therapists working with psychopathy in patients, facing our own is prerequisite, however it may appear and irrespective of the theoretical perspective or clinical approach.

Diagnostic Issues

Viewing psychopathy beyond a diagnostic category, as a *characterological* trait, means that any of us, perhaps all of us, carry elements of this emptiness within—a viewpoint that has implications for theoretical approaches and therapeutic practice. Although there are certainly those individuals who fit the prototypical profile of "a psychopath," many more individuals have psychopathic traits without that extreme level of severity. This is similar to the variations within any diagnosis. There is typically a checklist or gradated scale of characteristics that a clinical perspective associates with corresponding strategies and techniques for assessment and treatment—only some of which usually apply to given individual clients, who rarely fit neatly into diagnostic categories.

Cognitive, behavioral, or psychophysiological instruments are valid tools with which to assess and measure risk for legal purposes and community safety, usually called for when the primary reason for evaluation and treatment is inherently associated with danger to others. In other instances, when psychopathy is subtle and internalized, which is more likely for most of us, approaches ranging from history-taking to dream analysis may be a better way to unearth it. Diagnostic measures and tools are most useful to *guide* insightful perceptions and thoughtful questions about each individual case, not to replace that process with a preset conclusion in response to a checklist of criteria. Absolute judgments tend to split off or devalue other aspects of the individual. This is one area where the legal system and forensic psychology—where absolute judgments are fundamental—depart from the theoretical premise of analytical psychology and psychotherapy, where splitting off and devaluing aspects of personality are contraindicated, even antithetical.

There are numerous models for understanding the profoundly complex human psyche, including the dimension of psychopathy. Psychodynamic principles have been applied to the understanding of psychopathy since 1925, with the main emphasis placed on psychogenetic aspects. Psychoanalytical schools believe that psychopaths are fixated in an infantile stage of the first phallic phase.[1] That is, they suffered a developmentally normal crisis of sexual and hostile feelings in very early childhood that was essentially frozen in time and never resolved, resulting in failure to develop adequate conscience. Sociologists view psychopathy as a sociological problem, emphasizing social and cultural influences on behavior, such as conflicts between societal norms and expectations, subgroup influences, and family dynamics (including child abuse, for example). From a sociological perspective, such conflicts, combined with moral and/or intellectual aberrations, produce an individual lacking social conscience in relation to society. The field of psychology today is primarily oriented toward descriptive diagnoses and cognitive-behavioral social education, as opposed to dynamic psychotherapy or analysis, so the prevailing attitudes and beliefs about psychopathy reflect this orientation.

A current popular trend in the field of psychology is the use standardized treatment approaches validated by "evidence-based" research. Treatment manuals include protocols to be followed, corresponding to specific diagnoses and problems. Ostensibly, this will produce predictable outcomes. While such a generic approach may offer useful structure and guidance, this clinical strategy cannot possibly accommodate the vast range and complexity of real-life therapy cases or circumstances, leaving only a narrow window through which to view, and attempt to foster, healing.

---

1 Sigmund Freud, "Dostoevsky and Parricide." In Standard Edition of *The Complete Psychological Works of Sigmund Freud, Vol. 21* (London: Hogarth Press, 1928), 175–196 (quote on 178).

The core of a Jungian or depth psychology orientation emphasizes theoretical constructs (such as individuation) that guide the treatment and the use of a variety of approaches to meet the unique needs of individual patients. A Jungian attitude toward treatment is essentially introverted, by which I mean inner-focused, guided by the spontaneous, genuine, in-the-moment experience of the therapeutic interaction between patient and therapist. There are no set rules for applying externally designated strategies by rote to match categories of presenting symptoms or circumstances. The analytical therapist uses awareness of personal, immediate experience with the individual patient to identify the fitting approach, as opposed to focusing objectively on the patient and applying predetermined techniques in response to certain diagnostic categories. The depth-oriented therapeutic relationship is interactive and dynamic. This unpredictability creates a certain vulnerability for both participants, which is challenging but fundamental to the healing process.

Another way that a depth-oriented approach to therapy can be described as essentially introverted is that it emphasizes a flow of energy and action from inner to outer experience, rather than using externally applied strategies to deliberately alter cognition or conduct, for example. Rather than starting with the goal of behavior change, this inner focus can be associated with a corresponding life philosophy encouraging awareness and acceptance of our opposites within, thereby fostering the emergence of wholeness. Changing problematic behaviors and thinking patterns may still be the goal and result of treatment, but may be achieved through a more organic guidance generated from within the individual, through personal experience of healing eros.

We all need love, and we can all benefit from hard science; each approach to therapy has value in its context. A depth orientation brings a rich dimension to the therapy process, but evidence-based methods also represent significant contributions to the field of psychology. The two approaches are by no means mutually exclusive. Each approach to therapy, and there are many, can enhance the others. Coping with the broad continuum of issues we face in our clients and within ourselves substantiates the need for a range of approaches to understand and manage problems most effectively—including psychopathy.

Psychopathy and the Therapist

Broadening our definition and understanding of psychopathy may be uncomfortable, but as with many dark contents, doing so offers the potential for personal and professional growth. Limited to a psychiatric diagnosis, we can too easily dismiss patients who exhibit the classic psychopathic characteristics with the excuse that trying to work with them is pointless. If we seem to be getting nowhere despite all of our best therapeutic efforts, we can attribute this stalemate to limitations in the patient, concluding that the patient is a psychopath—a lost cause. This response is consistent with the popular opinion that psychopathy itself is amoral, even immoral, providing a handy rationalization for dismissing individuals who exhibit the traits, along with disavowing the possibility of our own.

An expanded conceptualization of psychopathy is relevant to how therapists recognize and work with shadow aspects, both their patients' and their own. When a therapist experiences aspects of a patient as psychopathic, that experience may indeed result from that patient's psychic gaps or moral depravity, but it may also be a more dynamic and blended process involving the therapist's own unacknowledged psychopathy within. As therapists, we inevitably contain our patients' projections, and our countertransference reactions to their psycho-pathic character traits may well express our own.

For example, a young patient with a history of childhood sexual abuse by her father might behave seductively toward her male ther-apist, manipulating him to reenact her abuse and transferring her mixed feelings of arousal, devotion, and fury onto him. If that thera-pist has unresolved incestuous desires for his own daughter, he might respond to the patient's overtures in a number of unhelpful ways: by disengagement, by sexualizing the relationship, or by blaming her for being devious, instead of retaining the objectivity needed to use her symptoms to help her heal. Although his countertransference reaction could have many origins, attributing it to psychopathy is one way to understand it. Jung described how difficult this kind of countertransference is for a therapist to admit, as well as how to work with it in terms of professional personas, which are deeply challenged by both the idea and the experience of engaging such an aspect of personality.[2] This professional "innate" response of denial, steeped in unacknowledged revulsion, may be another reason psychopathic patients are typically described as so difficult to work with. Put simply, their gaps lacking eros may mirror our own.

Guggenbühl-Craig cautions that often "therapists who, themselves, do not rightly know the meaning of relatedness are the very ones who claim relationship with psychopaths."[3] One of the reasons that psychopaths make challenging patients, even for therapists who envision themselves as fitted for the task, is that those therapists are "often helplessly manipulated by the psychopath; just as are the psychopath's other victims."[4]

Some therapy patients more than others—individuals with borderline or dependent personality disorders, in particular—seem to need to use the therapeutic relationship as a vehicle for becoming whole, for resolving their inner gaps. Working with the dreams of these individuals can eventually provide them with the means to do so independently. Dreams often manifest our struggle to reconcile the disparity between the reality of our day-to-day lives and our perceptions about what constitutes an authentic life: the life we believe, or

2   Jung, *Practice of Psychotherapy*, 73, 74.
3   Guggenbühl-Craig, *Emptied Soul*, 93.
4   Ken Magid, *High Risk: Children without a Conscience* (New York: Bantam Books, 1987), 193.

unconsciously know, we were meant to have. This uncanny power of dreams to reveal the gaps between the ideal and the real is one reason Jungian analysis encourages an ongoing relationship with our dreams for guidance in understanding all aspects ourselves and clarifying our unique life dilemmas.

Discovering and steadfastly confronting those areas within where we have, in effect, abandoned ourselves can be an elusive process. We humans are usually reticent to acknowledge the possibility that our reactions or behaviors may represent negative qualities within ourselves. This stance may be particularly entrenched in the ego-gratifying role of therapist. In our eagerness to promote healing, not to mention our own shadow drives for power and control, it is both tempting and distracting to bask in the glow of grateful patients. Even that gratitude may be a deceptive gauge of therapeutic outcome, however, since the patient who emerges from treatment with an easy, superficial success may be much happier in the short run—until the original presenting problem returns, now expressed through different symptoms. However, when the therapy process actually succeeds in engaging the core psychic upheaval inherent to major life change and healing, the patient is bound to be extremely uncomfortable, at least temporarily—and more likely to be furious, hate and project blame onto the therapist, or disrupt treatment—than to be grateful!

Although some types of problems can be adequately addressed by a structured, socioeducational or strictly cognitive-behavioral method, fundamental lasting change usually requires deeper therapeutic work. That being said, the reality of today's mental health field and market is that many patients, not to mention managed-care entities, expect simple strategies and quick, reassuring answers, regardless of the level of intervention needed.

Psychopathy is inevitably associated with terrifying, heartless serial killers, but on a deeper and more universal level, the struggle to deal with psychopathy is the struggle to deal with disconnections within the psyche. Accordingly, the therapeutic process to address the continuum of psychopathy necessarily ranges from a focus on eliminating dangerous psychopathic behaviors to addressing subtler problems with psychopathic characteristics that can be approached in the context of a far more open-ended search for wholeness. If, as depth psychology posits, the core dilemma of human existence is essentially how to foster a fully integrated personality realized through the process of individuation, then consciously identifying, accepting, and integrating our pockets of psychopathy within—the fragmentation within each of our psyches—is part of our human calling. Furthermore, the extent to which we attend to that suffering within our own psyches is inevitably reflected in the world we create around us.

The Process of Therapy

Whatever approach we think we are practicing as therapists, I strongly suspect that the gist of what is accomplished in each therapeutic encounter primarily reflects who we are, the work we have done on ourselves, and our ability to recognize the humanity in our patients.

The popular, illusory lure of an "instant cure" is in direct contrast to the kind of unpredictable, deeper process of therapy that includes accepting psychopathy—our inner gaps, as well as the content-laden shadow aspects, the difficult material—within each of us. In modern American culture we gravitate to extremes when it comes to mental health treatment approaches, although quicker is certainly most popular; if instant therapy was available, many would choose it, and in fact figuratively often do, via the pharmaceutical industry. Psychotropic medications are increasingly conventional; nearly everyone knows someone taking antidepressants or antianxiety medication.

At one end of the therapy spectrum is short-term cognitive-behavioral treatment that most resembles social education or life coaching. The opposite end is probably best represented by a new breed of psychoanalytic practice that suggests modernity by calling itself *"neo*-Freudian" but in its extreme form involves a demanding commitment, resembling much earlier models, for both the psychoanalyst and the patient.

One of my therapy clients had been previously convicted of a sex offense well before coming to me for a different issue. He spoke disparagingly of the structured cognitive-behavioral sex offender treatment program he had been court-ordered to complete previously. However, he also described having had a life-changing experience of individual therapy with a provider within that same program over several years, which had helped him to heal his inner wounds in a deep, lasting way. Although the methods and details were somewhat unclear, it was obvious that a caring relationship had developed between this therapist and the patient that genuinely improved his sense of himself; he remembered this fact better than the specific content of their interchange. Despite his complaints about the cognitive-behavioral program he had been required to complete, subsequent to his treatment he had no further problems involving sex offending, maintained his sobriety, established a healthy relationship with a partner, and was not suicidal for an unprecedented stretch. He fully attributed these successful outcomes to this meaningful therapeutic relationship, which had transpired "between the lines" within a cognitive-behavioral, socioeducational program. The core of any deeply healing therapy is the connectedness, the eros, between patient and therapist.

This is an era in the field of psychology (perhaps most evident in forensic psychology) of quick fixes and an application of the law that is prone to disconnection from individual ethics. As professionals, although we collectively emphasize adherence to laws and ethics more strenuously and elaborately than ever before, the foundation of ethics, the deepest stratum of morality— faithfulness to the self—is rarely considered. Yet our own integrity is fundamental to the therapeutic process.

Psychotherapy is both science and art, and although our interventions are aptly informed by science, the artful creativity of the therapeutic process is often unforeseen and even illogical, not unlike love itself. The healing, generative force of love, of eros, is inherently beyond our control. Arriving at a particular diagnosis may fulfill the purpose of guiding effective treatment or formulating prognoses, and yet the magic of eros, so fundamental to human nature and existence—our capacity for insight and change founded in connectedness and relationship—remains essentially unpredictable. In *The Tao of Psychology*, Jean Shinoda Bolen paraphrases a concept from John Lilly's autobiography, *The Center of the Cyclone,* thus: "We must transcend our own limiting beliefs in order to grow beyond them, or in order to have the experiences which allow us to grow." She adds: "This is what occurs in psychotherapy."[5]

There are certainly parallels between what occurs in psychotherapy and other creative processes, such as writing, along with some similar potential pitfalls: the work may become uninspired, shallow, stuck, or mechanical. There is only so much success we can premeditate in such endeavors—inspiration cannot be forced—and in fact, the best of what we produce often comes as an unexpected gift, at a moment's notice. Perhaps the planning has to pause for the solution to present itself. That is one reason handbooks on how to achieve self-improvement may seem to fall short, even if they make logical sense: Making a decision about how to change behavior is not equivalent to allowing it to happen—although making the decision can be a good start.

Offering the possibility of change to our patients is contingent upon our ability to step back from an ego investment in how that change occurs. As therapists, we can create a safe and protected environment, a *temenos*, which motivates patients to actualize their own process through differentiation and fuller integration of all aspects of the personality.[6] The temenos must withstand and contain the full range of patients'

---

5 Bolen, *Tao of Psychology*, 76.
6 C. G. Jung, "The Tavistock Lectures." In *The Symbolic Life. Vol. 18. The Collected Works of C. G. Jung,* 11th ed. (Princeton, NJ: Princeton University Press, 1976), par. 410.

material, including their inner psychopathy, those gaps in the psyche lacking eros. In order to heal the gaps, they must first be identified and illuminated in the far broader context of the patient's comprehensive personality. They are not the whole of an individual. As therapists, such a fundamental dimension of our work is to facilitate patients' fuller acceptance of themselves. Thus *our* ability to be genuinely accepting is instrumental to the context we provide for them. Dealing with psychopathy is particularly demanding in this regard because we must scrupulously differentiate between unconditional positive regard for the humanity of the individual and the entirely separate matter of how we may judge the individual's behavior. As an obvious but relevant side note, we cannot offer to others what we cannot realistically conceive or genuinely experience within ourselves.

It is tempting to objectify and intellectualize treatment or healing, talking *about* how things occur, rather than subjecting ourselves to painful uncertainty and living open to change for ourselves or others. Anyone who has been blindsided by unforeseen change knows such fears are warranted. However, by risking uncertainty and holding the tension of opposites within us—the characteristics we value together with our unwanted aspects—we allow whatever change we need to signal us from our own unconscious depths and to emerge: a potentially useful consideration, personally and professionally. Accepting this idea challenges us to loosen some of our safe assumptions about mental health and question our collective orientation toward being able to compartmentalize, quarantine, classify, diagnose, and treat problems in a measurable, finite, predictable way. Perhaps fortunately, in the final assessment of what works or does not, the label of the therapeutic approach, the required time frame, and even the cost matter less than the quality of the meeting.

CHAPTER 12

A Clinical Perspective: The DSM-5 and Beyond

There is no actual diagnosis of psychopathy in the previous *Diagnostic and Statistical Manual of Mental Disorders–Fourth Edition–Text Revised* (DSM-IV-TR, American Psychiatric Association, 2000). The most recent edition of the manual (DSM-5; American Psychiatric Association, 2013) condenses personality disorders into five clusters, one of which is *antisocial/psychopathic personality disorder*, commensurate with the common clinical and forensic understanding of psychopathy as nearly synonymous with antisocial traits. The *psychopath* is a well-studied and popularized label.

In general discussion psychopathy is often described as identical to antisocial personality disorder. Antisocial personalities may or may not be extremely psychopathic, and psychopaths may or may not fit the diagnostic profile of antisociality. This kind of subtle distinction is fundamental to the idea that the continuum of psychopathy is more insidious—and common—than generally assumed. Criminality aside, one way to visualize the inconsistencies in our character and conduct is that there are pockets of emptiness in the fabric of the human soul: our inner psychopathy. Brain chemistry may help to explain how serial murderers are different from the rest of us, but what mystery underlies those aspects of the human psyche that defy our conscious values in terms of character traits, motivation, and behavior in the *rest* of us?

The antisocial personality is characterized by a failure to respect the rights of individuals and the laws and rules of society. This attitude of disregard for collective social values represents the common ground between the antisocial psychopath and criminality and is an obvious dimension of psychopathy, but certainly not the whole picture. Psychopathy has a broader range of descriptors. At least in general psychological terms, psychopathy involves poor emotional intelligence, lack of conscience, and an inability to feel attached to people except in terms of their value as a source of stimulation or a new possession. Someone with pronounced psychopathy may be an expert at reading and mimicking the emotions of others, which the person then uses to exploit and manipulate, without actually experiencing any depth of feeling within.

This facet of psychopathy is featured in the generally accepted forensic and clinical definitions, and even overlaps with an analytical psychology perspective, as represented by Guggenbühl-Craig's ideas. Like most diagnostic terms, we explain what it looks like in an extreme form to make a point, but in this case, the idea is useful for understanding problems that are less pronounced and far more common. As Guggenbühl-Craig pointed out:

> The existing deficiencies in our soul, even the empty spaces, are important for psychology. It is important that we see them in our fellow human beings. . . . But it is even more important to see these empty spaces in ourselves and not fool ourselves by denying them. Many of the empty or half-empty spaces in our psyche do not have especially tragic consequences. . . . But the closer our empty spaces come to eros, the more tragic the situation becomes. . . . This applies . . . to the endeavors of everyone to know himself and herself. . . .[1]

---

1 Jung, *The Symbolic Life*, x–xi.

It is understandable why the American Psychiatric Association and the numerous editors and authors of the DSM-5 would reason that the two categories, antisocial and psychopathic, belong together; they include characteristics that frequently appear in those individuals who come to the attention of authorities and the media. However, the distinction between them is important to understand, because psychopathy within affects our lives even when it goes unnoticed by others. Simply because it often does *not* manifest in obvious criminal conduct or legal problems, the trait in its subtler forms eludes definitive measurement.

A personality disorder often represents an unhealthy exaggeration of nonpathological traits. Interestingly, there is considerable overlap in terms of diagnostic categories that include related symptoms. Elements of the psychopathic dynamic are recognizable in a number of personality disorder traits besides antisocial, as described in the DSM-5, including excessive distrust and suspicion (paranoid), relationship instability and impulsivity (borderline), and grandiosity masking a fragile ego (narcissistic).[2] My intention is not to add psychopathy as another category of personality disorder but to point out that psychopathy can be understood as a more general—and elusive—trait in *addition* to being a characteristic of extreme disturbances and recognized diagnoses.

The psychopathic character disorder appears irrespective of distinguishing personal descriptors: It shows up in the charming cons and sexual predators whom Hare (1993) describes; in the lower-class, substance-abusing sociopaths Black (2000) writes about; and also in individuals of "high social standing," as Guggenbühl-Craig (1999) suggests, because anyone who cannot love, whatever the social standing, wants power as a substitute.[3] One of the most prominent and influential psychiatrists of Jung's era, German-born Emil Kraepelin, described

---

2   American Psychiatric Association, *Diagnostic and Statistical Manual of Mental Disorders (DSM-5)*, 5th ed. (Washington, DC, 2013), 649, 663, 669, 670.

3   Guggenbühl-Craig, *Emptied Soul*, 92, 128.

several "types" of psychopaths in notably outdated language, but with obvious modern counterparts, as liars and swindlers, criminals, and morbid vagabonds.[4]

From Jung to Hare to the DSM-5, studies of psychopathy have variously explored and defined this shadow aspect of human existence and behavior. General psychology focuses on antisocial symptoms. Hare identifies psychopathy by measuring personality characteristics emphasizing risk factors to the community. Jung and others portray it in terms of unconscious dynamics—a conceptualization that can be helpful in the service of individuation.

The ego predictably avoids the whole idea of psychopathy, even though the concept has collective sensational appeal. We detect and loudly reject it in others; it terrifies us like a thrill ride through which we scream wildly and then return for more. Still, the word itself makes most people shudder. The term we now favor, *sociopathy*, is often used interchangeably with *psychopathy* and suggests a figurative diminishment of the meaning, perhaps reflecting our collective hopes that we can better control it. A psychopath is not the same as a sociopath, however, which more resembles an individual with an antisocial personality disorder. Sociopathy emphasizes the commission of crimes against society. Renaming and slightly redefining the entire syndrome so that *psychopathy* becomes *sociopathy* subtly alleviates some of the negative connotations—or at least the more *personal*, negative ones. The phenomenon under consideration becomes relatively benign, or at least more manageable, since one is no longer dealing with the profound vastness of the psyche in all of its imperceptible machinations, but with a conflict between the individual and *society*.[5] Thus, the focus is objectified and externalized, rather than describing more intangible limitations within an individual. The implied meaning has shifted from an automatic association with extreme

---

4   Theodore Millon and Roger D. Davis, *Disorders of Personality: DSM-IV and Beyond* (New York: Wiley, 1996), 430.
5   Guggenbühl-Craig, *Emptied Soul*.

violence—and terrifying characterological emptiness—to a version that is somewhat easier to understand and discuss without revulsion.

Developmental Origins of Psychopathy

A child might begin learning a psychopathic style in response to a perpetrator parent who enjoys alienating the child from the victimized spouse. A child who is alienated from the non-offending parent and required to be loyal only to the abusive parent may create false memories to secure the love of the perpetrator, since the other parent has been characterized as bad, undeserving, or weak. The victimized child may thus be manipulated, against vehement inner protests, into loyalty by a powerful offending parent to avoid abuse and survive. Often, as they grow older, these children mimic the parental dynamic, either by becoming perpetrators or forming relationships with them.

This effort to avoid an intolerable external reality also teaches a problematic internal coping mechanism of compartmentalizing genuine feelings from behaviors—an early precursor of a pattern of shallow emotional responses, self-sabotage, and false accommodation: inner psychopathy. Nonetheless, such a self-defeating automatic response hard-wired into the psyche has the potential to become an individual's primary challenge. A complex forms that must be illuminated and depotentiated over a lifetime, if the individual chooses this path. Such a process is somehow inextricably linked to the person's destiny—in addition to being a characterological impediment. From a Jungian perspective, such traumatic childhood events that appear to threaten the soul may not ultimately derail it but illuminate the first manifestations or seeds of the individual's destiny or basic temperament, albeit through a painful and challenging process.[6]

---

6   James Hillman, *The Soul's Code: In Search of Character and Calling* (New York: Warner Books, 1996), 63–91.

A split in terms of a child's learning to identify and experience true feelings could result from any number of early family experiences. Both parents may be either abusive or unavailable, such that the child creates a false reality of some kind, perhaps through compartmentalizing thoughts and feelings, withdrawing, or dissociating to survive and protect against the harshness of having no parent to love and be loved by. Or one parent may demonize the other, manipulating the child to disconnect. Children who are frustrated or denied the natural inclination to show and experience healthy love and compassion with parents will eventually recreate the psychopathic style in their own relationships, either directly or indirectly, in ways that can be either obvious or hidden.[7]

We tend to think of child sexual abuse—fertile ground for the development of psychopathy—in terms of dramatic criminal cases. However, child sexual abuse often occurs in ways that are hidden, far more subtle than overt physical offenses but no less impactful on the developing psyche. A child sexualized, stimulated, or violated in cases of emotional incest by an otherwise loving parent is faced with that parent's psychopathy in an irresolvable dichotomy, torn between the need for self-protection and maintaining instinctive allegiance to a parent experienced as untrustworthy at some deep level.

For example, an isolated single parent might use an only child as the sole outlet to meet personal adult needs for companionship, love, and even physical closeness. The parent might violate emotional boundaries by overloading the child with expectations that place the child in a double bind between loving the parent and feeling flattered by the attention, while at the same time feeling trapped and resenting the intrusive closeness. A victimized child who trusts personal core reactions may feel a terrible mix of feelings, caught between self and

---

7   Marian Trent, *Exposing, Healing, and Preventing the Sociopathic Style: A Look at Parent Alienation Syndrome* (Dallas: Intra Muros, 2013). Available online at http://www.sociopathic-style.com/parent-alienation-syndrome.

survival: guilty for hating the parent, conflicted about loving the parent, responsible, and revolted by the involuntary arousal—a mix ripe for the development of psychopathy to escape into soothing oblivion. I encountered such cases in my work with child protective services.

Sexually abused children are often physically and emotionally stimulated by the molestation or incest at the same time they abhor the abuse, whether or not they are old enough to consciously understand it, and a wrenching conflict between true feelings, survival instincts, and attachment is created and internalized. Such dynamics may occur before a child has any means to conceptualize what is happening. Thus the seeds of psychopathy—along with other disorders—may be sown very early in life, at a stage before language can capture and express the inner conflict.

The child victim inevitably internalizes that toxic energy from the abusive parent in some way, often relegated to the unconscious where it may manifest unpredictably, perhaps with uncharacteristic acting-out behavior, early hypersexuality and promiscuity, and/or substance abuse. Later in life such an early experience may influence relationship choices. Children are more likely to blame themselves than take on the overwhelming struggle to resolve such coexisting opposites in perpe-trating but also caring adults, whom they love and hate, and in whom they need to believe for their own psychic equilibrium and survival. Thus, the psychopathy of the parent generates a complementary gap in the child.

One approach to understanding the origins of psychopathic development is through the concept of projection. Early in life, the self is projected onto parents or parental figures. In essence, a small child develops an identity from the responses of caretakers, and then introj-ects, or internalizes, parts of these characters as the child experiences them. If personal needs are responded to with consistency and care, the child will most likely feel secure and receive the message of being valued and safe in the world. If the caregivers are angry, depressed, or erratic, a corresponding lesson and lower expectations about self-worth and the environment are learned and deeply rooted. This unconscious process triggers both constructive and destructive aspects within us. In this way, fundamental archetypal constructs within our personalities are activated, representing this earliest experience of relationship and identity, from the inner psychopath to the inner good mother, for example. Understanding this phenomenon is another route to perceiving our psychopathic gaps, those ultimately destructive blind spots developed early in life to help us survive.

Hillman's Theories of Psychopathy

As Jungian analyst, scholar, and author James Hillman states in his chapter on "The Bad Seed" in *The Soul's Code: In Search of Character and Calling*, extreme psychopaths such as Adolf Hitler and Mary Bell—a British "bad seed" who, at the age of 11, killed two young children—manifest an "odd coldness. . . . There seems to be . . . some lack in their souls, or a lack of soul altogether."[8] Hillman identifies eight models that explain psychopathy, as follows: as early traumatic conditioning, as hereditary taint, due to group mores, as a product of the choice mechanism, through the forces of karma and zeitgeist, as part of the shadow, as lacuna, and due to a "demonic call."[9] The titles of these models suggest the general thrust of each. As with most theories to explain a conceptual phenomenon, there is some overlap but varying emphases. Hillman's analysis is particularly helpful here as a comprehensive and representative synopsis of the range of existing theories that attempt to explain the nature and origins of psychopathy. Perhaps most relevant to this writing, Hillman distinguishes between the concept of psychopathy as the shadow aspect of the human soul or character, and the idea presented in Adolf Guggenbühl-Craig's theory of lacunae: that psychopathy essentially reflects an absence of eros.

---

8   Hillman, *The Soul's Code*, 230.
9   Hillman, *The Soul's Code*, 227–238.

Hillman also suggests that the kind of either/or logic we tend to prefer in the Western world falls short when considering complex phenomena such as psychopathy. Each of his alternative ways of describing psychopathy holds merit, and they are not mutually exclusive. Most of the models on this list of theories differ from the idea of psychopathy as existing along a continuum. Hillman's theories point to an individual who is born or influenced a certain way that is *primarily* characterized by psychopathy, such that this person *is a psychopath*, different from the rest of the human race, rather than acknowledging varying degrees of psychopathy in a wide range of subtle—and more universal—ways.

The expression *bad seed* in the title of Hillman's chapter on psychopathy brings to mind William March's gripping novel by the same name, about a child serial killer, who, March suggests, inherited her murderous tendencies from her maternal grandmother—also a serial killer. Even the idea of a child with such a horrific trait violates our every cultural value about the presumed natural innocence of childhood. March's "bad seed" is a chilling example of genetically transmitted psychopathy in its extreme form: Evil dominates the personality of 8-year-old Rhoda. She is the fictional prototype for psychopathy: cold-blooded to the core, unaffected by love and compassion, and cut off from all others.[10]

March's book presents the classic example of either/or thinking about psychopathy, depicting an individual who is *a born psychopath* and therefore inherently different from the rest of the human race. It is important to note that while this either/or model differs radically from psychopathy defined as lacunae or gaps—as aspects of personality and character that are devoid of eros—our broader definition does not preclude due recognition of dangerous "bad seeds" among us or the grave consideration they warrant.

---

10   William March, *The Bad Seed* (New York: Rinehart & Company, 1954).

The dangers of polarized thinking notwithstanding, it can be equally ineffective to create such broad definitions that no distinctions are possible. If we are all psychopathic, the word can become meaningless, or at least nebulous. However, as illogical as it may sound from our normal frame of reference, Guggenbühl-Craig's observation that *in some regard,* "We are all psychopaths," is resonant with the premise of this writing, from his quote: "I am not speaking of 'us' and of 'them,' of us as integrated, balanced, or whole and of the others who are missing something—the psychopaths. . . . It seems to me far more important that, in speaking of psychopathy, we strive to realize in what way we are [all] psychopaths."[11]

Psychopathy as a characteristic of the human condition inevitably includes the existence of the blessedly uncommon extreme—but is not confined to it. The problematic versions are a matter of too much of something that is common, rather than the presence of an unusual, clearly definable disorder that allows a simple us–them dichotomy.

The definition of the word *psychopath,* from its Greek origins, is literally *suffering psyche,* which is somewhat ironic since the extreme psychopath is unlikely to suffer at all, given the absence of eros. One way to interpret this translation is that the psyche might be suffering in the sense of having a deficit, lacking some crucial element of pathos: a missing piece where something is needed but absent, manifested by thoughts, feelings, or behaviors that are devoid of warmth, sensitivity, humanity, and compassion. This concept of the damaged psyche is consistent with the idea of psychopathy as a characteristic of human existence and experience, affecting us personally and collectively: a somewhat amorphous quality that cannot be confined within a segregated classification of individuals. As a psychologist and therapist, but also as an individual, when I settle for a safe definition of human characteristics, hoping to be able to make judgments based on fixed and

---

11 Guggenbühl-Craig, *Emptied Soul,* 79.

discrete categories, I know that I risk compromising the tremendous healing power of my capacity for genuine reflection.

An expanded definition of psychopathy summons awareness of our own gaps. Such areas of emptiness, as suggested by Guggenbühl-Craig, and as I propose here, may manifest as characterological vulnerabilities. Emptiness described in this way does not equate to a total absence, which would mean *nothing*, but instead refers to a part of the personality that is unformed. Such gaps may be unexpected or inconsistent with other, more obvious aspects of an individual's personality and functioning. Conscious awareness of such inner aspects can potentiate our ability to heal them.

An expanded interpretation of psychopathy opens the possibility of greater understanding in a realm where our judgment is so readily informed by extreme reactions—charged emotional reactivity or statistical cutoff scores—neither of which fully reflects the scope and depth of the concept. The continuum concept roused my broader curiosity about psychopathy in more general terms and colored my perceptions of the world. I began to recognize psychopathy manifested culturally and collectively.

Eons before the advent of any diagnostic and statistical manuals of mental disorders, the character traits and conduct associated with psychopathy challenged humankind. Shortly following my father's death, when I had just begun deeply questioning my forensic and clinical understanding of psychopathy, I attended training at the C. G. Jung Institute in Küsnacht, Switzerland, and recognized the concept presented in an unexpected form, in mythology, reiterating the universality of this theme.

CHAPTER 13

Psychopathy in Mythology

In the summer of 2010, I attended lectures by Italian Jungian analyst and prolific author Luigi Zoja at the C. G. Jung Institute, Küsnacht, Summer Intensive Study Program (ISP). His topic: "The Two Poles of Masculine Identity." At one point during one of his lectures as he was discussing centaur myths, I experienced a breathtaking realization: I was struck by the resonance between Zoja's topic and my understanding of psychopathy. Immediately after the lecture, I ran into the institute office and feverishly scribbled notes.[1] Encountering Zoja's concept of the centaurs at this formative point in the development of my thinking about psychopathy felt like startling synchronicity to me. Suddenly and unexpectedly, the lecture evolved from an academic presentation to a personal message that resonated with the very subject I had been wrestling with in my writing, cracking wide open my understanding of psychopathy to include a broader historical and mythological perspective with rich portent.

The content of the following two chapters reflects Zoja's presentation, in particular his exploration of the centaur, which I recognized as an archetypal symbol for our human struggle between higher

---

1 Luigi Zoja, Lectures: "Two Poles of Masculine Identity." Based on notes from his lectures at the C. G. Jung Institute Zürich Summer Intensive Study Program, July 2010.

consciousness and the inner beast: an embodiment of the challenge to integrate our psychopathy within. Bridging from Zoja's ideas about history and mythology to our current cultural dilemmas, this chapter includes a discussion of the powerful similarities between character- istics of the centaurs of age-old Greek–Roman tradition and modern forensic indices measuring psychopathy.

My experience of entering the spacious upstairs lecture hall at the C. G. Jung Institute in Küsnacht felt like entering a storied time capsule, fantastical yet oddly familiar. The well-oiled wooden floors creaked comfortably with the footsteps of this season's international students and seekers, most gazing around with unabashed delight at the elegant design of the vast, high-ceilinged classroom, basking in the ambience of this place and its splendid history. Lake Zürich sparkled through a promenade of statuesque windows lining the long walls, opened wide to invite the warm summer breeze.

Dr. Zoja was perfectly cast for this setting as the distinguished lecturer—a lean, tall Italian scholar with a spontaneous wit and a kind, engaging, humble manner that belied his intimidating credentials. Initially distracted by the sonorous timbre of his voice and the general ambience, it took me a while to focus on the content of his lecture, as he described the rich imagery of the centaurs in their mythological world, in the context of opposite historical images and aspects of masculine identity: the father versus the competitive male.

In a central way, Zoja's point about fathering was about modern-day role confusion: our having lost the old image of the father as head of household, leader, protector, and sole or primary provider, and replacing it with a compensation that cannot quite stand alone—a new man not yet clearly defined. This confusion about roles reflects more generalized confusion about tradition, change, and values that seem discordant. Collectively, modern society is fraught with mixed messages. Confusion is evident universally in our world culture, not just in terms of gender roles, which are anything but simple. A prime example is to be found in the duality of our attitudes about violence. It may be politically correct to abhor and decry violence, but after all of these centuries, in our sophisticated era, still nothing declares power more universally or provides more popular entertainment to the masses. Rape, sexual abuse, and other forms of radical oppression certainly continue worldwide. I am reminded of the following lines from Yeats's prescient poem "The Second Coming":

> Turning and turning in the widening gyre
> The falcon cannot hear the falconer;
> Things fall apart; the centre cannot hold;
> Mere anarchy is loosed upon the world,
> The blood-dimmed tide is loosed, and everywhere
> The ceremony of innocence is drowned;
> The best lack all conviction, while the worst
> Are full of passionate intensity.[2]

Chaos and confusion about values in our world culture create vulnerability to more of the same. This kind of disequilibrium reflects a struggle between extreme opposites, manifested individually and collectively, inviting the *centaur archetype*, as I am using the term here: as an archetypal representation of the inner psychopath.

The Centaur Archetype

The patriarch, as depicted in ancient Roman lore, is essentially a good citizen, an ethical man, a provider. The opposite aspect to the patriarch—the nonpaternal, violent male—is aptly symbolized by the centaurs of Greek–Roman tradition, those half-human, half-animal gangsters of antiquity. Their relationships with females were unstable at best, and they were known for wantonly engaging in abduction, drunkenness, and rape. As Zoja described these characters, they were

---

2   William Butler Yeats, "The Second Coming." In *Collected Poems of W. B. Yeats*, ed. Richard J. Finneran (New York: Simon & Schuster, 1983187.

clearly missing the emotional depth and integrity associated with love, and their blatant misconduct reflected an obvious *absence of eros*: that is, psychopathy.[3]

As described in many myths, centaur behavior is generally ruled by base instinct rather than reason. The centaur's horse loins symbolically suggest aggressive sexuality driven by instinct without conscience, while the upper body is that of a man, symbolically suggesting the potential for higher consciousness, refined sensibilities, and morality.

(As a caveat, identifying the centaur's half-animal nature as representative of psychopathy draws solely upon our human projections regarding animal consciousness as inferior to that of humans. Given the blight on this planet inflicted by humans, the arrogance we display in our contention that we hold such a higher status than animals is irrational. We have no idea of the levels of consciousness living, breathing animals inhabit; different than ours, certainly, but "baser" could be easily contested, given how we humans behave. The comment that one is acting "like an animal" by being brutish reflects our tendency to project our own baser instincts onto the animal kingdom, yet we so often do not conduct ourselves like the noblest of creatures. The mythological centaur is a symbol that represents the inevitable human struggle between the polarities of consciousness and *our* baser instincts. Real animals are incapable of psychopathy.)

The centaur archetype embodies the process of the innate human struggle to contain the opposites within us, spanning our best sensibilities and conscience, our noblest aspects and potential, and our lesser qualities, those aspects devoid of honor, morality, or eros. The centaur provides a vivid symbolic representation of the psychopath within—in the bound context of everything else we contain, including the potential for integration. The violence and mayhem on this planet provides its own literal substantiation that the centaur archetype is alive, repre-

---

3   Guggenbühl-Craig, *Emptied Soul.*

senting a human struggle that is perhaps forever unresolved but still endlessly compelling.

The centaur is a lawless, remorseless aggressor. The struggle to contain that kind of archetypal energy is a personal and societal predicament irrespective of gender: a timeless challenge for collective humankind. Zoja's lecture that afternoon in Küsnacht brought these ideas to life for me, as I recognized the themes of the ancient myths he described in my own journey, my studies, and my personal and professional experiences of psychopathy. Ancient Greek and Roman mythologies are replete with classic examples of the centaurs' psychopathic behavior and the frustrated efforts of humans to cope with it.[4] Indiscriminate elimination does not work, and attempts at conventional socialization seem to backfire as well. Some such examples follow.

Ixion

Ixion, the Greek mythological character who fathered the race of centaurs, represents the lawless man. Ixion was king of the Lapiths, the most ancient tribe of Thessaly. Ixion married Dia and promised her father, Deioneus, a valuable present as the bride price. However, Ixion neglected to pay the bride price, so Deioneus stole some of his horses in retaliation. Ixion concealed his resentment and invited his father-in-law to a feast. When Deioneus arrived, Ixion pushed him onto a bed of burning coals and wood, killing him.

The neighboring princes were so offended by Ixion's act of treachery that they refused to perform the rituals that would cleanse him of his guilt and allow him catharsis. Thereafter, Ixion lived as an outlaw and was shunned. He subsequently went mad, defiled by his own act. Although his violent conduct was obviously callous, demonstrating a serious lack of integrity, the fact that he felt conflicted and remorseful about it afterward at least suggests an inner split, some complexity of

---

4   Zoja, "Two Poles."

character. By killing his father-in-law, Ixion was considered the first man guilty of kin-slaying in Greek mythology. That alone would warrant a terrible punishment for him.

The mighty Zeus took pity on Ixion, brought him home to Mount Olympus, and introduced him at the table of the gods. However, instead of remaining grateful for this mercy, Ixion grew lustful for Hera, Zeus's wife, and tried to seduce her—a blatant violation of guest–host relations and another illustration of his character flaws. Zeus discovered Ixion's intentions and created a cloud in the shape of Hera. He then tricked Ixion into raping the cloud instead of his wife. From the union of Ixion and the false-Hera cloud, Centauros was born. He was deformed, hunched over, and never found peace with humans. The only place he felt loved was roaming on the Pelion Mountain with the Magnesian mares, with whom he mated and spawned offspring, thereafter called *centaurs*: a violent life form embodying unresolved opposite character traits!

The centaurs conducted themselves much like our urban gang members, manifesting some similar group traits, problem-solving strategies, beliefs, and behaviors, although less is known about their loyalty to each other, which is a predominant value in modern gangs. Even the most evolved centaurs had obvious character deficits, pockets of psychopathy, across circumstances: inability to delay gratification, low to no impulse control, lack of integrity, and anger management issues—characteristics that are *all* identical to items on the modern psychological risk assessment tools we employ to identify and measure psychopathy.

Hercules

Hercules is the Roman name for the Greek divine hero Heracles, who was the son of Zeus (Roman equivalent, Jupiter) and the mortal Alcmene. One of his unique characteristics is that he is half-human. Hera, Zeus's wife, was jealous and spiteful toward her husband's many mistresses, and because Hercules was the product of one of Zeus's many extramarital affairs, he became a target of her wrath. In classical mythology, Hercules is famous for his strength and for his numerous, far-ranging adventures. A myth about Hercules illustrates the problems created by attempts to engage or befriend the centaurs, even with the best of intentions. Some accounts suggest that Hercules was visiting his centaur friend, Pholus, and the two were having dinner. After eating, Hercules was thirsty and helped himself to some wine; however, he mistakenly began drinking the sacred wine reserved for special occasions. Pholus saw that Hercules was drinking this wine but could not gather the courage to tell him to stop. The sacred scent quickly reached the other centaurs, who promptly grabbed their weapons and charged Pholus' house. Pholus fled and left Hercules by himself to fight off the angry centaurs, which he did with little effort. After Hercules killed some of them, the rest ran away in fear.

A slightly different version of this story is that Hercules tried to befriend a couple of the most decent centaurs and invited them to dinner, but when he brought out the wine, the other centaurs picked up the scent of the alcohol with their heightened animal instincts and came uninvited to disrupt the party. They became wild and intoxicated, leaving Hercules no choice but to kill them (the moral of the story being that a civilized approach was not a viable alternative where centaurs were concerned). This event generated an attitude of extreme repression within the ancient culture; the local citizens concluded that the only way to deal effectively with centaurs was not to try and find the good in them or educate them, but to kill them. Needless to say, the attitude pertained to all centaurs, ignoring the variance within that population.

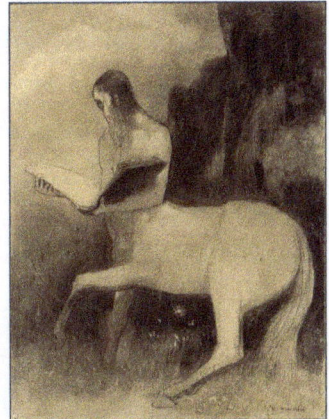

ODILON REDON
(1840–1916),
CENTAURE LISANT
(CENTAUR READING)

Strikingly apparent to me was the similarity between how our modern society is struggling to deal with "sex offenders" as a blanket category and these stories of how ancient cultures attempted to deal with the mythological centaurs among them. Although we are certainly faced with other criminal categories that challenge our society, including other kinds of violent offenses and offenders, the broad category of sexual offenses and the corresponding label of "sex offender" have acquired a far-reaching "pariah" portend that is unique, suggesting a categorization and stigma resonant with the stories of the centaurs in their ancient mythological context. The oddly similar descriptions of public attitude toward centaurs then and toward sex offenders now suggested parallel themes between our responses to psychopathy in ancient times and today: avoiding intolerable aspects of human nature and attempting to consign them to an identified population that can be ostracized.

In the modern example, it seems we are attempting to widen the boundary between *us* and *them* by adopting a generic, polarized response to individuals convicted of a plethora of sexual crimes. This approach at least figuratively represents a modern version of the ancient outcome of Hercules' conflict with the centaurs, when the Roman citizens concluded that the only way to effectively deal with centaurs was to treat them identically, as *a priori* offenders, to cease efforts to redeem or teach any of them, and to uniformly kill/repress them.

In ancient Roman mythology, no solution to Hercules' battle with the centaurs is described in terms we can emulate as a society; their conflict was never resolved. Hercules' life on earth ended due to centaur trickery, as he put on a shirt soaked in poisoned blood, burning his flesh to the bone. Half-mortal Hercules could not die, per se, so he built himself a funeral pyre, spreading his lion skin cloak upon it and lying down to burn. The flames consumed the mortal part of him, while the immortal part ascended to Mount Olympus. There Zeus set him among the gods, where he was reconciled with his tormenter, the queen of the gods, Hera. She allowed him to marry her daughter, Hebe, and live among the gods thereafter.

This Hercules myth depicts a clear separation between the centaur/mortal and the godlike/immortal aspects of existence, but of course we have no such option to separate these polarities in real life. The story of Hercules and the modern saga of our dealings with sex offenders represent situational expressions of a dilemma endemic to humankind. Individually and collectively, we bear the universal task of integrating our opposites within and coping with the opposite contents in each other and the world we create. Stories of the centaurs illuminate that archetypal struggle.

Centaur Psychopathy

Ovid's *Metamorphosis* includes stories about the mythological war between the Lapiths and the centaurs that further illustrate centaur psychopathy, amplifying the potential consequences and describing different responses to manipulation, deception, rape, victimization, and violence.

Nessos is one of the Thessalian centaurs who flees his homeland after the Lapith war. Making his way to the Aitolian River Euenos, he establishes himself as a ferryman. When Hercules later passes by with his new bride, Deianeira, Nessos meets them. Somehow the couple becomes separated and Nessos is left alone with the woman, clearly foreshadowing problems. It is significant that psychopathy prevails once the newlywed partners are apart. With Hercules and Nessos no longer in view of each other either, the polar masculine opposites are symbolically separated as well, portending extremes and conflict. Nessos takes Deianeira upon his back and appropriately (given his job) ferries her across the river. However, ultimately, his centaur nature prevails: He becomes inflamed with desire for the beautiful woman and attempts to rape her. Zoja captured the essence of this scene by describing Nessos putting "crazy, lawless hands on her . . . the violence of the centaur has to do with manipulation and perverted use of the hands."[5]

Deianeira struggles with the centaur and cries out. Hercules spots them, presumably from a distance, throws his bow like a boomerang, and miraculously strikes Nessos in the chest with it. Other versions say he strikes him with his poisoned arrows. Nessos feels death coming but still recoups enough to violate his victim in a different kind of perverse manner, as his physical strength wanes. In a classic psychopathic maneuver, he emotionally manipulates her, telling her that he repents, undoubtedly crying false tears. He plays on her sympathies and begs her not to let all of his blood be wasted in the river, urging her to take some of it and use it as a love charm. If Hercules should ever prove unfaithful, she is to tell him to clothe himself in material soaked in Nessos' blood and the problem will be solved. Of course, she is moved and takes the blood as he implores her.

Subsequently Hercules and Deianeira live happily enough together until he goes off to war and defeats another king, who happens to have a beautiful daughter. Hercules arranges to bring the king's daughter back with him as a concubine. He sends a message home to get his clothing.

The myth of the *Women of Trachis,* an Athenian tragedy by Sophocles, begins with Deianeira's lament about her difficult life. She tells of Hercules marrying her and rescuing her from the centaur, only to subject her to further suffering because he is so frequently away from home. She discovers Hercules' infidelity with the conquered king's daughter, and her feelings are hurt, so she soaks his clothing with the dead centaur's blood, as he had suggested, and ensures that Hercules dons it. This turns out to be a fatal trick on them both. The clothes suffocate him and tear his flesh. Once Deianeira realizes she has been naïve and duped by the centaur, she kills herself.

---

5   Ibid.

Nessos manages to rape her once again in a figurative way, ravaging her mind long after her body has recovered from his physical abduction and causing her eventual demise. This myth symbolically represents how the damage caused by psychopathy is contagious and pervasive. Various efforts to win a battle with it easily fail, resulting in some form of loss or death, literal or figurative, body or soul. The next mythological example represents a form of the latter, where a victim's strategy to survive requires sacrificing an aspect of self that can never be retrieved.

Caenis: Identification with the Aggressor

In the ancient myth about Caenis, from Ovid's *Metamorphosis*, Caenis defends herself through her identification with the perpetrator in a most radical manner. She does not fall in love with the aggressor; instead, she chooses to become one, interestingly prescient of the modern concept of the *Stockholm syndrome*: identification with the aggressor.

As the myth begins, Caenis is a beautiful girl living in Thessaly, Greece. Many suitors want to marry her, but she is in no hurry and rejects them all. One day when she is walking by the ocean, Neptune emerges, attacks her, and brutally rapes her. He then makes a conciliatory gesture, expresses halfhearted repentance, and tells Caenis that because he is a god, he can grant any wish for her. She answers with only one desire: that something like this absolutely never happens again. She asks him to transform her so that she would never again be a victim—or a woman.

As well as granting this request, Neptune makes her invulnerable to attack. Thus, Caenis became Caeneus, a brave and steadfast warrior. She/he fights the centaurs with fierce aggression at the wedding of Pirithous, which turns into a bloody conflict. Transformed into an invincible and fearsome warrior, she/he kills many men in battle, exacting revenge against the sex that had harmed her, symbolized by the male god Neptune. The story depicts a classic concept: The response to sexual violence is often to inflict upon the self or others some form of the harmful experience. In this case, Caenis does both; she becomes the violent male perpetrator instead of the female victim, but these two identities remain two aspects within her/him that can never be integrated. The price of this solution is that her/his feminine is forever lost, leaving her/him with a tenuous victory at best.

This story also symbolizes a general principle relevant to psychopathy, which affects both outer experience and inner process: The psychological scars from sexual violence often long outlive the visible repercussions to the body, buried deep within the psyche, where fear, shame, and secrecy further diminish or eliminate the hope of healing.

To illustrate the universality of this theme, here it is described from a completely different context and era, but touching upon the same enduring dynamic, in D. H. Lawrence's *Lady Chatterley's Lover*:

> And dimly she realised one of the great laws of the human
> soul: that when the emotional soul receives a wounding
> shock, which does not kill the body, the soul seems to recover
> as the body recovers. But this is only appearance. It is, really,
> only the mechanism of re-assumed habit. Slowly, slowly the
> wound to the soul begins to make itself felt, like a bruise
> which only slowly deepens its terrible ache, till it fills all the
> psyche. And when we think we have recovered and forgotten,
> it is then that the terrible after-effects have to be encountered
> at their worst.[6]

Psychopathy expressed through overt behavior is usually easiest to recognize, but as suggested by the above examples, the inner manifestations and psychic repercussions of psychopathy are far more elusive—and no less devastating. The Stockholm syndrome illustrates a strategy that might not be recognized as psychopathic, since the victim

---

6   D. H. Lawrence, *Lady Chatterley's Lover* (New York: Penguin Books, 1993/1928), 49.

appears to be choosing to align with the perpetrator voluntarily—but in fact may, indeed, be the result of a psychopathic gap.

Stockholm Syndrome

Stockholm syndrome is probably our best-known modern example of coping with psychopathy through identification with the aggressor.

The syndrome is named after the 1973 robbery of the *Kreditbanken* at Norrmalmstorg in Stockholm, Sweden. The robbers held bank employees hostage for five days. The victims became emotionally attached to their captors and even defended them after they were freed from their ordeal. The term *Stockholm syndrome* was coined by criminologist and psychiatrist Nils Bejerot, who assisted the police during the investigation and subsequently referred to the syndrome in a news broadcast. It was originally defined by psychiatrist Frank Ochberg to aid in the management of hostage situations. Stockholm syndrome describes a paradoxical psychological phenomenon wherein hostages express adulation for their captors and develop positive feelings toward them. Such feelings appear irrational in light of the danger and risk endured by the victims, also suggesting their attempts to integrate their experience through identification with the aggressor aspect within themselves. The FBI's Hostage Barricade Database System shows that roughly 27% of crime victims show evidence of the syndrome.

Patricia Campbell Hearst ("Patty Hearst"), now Patricia Campbell Hearst Shaw, is a renowned example of Stockholm syndrome. Born in 1954, she is an American newspaper heiress, socialite, actress, kidnap victim—and convicted bank robber. The granddaughter of publishing magnate William Randolph Hearst and great-granddaughter of millionaire George Hearst, she gained notoriety in 1974 following her kidnapping by the Symbionese Liberation Army (SLA), when she ultimately joined her captors in furthering their cause. Apprehended after participating in a bank robbery with other SLA members, she was imprisoned for almost two years before her sentence was commuted by

President Jimmy Carter. She was later granted a presidential pardon by President Bill Clinton in his last official act before leaving office. She subsequently married her former body guard, Bernard Shaw.

Both of these stories, worlds apart—that of Caenis and of Patty Hearst—represent attempts to resolve psychopathy experienced at the hands of external perpetrators with an inner adaptation—at a cost. These roughly parallel examples of identifying with the aggressor, illustrated by an age-old myth and a modern-day syndrome, suggest a timeless universal theme of humanity struggling to cope with this dark aspect of human character through various means.

These examples both feature female victims at the hands of psychopathic male perpetrators. However, the struggle to deal with psychopathy, which can be symbolized by the centaur aspect within us, is by no means gender-specific.

The Centaur Animus: Identifying Psychopathy in Women

The two poles of masculinity—the good father and the centaur aspects—are also relevant to females in terms of their animus, or the masculine aspect within them. The animus may manifest in a number of ways. For example, a woman's good-father animus energy is observable when she acts responsibly, accomplishes her goals, and interacts ethically with others. Her centaur animus energy, in contrast, might be evidenced when she slips into playing a willing pseudovictim role to a man's centaur overtures, using his own mindless instincts to deceive and manipulate him for her own purposes. Or she may act out her own violence and sexuality in overtly aggressive or promiscuous conduct. An example from my private therapy practice illustrates how the centaur animus might manifest.

The patient is an attractive, married, middle-aged professional woman. During therapy, she described an experience she had while on vacation in another state. She had met a man who was clearly interested in her and toward whom she felt a kindred spark. She wanted to connect with him but did not trust herself, worrying that she would lapse into old promiscuous behaviors and sexualize the mutual interest, so she talked with him briefly and avoided extended contact. The night before she was scheduled to return home to her husband, there was a party at the resort center where everyone was drinking. She had some wine and decided to leave. She went to hug the man goodbye, and he grasped her tightly, even after she started to pull away. She felt familiar arousal emerge in that moment and lingered in the hug until his grip softened, then they exchanged parting comments and she returned to her hotel room.

Later that evening, she was downstairs in the lobby when another guest approached and invited her to rejoin the same group in the hotel bar for a drink, where they had reconvened to prolong the farewell party. She agreed and walked to the table where the others were gathered. The man was there across the table and brightened as she joined the group. Her heart leaped, but she deliberately downplayed her reaction. She was about to order another drink but noticed herself slipping into a former problematic behavior pattern, so she made a conscious choice not to place that order. Knowing she had already said goodbye, she left quietly, returned to her room, and prepared for bed alone. She felt calm and strong. Later, she reflected on what had transpired and although she realized that her response had been true to herself, she was also keenly aware that she had suffered an inner struggle.

In session, as she described this process, I imagined the centaur within her having roused himself with an animal grunt, lifting his sensuous head from crossed arms where he had been dozing, one eye slowly opening, tail twitching, suddenly alert to the scent of pending action, ears perked—only to be ordered to go back to sleep. He almost had her.

After she returned home to her husband and her life, she continued to fantasize about this man. She caught herself in wild musings about what life would be like with him, or at least what sex with him would be like, amplifying in her imagination the energy that had transpired between them so briefly. She could laugh a little at herself when she caught herself engaging in this self-delusion. Long afterward, she found herself trying to rationalize indulging the seductive enticements of the centaur animus, fantasizing such logical and benign-sounding excuses to contact the man that she nearly succeeded in fooling herself. That inner centaur energy can be both elusive and tenacious. In this case, her deliberate acknowledgment of its presence allowed her make a conscious decision to ignore its calling.

The centaur animus archetype may operate subtly, as when a woman either repeatedly chooses mates who are unavailable on some level (whether emotionally, logistically, or legally) or when she herself engages in behavior that sabotages her relationships, and then makes exaggerated efforts ostensibly trying to "make it work." Such a woman might only select and ardently pursue married men or long-distance relationships, or she might have secret serial affairs while presenting a flawless appearance of enthusiastic devotion and commitment to her husband.

False Accommodation

A woman experiencing her centaur animus has trouble being true to herself and connecting with her inner integrity, even if she surmises it must be there somewhere. Her efforts to mine it come up empty on occasion, revealing only a gap in her psyche—her inner psychopathy. One relatively inconspicuous way this centaur animus energy may manifest is through false accommodation.

Under the influence of a psychopathic animus aspect, a woman may conduct herself in ways that unwittingly repeat the wounding that caused her initial suffering. For example, in my case, in younger years I adopted an attitude of faux emotional toughness in relationships. I was drawn to males who were unavailable or difficult, not unlike my father in some ways. If a woman has had an experience of rejection or worse from a significant male, she may attempt to protect herself indirectly from the pain and vulnerability that are her true responses to such treatment by adopting a compensatory defense: She may tell herself that hurtful behavior does not affect her or that she deserves it in some way. With this underlying attitude, *false accommodation* is likely, meaning that she acts as though she accepts situations or treatment she experiences as absolutely intolerable at her unconscious, hidden, or avoided core.

Managing this unconscious conflict requires a disconnection from her own true thoughts and feeling responses: in essence, she abandons herself, however unwittingly, to maintain approval or the illusion of peace with others. This defense may evolve into a coping strategy that she uses in a wide range of life situations. She may appear able to tolerate circumstances or behavior antithetical to her best interest. She may make amplified efforts to misrepresent her feelings, concealing the truth even from herself, by overcompensating and behaving in polar opposite ways. For example, an angry employee might overzealously compliment the boss she secretly blames for her failure to advance in the company as she deserves, or a jealous wife who finds out her husband is having an affair with his attractive new secretary might pressure him to give the woman a raise and invite her to dinner at their home.

This protective shield of falsely accommodating others inevitably precludes the genuine intimacy she may profess to want, but of which she is secretly terrified. The result is a kind of pseudoexistence that ironically blocks her experience of the very love and connection that might actually help to heal her. This dynamic may be well hidden under an apparently healthy exterior. Women who seek abusive partners whom they glorify, while blaming themselves for the maltreatment and preserving an airtight family image at all costs, provide an extreme example of this problem.

Beyond intimate relationships, false accommodation may be expressed when one makes exaggerated gestures to appear generous,

thoughtful, or tolerant, despite feeling otherwise; to do so can potentially intensify inner detachment, building frustration and resentment.
Even for those of us who would never identify with *inner psychopathy*,
there may be ways in which we manifest our gaps, inconsistent areas of
the psyche devoid of conscience or morality, untouched by eros—even
if our behavior hurts no one other than ourselves.

To further broaden our exploration of psychopathy through the
centaur archetype, from individual to collective cultural examples, in
this next section we return back in history to mythological manifestations.

The Mythological Origin of Rome

The mythological origin of Rome includes a story that illustrates one
way conflicts generated by psychopathic behavior are resolved within
a culture.

Rome was founded by the twin brothers, Romulus and Remus.
Following the death of his twin brother, Romulus completed the city
and named it *Roma* after himself. He then divided Roma's fighting
men into regiments of 3,000 infantry and 300 cavalry, which he called
legions. From the rest of the populace, he selected 100 of the noblest
and wealthiest men to serve as his council, whom he called *patricians*.
They were the representative fathers of Rome, not only because they
cared for their own legitimate citizen-sons, but because they maintained a paternal love for the city and all of its inhabitants. They
were also Rome's elders and were known as *senators*. Romulus thereby
inaugurated a system of government and social hierarchy focused on
the patron–client relationship, characterized by compassionate caring
and responsibility. The patricians generally represented the values of
the good father: reliability, honor, protection, and provision.

However, the burgeoning empire of Rome drew exiles, refugees,
the dispossessed, criminals, and runaway slaves. The city expanded its
boundaries to accommodate them, and five of the seven hills of Rome

were settled. As most of these immigrants were men, Rome found itself with a dire shortage of marriageable women. For all intents and purposes, it was an all-male population.

At the suggestion of his grandfather, Romulus held a solemn festival in honor of Neptune (according to another tradition the festival was held in honor of a different god, Consus, the protector of grains). In one version of the story, Romulus lied and spread the rumor that the bones of a god had been discovered in Rome, hoping to entice their neighbors, the Sabines—who arrived en masse, along with their daughters, in response to the trick. The Sabine women, who happened to be virgins—683 of them, according to ancient Roman historian Livy—suddenly appeared in the city. The Romans responded by raping them and subsequently kept them afterward, which also required killing or fighting off the Sabine men.

The overriding Roman intention was apparently to create a society—basically an honorable motive—but the method included abduction and rape, certainly absent eros, and thus psychopathic in nature. Understanding the nature of eros is fundamental to understanding the nature of its absence as psychopathic: a prevailing theme of this writing. Guggenbühl-Craig describes the Greek god Eros as the archetypal representation of a wide-spectrum definition of love, here presented as a reminder of how the god image symbolically impacts society:

> According to Greek mythology, Eros is the oldest of the gods, although there are some tales which make him the youngest. Whether oldest or youngest, it is clear that he is a special god different from the others. He is the god of love. Here love is understood to include the entire spectrum of emotional attachment, from sexuality and friendship to involvement with profession, hobbies, and art. Eros is at work in the love which men have for women and women for men. Eros is also present in politicians whose "love" is politics, or in mathe-

maticians whose passion is mathematics, or in flower fanciers who live for their roses. It is to Eros' credit that gods and goddesses, gods and mortals, come together as lovers so that new gods and demigods are born. Without him there would be no movement among the gods; in fact, there would be no gods at all. It is Eros who makes the gods—the archetypes— loving, creative, and involved. Only through Eros can gods or archetypes be loving. As far as we mortals are concerned, gods are neutral, inhuman, distanced, and cold. Only when they are combined with Eros do we sense their movement, do they become creative, intimate, and stimulating.[7]

After a considerable length of time elapsed, the Sabine men returned to Rome to fight for their women and their honor. They attacked the Romans and thus ensued the War with the Sabines. However, by that time the Sabine women had conceived babies with their captors and adjusted, perforce, to life in their new home, although it was a relocation into which they had initially been forcibly abducted. Undoubtedly motivated by their revised practical priorities, the Sabine women walked onto the battlefield and stopped the mutual destruction, realizing the conflict would be a loss for them either way it ended, if allowed to continue.

This action was pivotal in determining the subsequent course of history and essentially preserved Roman society, with the many possibilities created by then—albeit originally through violence and deception. Further, as Zoja put it, this myth "invented the melting pot," noting that often the way racist barriers are dissipated is through inter- marriage.[8] This example also shows that the resolution of psychopathy may arise through the expression of eros in unanticipated, indirect ways. Although the original ancient Roman conflict depicted here involved psychopathic behaviors in the form of violence and deception, the final outcome, achieved through such a dark, circuitous route, was

---

7 Guggenbühl-Craig, *Emptied Soul*, 25, 26.
8 Zoja, "Two Poles."

the creation of family, community, and civilization, manifesting eros in the form of redeeming human propensities and priorities.

This example from ancient mythology suggests that the struggle to contain our inner opposites, individually and collectively, is inarguably endemic to the human race. When we lose the battle to the inner centaur, that aspect prevails, manifesting with absent or compromised conscience, disregard for potential consequences, wanton violence and sexual misconduct, psychological and emotional manipulation, deception, callousness, and behavior driven by thoughtless animal instinct: psychopathy within. When the better, more conscious, and evolved aspects of ourselves figuratively win that battle with the inner centaur, the victory is likely to occur through healing eros, operating less through direct action and intention than in unforeseen ways, reflecting a spontaneous emergence of the integrity and compassion that also characterize humanity. Further understanding of psychopathy is most useful if doing so informs and guides our potential to heal it.

The centaur as an ancient archetypal symbol represents not only the potential domination of brute instincts but, perhaps most importantly, the unconscious hope for *healing* psychopathy. Instead of mastering or taming their worst instincts—violent lust, adultery, vengefulness, etc.—centaurs are typically ruled by them. Interestingly enough, however, their king, Chiron, manifested the polar opposite of this characteristic brutality. In its entirety, the centaur myth symbolically represents the challenge that pervades our human existence: the challenge within and between each of us to somehow contain both our worst instincts *and* our innate human capacity for their opposites, including consciousness, wisdom, and justice. As a symbol, the centaur embodies both polarities and the inherent struggle between them—as well as the potential we all hold for healing through love.

Chiron: Hope for Healing Psychopathy

Chiron, king of the centaurs, was Zeus' half-brother, and unlike the rest of his race, was reputed to be intelligent, wise, and a renowned healer. Born of a violent rape, abandoned and rejected by his parents, he was a god and a nymph who was eventually lauded primarily as a healer, but also as a teacher and a prophet.

As previously described, Chiron had become friends with Hercules. In the violent confrontation that erupted between Hercules and other centaurs who came to disrupt his dinner with Pholus, a centaur and a friend, a poison arrow grazed the knee of Chiron, who was not involved in the fight but had come to try and stop it. The immortal Chiron could not die from his wound but would have been doomed to live in great pain forever. He cried to Zeus to give him relief and end his life. Zeus took pity on Chiron and let him die. The Greek god of healing, Asklepios, was taught the art of healing by Chiron, an ideal representative of this archetype, having himself suffered an incurable wound.[9] To honor Chiron, Zeus gave him a place among the stars, where that constellation eternally symbolizes the integrity and power of the wounded healer. The essence of the healer–patient relationship is expressed by the archetypal symbol of the wounded healer: "Chiron, the centaur and wounded healer of ancient Greece, expresses consciousness rooted in the body, and reveals the medicinal seeds of light in the psychosomatic darkness."[10]

The battle of conflicting forces within the human character may appear irresolvable, without much possibility of integration; however, this chaos may also contain an unexpected, creative solution in the form of healing love. As Shinoda Bolen suggests, such a transcendent outcome is most likely when we "live with a hopeful assumption that

---

9   Anthony Stevens, *Ariadne's Clue: A Guide to the Symbols of Humankind* (Princeton, NJ: Princeton University Press, 1998), 275.

10 The Archive for Research in Archetypal Symbolism (ARAS), *The Book of Symbols: Reflections on Archetypal Images* (Cologne, Germany: Taschen, 2010), 738.

what we do with our lives is important and has meaning, and if we act accordingly with integrity, hope, courage, and compassion." This stance toward life allows *eros* to guide us and infuse our circumstances—to heal our inner psychopathy.[11]

The more we understand how psychopathy plays out on collective levels, the better our chances of recognizing the potential for healing it. It was when the idea of a gradated definition of psychopathy was beginning to jell in my thinking that I noticed dimensions of my forensic, Jungian, and clinical work had an unexpected congruence with the broad theme of psychopathy in some of the ancient myths. As noted previously, most striking to me was how our modern struggles to effectively deal with sex offenders in some ways seemed to parallel the myths about our ancient Greek forebears contending with the centaurs, reflecting the timeless human struggle to cope with inner and outer polar opposites through the creation of broad-brush scapegoat categories, and suggesting our collective avoidance of the perpetrator and victim within each of us. I was strongly reminded of this dynamic by several of Zoja's lecture topics that summer in Küsnacht, which further aroused my curiosity and enhanced my understanding.

---

11 Bolen, *Tao of Psychology*, 81.

CHAPTER 14

Concepts Related to Psychopathy

Zoja's lecture touched on various concepts and principles relevant to understanding psychopathy in human nature and experience, including *pseudospeciation, enantiodromia,* and *compensation.* I was surprised when I recognized the relationship between these ideas and our unifying theme, a gradated definition of psychopathy and its ramifications.

Pseudospeciation

Pseudospeciation was one of Zoja's topics that enriched my perception of psychopathy as a broadly defined human characteristic. Pseudospeciation tills dangerous, fertile ground for psychopathy and warrants our wary attention. According to the Oxford English Dictionary, *pseudospeciation* refers to the tendency of members of in-groups to consider members outside their groups to have devolved into genetically different, separate—and inferior—species to their own.

The term was first used by psychologist Erik Erikson in 1966. Dehumanization is one possible outcome of pseudospeciation. Discrimination and genocide are others, since the distorted perspective promotes a disparaging view of other groups, races, and ethnicities as comprising inferior species. Such a belief system creates a *collective psychopathic mindset* characterized by failure to experience or even recognize eros or to register feelings of guilt. Killing animals without conscience is rationalized in this manner, and political movements enlist this philosophy to allow one human being to feel no guilt for killing another, as occurred in Nazi Germany and is still occurring in all the various genocidal travesties that are taking place in various parts of the world.[1]

Pseudospeciation as a rationalization has been applied by military and political leaders in many countries to legitimize callous disregard, brutality, and sexual abuse of women. Modern-day racial, ethnic, religious, or political conflicts that erupt in the streets of many countries quickly escalate into widespread rape and violence, reflecting a similar mentality. In both examples such conduct is literally thoughtless. This kind of behavior expresses a mind–body–soul disconnection: psychopathy within.

In his infamous manifesto *Mein Kampf*, Hitler first began referring to other ethnicities as another species, thereby rationalizing his killing of them and suggesting that mating with them was a horrible perversion against nature, comparable to a human mating with an animal. Removing conscience and the feeling of guilt justified extermination. Paranoid perceptions about other humans feed this propensity.[2] This kind of extreme prejudicial behavior evinces archetypal psychopathic characteristics of deception, manipulation, violence, and the stark absence of eros. The power of the archetype overrides what we now know: that seeking mates from other human groups is biologically *beneficial* because it increases genetic variability and survival.[3]

Pseudospeciation as a strategy to protect us or to avoid aspects of others/ourselves is flawed and doomed to failure. We are unable to identify a specific target group that alone suffers from psychopathy—

---

1   Zoja, "Two Poles."
2   Ibid.
3   Ibid.

psychic leprosy—and colonize its members into seclusion. There is no realistic way to distinguish such a population because, consistent with the gradated definition, psychopathy presents in degrees, not absolutes, as described poignantly in the following quote by Russian novelist, historian, and activist Aleksandr Solzhenitsyn:

> If only it were all so simple! If only there were evil people somewhere insidiously committing evil deeds, and it were necessary only to separate them from the rest of us and destroy them. But the line dividing good and evil cuts through the heart of every human being. And who is willing to destroy a piece of his own heart?[4]

Psychopathy appears across cultures and throughout world history as a human characteristic on a continuum. Differentiating it is further confounded by the fact that even most obviously *bad* people do good things sometimes, and most *good* people err at least occasionally.

An illustrative historical example of the psychopathy continuum occurred when the Russian Red Army conquered Berlin in 1945; during that time period, more than two million women were raped in Berlin, often including multiple assaults on each victim. *A Woman in Berlin (Eine Frau in Berlin)* is an account of the period from April 20 to June 22, 1945: the Battle of Berlin. At the author's request, the work was published anonymously, for her protection. The book describes the writer's experiences as a rape victim during the Red Army occupation of the city. Two years after the death of the anonymous author in 2003, Jens Bisky, a German literary editor, identified her as Marta Hillers in the *Süddeutsche Zeitung*. Bisky said that Hillers had been a journalist who worked on magazines and newspapers during the Nazi era. She had also been a small-time propagandist for the Third Reich, writing a Navy recruiting brochure, but she was probably not a member of the

---

4   Alexander Solzhenitsyn, *The Gulag Archipelago: 1915–1956* (New York: Harper & Row, 1974), 168.

Nazi Party. Hillers' account describes her personal experiences during the occupation of Berlin, explaining many of the horrors she faced and the struggle of the city's inhabitants to survive. Of course, caution was warranted in releasing such material, since it sounded pro-Nazi; sympathy for a female Nazi rape victim was unlikely, despite the legitimacy of the suffering she described.

Collectively, our automatic intolerance of all Nazis is now endorsed as politically correct, for obvious reasons. Ironically, the Nazis' absolutist generic mindset, which led them to depersonalize all Jews (and other minority groups) and justify their horrific treatment, was essentially a similar kind of groupthink rationale, suggesting that the human capacity for pseudospeciation is more ubiquitous than we might like to believe—although we judge it differently if it represents a popular or politically correct attitude with which we agree.

The German writer Kurt Marek (C. W. Ceram) was responsible for the book's initial publication in America in 1954. A movie was made of it in 2008, *A Woman in Berlin* (*Anonyma—Eine Frau in Berlin*; translated by Nina Hoss), directed by Max Färberböck. The theme of the story reflects the healing of psychopathy by eros. After being raped by a number of Soviet soldiers, the film's protagonist, Marta Hillers, petitions the battalion's commanding officer for protection. After an initial cold refusal, the officer finds himself moved. He shows her pictures of his children and subsequently protects, feeds, and celebrates with the inhabitants of her entire apartment complex—at what turns out to be a great personal cost. These two individuals discovered each other's mutual humanity, so the objectification fundamental to an attitude of pseudospeciation became impossible. The benevolent opposite within the Soviet officer was activated. Another way of describing this is to say simply that eros prevailed.

Enantiodromia and Compensation

Zoja discussed the principle of *enantiodromia* in relation to the appearance of extreme opposites such as psychopathy and the healing power of eros, within and between us, in our collective cultural experience. Jung used the term (Greek: *enantios* = opposite + *dromos* = running course) to signify that an abundance of any force inevitably produces its opposite. Enantiodromia is equivalent to the principle of equilibrium in the natural world, in which any extreme element triggers a system to produce opposition in order to restore balance. This concept is associated with Jung's other ideas about finding the midpoint between the opposites within us to become who we truly are, which can be associated with identifying and accepting the range of characteristics within us—including our psychopathy.[5]

Although the term *enantiodromia* was popularized by Jung, as he did with so many terms and meanings, he dredged it from the ancient caverns of world history. This idea was even much earlier implied in the writings of the pre-Socratic Greek philosopher Heraclitus, to whom Jung often referred. Heraclitus made signature statements such as "Cold things warm, warm things cool"; "wet things dry and parched things get wet." This style of describing and understanding opposites is typical of Heraclitus, for example:

War is father of all, king of all.

They do not know that the differing/opposed thing agrees with itself.

Harmony is reflexive . . . like the bow and the lyre.[6]

---

5 *C. G. Jung Speaking: Interviews and Encounters.* William McGuire and R. F. C. Hull, eds. (Princeton, NJ: Princeton University Press, 1977), 428.
6 Charles Kahn, *The Art and Thought of Heraclitus: Fragments with Translation and Commentary.* London: Cambridge University Press, 1979), 1–23.

Heraclitus articulates the coincidence of opposites in a character-istic riddling style, conveying the dynamic interchange between two oxymoronic images, generated especially by opposition and conflict. This interchange between opposite images parallels one of Jung's central ideas: the concept of *compensation*.

Jung believed that any exaggeration, any one-sidedness in one's conscious attitude, would generate an unconscious compensatory reac-tion. Those aspects of the public's emotional and legislative reaction to sex offenders that are fear-driven and impractical, for example, suggest a compensatory attitude: projecting all of our unwanted sexual propensities onto a separate category of human being that can be neatly ostracized, an extreme compartmentalization, thereby protecting— and implicitly absolving—the rest of us.

If I listen to my unconscious, however, in balance with my conscious thoughts, it will help me to avoid exaggeration and find my center—my true self. This challenge applies to both individual and collective development: aspects within the personality as well as cultural roles and functions. The latter was the focus of Zoja's reference to the idea, which he tied to his theme of different styles and aspects of fathering, because the role confusion we experience suggests problems with balance.

"One must be what one is," said Jung, "one must discover one's own individuality, that center of personality, which is equidistant between the conscious and the unconscious; we must aim for that ideal [mid]point towards which nature appears to be directing us."[7] Jung's idea of finding the ideal midpoint within is related to our universal challenge of containing the opposites in human nature, which we will now explore further.

This next chapter bridges from ancient Greek mythology to a broader discussion of *the opposites*, including some examples from my

---

7   C.G. Jung Speaking: interviews and Encounters, Princeton University Press, 1977, p. 463.

therapy practice and then a relatively modern, cross-cultural example depicting the universal human challenge of coping with polarities, a story with a similar motif from a very different time, country, and culture: the Huichol Mexican Indians and their "Path with Heart."

CHAPTER 15

The Opposites

Without Contraries is no progression.
—William Blake, *The Marriage of*
Heaven and Hell, 1790

The idea of opposite characteristics within us is fairly commonplace, but usually we emphasize the separation between these contents. We validate what we consider positive qualities and we discourage, avoid, or deny the darker ones, rather than acknowledge the potential benefits associated with accepting that *totality*. The challenge to integrate these inner opposites is inescapably human, whether or not we like the idea—or the process. The basic struggle of reconciling opposites is a timeless concept, alive within and between us as citizens of the world, representing an archetypal theme. If the potential for healing inner psychopathy requires understanding it, integrating it, and somehow finding love in the equation, one way to visualize this process is in terms of illuminating our inner opposites.

My life experiences of this dynamic—of the polarities of human character—familiarized me with the theme long before I began exploring its associations with psychopathy. My frame of reference was immediately personal given my contradictory relationship with my father, and my thinking about the topic was further inspired by the world literature I studied early in my academic career, spanning the course of history. Expressed in a multitude of ways, the wisdom of this fundamental concept always struck me as not only unavoidable but clearly relevant within a far broader context than my own limited experience.

The struggle between the polarities within is an obvious human challenge that prevails across socioeconomic groups and class lines, religions, ethnicities, and races. Communities and individuals world-wide suffer from violence, substance addiction, and deviant sexual compulsions and proclivities. Although this reality is observable in a concrete, external way, evident in any newscast, most of us occasionally experience some conflict between the opposite aspects within our own psyches and lives, in a wide variety of contexts: in our relationships; in our professional decision-making; or even when we need to expand our thinking, question preconceived assumptions, and integrate contrary personal and collective opinions to form or reform our own.

As a personal example, a good friend of mine told me that she was trying to let go of lifelong and generally fruitless efforts to please her aging mother, who had been raised as a Nazi youth in Germany. Of course, my friend was aware of the prevailing American cultural atti-tude that Nazis epitomize the most heinous conduct against humanity, but she struggled to see the "other side." Initially, I could not make sense of what *other side* there could possibly be, but it gradually became obvious to me that her struggle was not to rationalize or justify the horrible history of genocide represented by the Nazis, but to reconcile the opposites within herself, including her mother's history and all that meant for her in her own psyche and attitudes. Part of what she needed to do was to see the universality of the human potential for evil, including within herself—only then could she fully experience her softer side!

As my friend began to allow this difficult process to unfold, the positive feminine aspect within her was somehow released and acti-vated. As she consciously worked on reconciling the inner opposites, represented by her relationship with her mother, her harsh, negative animus energy—her inner critic—was depotentiated. She grew able to tolerate and even welcome some of her own ambiguities with newfound grace and softness. She ceased feeling so driven and made some major decisions to alter her personal and professional life in ways that brought her hope, expressed her creativity, and granted her freedom. My initial resistance to her seeking to understand the Nazis, based on my automatic impression that she was somehow siding with them, was transformed. I became aware of my own extremist knee-jerk reaction, which was healed through eros, yielding new insight as I witnessed her personal integration of these difficult inner contents.

Before we consider another collective cultural example, on a smaller scale many of my private and forensic therapy cases exemplify this intrapsychic dynamic involving opposite tendencies/forces. Below I offer two case examples I find particularly illustrative of this struggle.

Psychotherapy Examples

I mentioned Zoja's topic, the two poles of masculine identity, to a male patient; this man had originally come to me as a forensic therapy referral but he had later voluntarily transitioned to become a private client. He was immediately struck by the way Zoja's description of the good and the lawless resonated with his own inner struggle. He identified the two opposite aspects of himself that he continued to labor to contain, understand, and reconcile. He had committed a serious federal offense resulting in his incarceration—he had manipulated and deceived others, even those closest to him, for financial gain, callously disregarding professional ethics and personal relationships. However, in treatment he was also becoming increasingly aware of the opposite aspects within himself, discovering that he had an innate sense of conscience and yearned to function as a provider and responsible adult, partner, and parent. The latter aspect was the subject of much of our work in therapy, as he discovered the painful early origins of his inner psychopathy and identified the harsh, abusive critic he was to himself, in the absence of drugs and expensive toys to distract him from the truth. It was no surprise that he came into my office initially suffering from severe depression, with a history of multiple hospitalizations for suicide attempts and drug addiction. In a symbolic sense, the ancient battle between patriarch and centaur was raging under his breastbone.

In a different case, a male inmate I interviewed in a local prison described the tension of the opposites in a vividly concrete, graphic way. He was a handsome man in his late 20s who had been convicted of lewd and lascivious conduct with an underage female: He had molested his 12-year-old paternal half-sister, whom he had never met previously because she lived in a different state. The girl came to meet his family one summer and was staying with him and his wife and baby. He told me how the illicit contact began. He would come downstairs exhausted from a long workday, often a little tipsy after a few beers, to sit on the couch with his young sibling. She was bubbly and affectionate. She would tease him by putting her legs up on his lap, which stimulated him. Each time his wife crossed through the room just before she could have observed this behavior, his young half-sister would remove her legs playfully, toying with him. This sequence happened repeatedly. I asked him what he was aware of feeling as this pattern was enacted, and he said it was an irresistible "tension." This toying eventually led to intercourse. After the sexual contact occurred, and certainly after he was arrested and convicted and his life was shattered, he felt remorse. He had been raised Catholic, and living with the exposed truth of his own behavior was absolutely torturous for him, even more devastating than the undeniable reality of the harsh legal consequences he suffered as a result and his grueling life in prison. The tension he described was in his groin but also in his psyche, as he struggled with the opposite drives and characteristics within himself.

The Huichol Indians and the Path with Heart

The human struggle to resolve the psychic tension of the opposites within us is manifested culturally in widely variant ways. As I noticed this theme played out in my own life, with ever-expanding lenses, a cross-cultural example from a very different context came to mind. Many years ago I encountered the Huichol Mexican Indians and their Path with Heart. The Huichols provide a uniquely fitting example of coping with the opposites in a collective cultural framework. Like many indigenous peoples, they have commonly accepted practices for dealing directly and symbolically with those opposite aspects of life and human nature that they consider to be *both* sacred and profane. This centuries-old Mexican Indian tribe demonstrates a special communal relationship between concrete and symbolic experience, central to their culture. Their traditional way of containing the opposites is infused with art and creativity to consciously invite and preserve the healing power of eros to guide their people—and, as they believe, the world.

My experiences with the Huichols occurred decades ago, long before I conceptualized these thoughts about the opposites and psychopathy within. Upon reflection, I realized the synchronicity of themes and thus offer these stories as illustrative. Apparently, my psyche was working on this topic long before I realized as much. My descriptions of the Huichol pilgrimage to Wirikuta and other details may not reflect the most current practices. The reader is referred to the Dance of the Deer Foundation website for further information.[1]

The 30,000-year-old Huichol Mexican Indian tribe believes in what its members call the *Path with Heart*, an approach that gives precedence to eros and is expressed through their rituals, their unique art, their spiritual beliefs, and their community values. A series of

---

1   Dance of the Deer Foundation, Center for Shamanic Studies, http://www.danceofthedeer. com/foundation/center-for-shamanic-studies.

relatively recent historical events involving the Huichols illustrate Jung's ideas about synchronicity—that there is no such thing as coincidence—and the alchemical magic that is constellated when eros is allowed to prevail, often unexpectedly. As a result of these events, described below, information about the remote Huichol Mexican Indians—their culture, healing practices, and belief system—is now shared internationally.

In the 1970s, Brant Secunda, a young Jewish spiritual seeker from New Jersey, was having a Carlos Castaneda-like experience deep in Mexico and became deathly ill in the desert. Don José Matsuwa, a 104-year-old Huichol Indian shaman, discovered him, saved his life, and subsequently took him in as his adoptive grandson, training him intensively for 12 years to become a Huichol shaman.[2] Brant later brought Don José and other Huichols with him to Esalen Institute at Big Sur, California, an international retreat center dedicated to humanistic education.[3] They began spreading their teachings, which were warmly welcomed and found to be strikingly synchronous with the mission and spirit of the institute.

In 1979, Brant formed and subsequently administrated the Dance of the Deer Foundation, dedicated to Huichol cosmology, in Santa Cruz, California.[4] Decades ago, he and some Huichol counterparts began leading small select groups of "pilgrims" from the United States and other countries through Wirikuta, Mexico, a site sacred to the Huichol Indians high in the mountains of central Mexico. Brant continues to hold Huichol spiritual retreats all over the world. Thus, universally relevant training framed in the rich traditions of this ancient culture is offered internationally by someone who might appear a highly unlikely messenger, given his original roots. However, at his own deeper level,

---

2   Carlos Castaneda, *The Teachings of Don Juan: A Yaqui Way of Knowledge*. (Berkeley and Los Angeles: University of California Press, 1969).
3   Esalen Institute, http://www.esalen.org.
4   Dance of the Deer Foundation, Center for Shamanic Studies, http://www.danceofthedeer. com/foundation/center-for-shamanic-studies.

apparently Brant was able to recognize and follow his eros within, his true individual calling—his personal Path with Heart.

The ceremonies and activities on the pilgrimages to Wirikuta are largely symbolic. The journey occurs mostly on foot and is often treacherous and dusty. On their travels, the pilgrims stop periodically to take turns telling each other jokes and stories. One interesting feature of this storytelling is that it is done *backward*: The narrator has to report the events being described in reverse order, while preserving the contents, producing a kind of nonsensical prose that mimics and pokes gentle fun at the way we conceptualize the neat, chronological order of life.

Once the travelers arrive at their destination in the desert, their objective is to spear the peyote in a ritual, symbolic gesture that represents bounty and beautiful visions for the tribe. The peyote is ingested thoughtfully and in measured quantities, not with the intention of intoxication or entertainment, but to invite visions that have symbolic meaning and utility for the Huichols, inspiring their well-known colorful yarn paintings and reinforcing the tribal community values.

JOSÉ BENÍTEZ SÁNCHEZ (1938–), SACRED DEER (UNDATED)[5]

5   This yarn picture depicts a vision of the deer with two heads, symbolizing dualities such as up and down—the innate balance of all things. In this two-headed deer figure both male (left) and female (right) are represented. The shaman is blessing and honoring the deer with his healing feathers, which are used to honor the gods. The shaman takes the offerings to the sacred deer, Kuyumari, represented by the central deer head. The offerings are sent by way of healing feathers and prayer arrows that are purified by fire, the gift from Father Sun. The gift of fire is a symbol of spiritual enlightenment, representing the eternal light that is necessary to keep humans warm and protect them from evil spirits. In this ceremony the shamans give and bless the offerings in communion with the gods, which represent duality. The stars and dots represent the ancestors that are present in all yarn paintings. Images can be viewed online at www.cunacueva.com/cc02b.php.

A special friend of mine had an experience that illustrates the synchronicity of the Huichol symbolic world juxtaposed with tangible reality at a personal level. He was a participant in one of those early pilgrimages and endured a long, arduous hike with the group back to Puerto Vallarta after leaving Wirikuta. When he took off his filthy shirt, a large scorpion tumbled out. The Huichols believe that the scorpion will not sting one with a true heart. My friend had carried the dangerous insect safely, right on top of his heart for many hours, unaware that it was there, of course—and the integrity of his character corroborated the Huichol belief. Simultaneously, he also just happened to be carrying a colorful Huichol yarn painting he had purchased days before from a tribal artist to bring home, at the corner of which was depicted a scorpion! That yarn painting is still in my living room, a reminder of the synchronicity of this story about the endurance of eros.

Yelapa

During the period when Brant Secunda was first leading Huichol pilgrimages to Wirikuta, in 1987, I met the group in Mexico and took a side trip to Yelapa, a tropical island on Banderas Bay near Puerto Vallarta. There I experienced the opposites in a way that was uniquely inner and outer, reflected in the place and the meaning that unfolded during our brief stay. My friend and I took the tourist boat over to Yelapa from the mainland, landing on the narrow beach where we were aggressively welcomed by a crew of grinning island locals holding enormous green lizards, zealously entreating us to take and buy photos. We soon realized that this display was also an attempt at distraction, to lead us to the tourist side of the island. Pigs roamed contentedly and junk was scattered on the tourist beach, but there were crowded rows of souvenir shops, bars, and restaurants to lure the boat passengers. A strikingly different atmosphere prevailed in the verdant jungle area that encroached, wild and tangled, humming and crawling with unseen tropical life, closest to our landing site. The two of us escaped the tourist route and instead dived into the jungle. After a long hike, we arrived high on a bright green hill, at a "hotel" unlike any I had ever seen.

The place consisted of a small group of rustic, wood-and-canvas cabañas run by an impeccably dressed, very tan gentleman with silver hair and a strong German accent, together with his Australian side-kick, who was much less serious but clearly subordinate. They offered us fresh homemade jam and bread, and stories. The Australian had a quirky sense of humor and an entertaining, unique style of banter, like a script perfectly delivered by a professional comedian—albeit in a most improbable setting. Our German host was polite but remote in contrast. In some way, their cockeyed partnership foreshadowed the contrasts within the odd experience we had later.

This was truly a jungle paradise, primitive but pristine, and yet for inexplicable reasons something profoundly disturbing occurred that night in our little half-tent, with the balmy breezes blowing and the diamond stars plentiful in the black sky. We both felt crazy, unsettled, and mortally endangered. It was as if the ground beneath us rever-berated with a powerful, dark energy, enough to rattle our senses and potentially dismantle our minds. We were both mental health profes-sionals, but maintaining sanity became an effort. In a conscious attempt to manage the unrest with some kind of symbolic ceremony, my friend suggested that I create a design in the dirt, which I did, to no avail. We struggled to fall asleep, and when we began to drift into dreams, vivid, horrific, violent images awakened us, seemingly generated from the black earth beneath us. We were pouring with sweat. We both felt ill. His watch stopped suddenly.

During the worst of the night, my friend suddenly made the obser-vation that no doubt the tourists and residents on the other side of the island, teeming with the squalor and junk of civilization, were sleeping peacefully under their streetlights and flashing neon bar signs. Ours was the opposite in terms of place and spirit: a paradise with a demonic underbelly.

The next morning at the barest crack of dawn, we made a hasty escape, plunging down the backside of the island away from the hotel, climbing through an unanticipated barbed wire fence at the rear of the property and stringently avoiding the way we had entered, both feeling inexplicably that we were fighting for our lives. During the previous evening, we had learned enough detailed information about our mysterious German host to construe that he may well have been an absconded Nazi war criminal, sequestered in this jungle retreat of his own elaborate creation. My friend and I were both half-Jewish, a subject that had arisen in our conversation with him. Afterward, we discussed our shared sense of intangible but intense danger only briefly, half-heartedly attempting to rationalize an episode so eerie it simply did not lend itself to ordinary logical analysis.

I never did calculate a more satisfying explanation for this hair-raising experience and have let the memory remain one of my life's permanently unsolved mysteries. I trust the reality of the strange feelings I had, however, and know that I inadvertently trod upon something real and greater than my own simple consciousness that night. What I also remember and treasure from that living, blessedly temporary nightmare was my conviction that this was a message from the unconscious about the opposites: the inevitable juxtaposition of inner and outer, appearance and substance, and the prevailing logic of faith when rational thinking falls short. If our sinister host and his jungle retreat carried the energy of the psychopath archetype, as was our impression, then perhaps surviving the ordeal of our encounter and our early morning exodus reflected the ultimate triumph of healing eros.

CHAPTER 16

Noticing Inner and Outer Psychopathy

You don't understand. I coulda had *class*. I coulda
been a *contender*. I coulda been somebody, instead
of a bum, which is what I am, let's face it.

—Terry Malloy (Marlon Brando), *On the Waterfront*

Psychopathy within can undermine our ability to know what we really want, to strive for it, and to experience the warm inner glow of accomplishment. In a related manner, at a collective level, our culture reinforces the natural human susceptibility to feeling inadequate.

We all have unique, passionate hopes and ambitions, whether or not we are consciously aware of a calling, path, or life purpose. Psychopathic gaps within are like hidden saboteurs, interfering with our capacity for introspective clarity and affecting outer functioning, sometimes rendering true peace and contentment mysteriously elusive, despite the appearance of comfort and evident success. One may achieve goals but still feel vaguely unfulfilled and fraudulent—a fairly common dynamic.

In an associated manner, the condition of psychopathy can be described as losing connection with one's self, one's inner life: a wound or gap in the psyche that may manifest in feelings of hopelessness, depression, and anxiety. As noted previously, such feelings are widespread, as evidenced by the disproportionate influence wielded by the massive pharmaceutical industry that supplies chemical antidotes to these unwanted states. We attempt to address this phenomenon with a potpourri of psychotropic medication and turn to charismatic self-help media mentors offering quick-fix advice. Still, the reality of inner process remains an uncomfortable anathema for most of us in today's Western culture. On the contrary, the concept of soul loss, of disconnection from one's self resulting in illnesses and emotional ailments, is considered normal—and treatable—within many indigenous cultures. Accepted methods to address such problems might include calling upon a shaman to restore spiritual—and physical—equilibrium.

Cultural and Collective Psychopathy

Discrimination can serve a healthy purpose by reinforcing strengths or common interests, but it can also be symptomatic of a kind of collective psychopathy, ultimately creating a dynamic of polar opposites: in-groups and outcasts. Feeling special at the expense of others reflects a lack of eros.

A broad example at a cultural level is illustrated by a personal experience I had years ago. I will always treasure the experience of teaching Shakespeare to an English class composed of inner-city African American high school students in the late 1970s. The language required some translation, but the meaning was readily understood because Shakespeare's themes and observations about character, conduct, and relationships are timeless. Being part of that recognition with my surprised class was a heartwarming epiphany. Collectively, we insulate "classical" art, music, literature, and the works of great scholars with a proprietary attitude, signaling that these highest achievements are only for a select audience at a high price. Ironically, this ubiquitous "in-group" stance ultimately reinforces the very kind of narrow thinking from which these luminary works potentially emancipate us.

The world's most brilliant thinkers and visionary artists enrich humanity with their contributions, guiding us toward expanded consciousness and stimulating creative development. However, the original message—the *heart* of it—may be eclipsed by the very organizations ostensibly designed to protect it. This is *psychopathy at the collective level*: eros institutionalized. The eros in these great works could be considered deactivated as they are rendered unavailable to many whose lives might be touched by them beyond the exclusive circle of their devotees.

Despite the dynamic that occurs once they become venerated, "classical" discoveries across diverse fields are fundamentally significant *not* because they are the purview of a privileged elite subgroup, but quite the opposite qualification. They represent the best of our collective creative possibilities by revealing, expressing, and celebrating human experience in ways that are innately *inclusive* and *universally* relevant to our inevitably shared existence. A form of exclusivity occurs at the hands of the social strata that institutionalize such works, representing a collective psychopathy among those groups—not a collective psychopathy in terms of all of us, per se, but manifesting the "haves" versus the "have-nots" theme played out in so many ways in our culture. When we liberate classical contributions from the exclusivity that so often surrounds them, limiting their broadest accessibility and meaning, we *free their eros*. Their great transformative potential is more accessible to collective humanity—which can help to heal our collective psychopathy.

Along with my propensity to notice psychopathy in my personal and professional life, my therapy cases, and in the collective realm, I began to question how this awareness was serving me constructively and to consider how I was already working to heal the gaps. I sought to consciously identify ways that I was already engaged in efforts to maintain my consciousness about this inner world where there was such a range of contents. I had not previously recognized these familiar, even automatic strategies for personal well-being to be related to my work with psychopathy.

Conscious Work to Heal the Gaps

One way I was habitually trying to invite healing, in addition to my deliberate professional and scholarly pursuits, was through my body. As much as I loved Jung's ideas and honored my thinking function, there was something profoundly liberating about my yoga practice and its unstated but deep philosophical underpinnings. Jung, too, was intrigued by Eastern religion and philosophy, and I felt an affirming compatibility between my appreciation of Jung and my delight in the simple reverence for life, breath, and the moment that I experienced doing yoga. Thich Nhat Hanh, a Vietnamese Zen Buddhist master, beautifully describes the connection between our breathing and our minds and bodies:

> Your breath should be light, even and flowing, like a thin stream of water running through the sand. Your breath should be very quiet, so quiet that a person sitting next to you cannot hear it. Your breathing should flow gracefully, like a river, like a water snake crossing the water, and not like a chain of rugged mountains or the gallop of a horse. To master our breath is to be in control of our bodies and our minds. Each time we find ourselves depressed and find it difficult to gain control of ourselves by different means, the method of watching the breath should always be used.[1]

Thich Nhat Hanh has helped create what he calls *engaged Buddhism*. My yoga teacher read the above quote one day at the end

---

1   Thich Nhat Hanh, *The Miracle of Mindfulness: An Introduction to the Practice of Meditation.* (Boston: Beacon Press, 1987/1976), p. 20.

of class, during *savasana*, the final relaxation pose. Engaged Buddhism is essentially aimed at building compassion and easing suffering to make the world a better place for humanity, through shared active intentionality. Paying conscious attention to ideals, even unattainable ones, can provide a valuable compass, at least pointing us in the right direction—in this case, a spiritual as well as practical destination. Jungian thought, at its core, also opens upon a deeply spiritual realm through its interiority.

From my limited understanding of the theologies and philosophies of Eastern religions, our earthly existence is a state of *samsara*, a kind of no-man's land between death and rebirth characterized by the endemic suffering, ignorance, anxiety, and dissatisfaction associated with the inherently limited range of activities that preoccupy ordinary human beings. Aspects of this Eastern religious belief system seem compatible with Jungian ideas about the duality within us and collectively, the limitations of collective consciousness, and the potential for liberation through expanding individual awareness. However, in contrast to a Jungian orientation, there is an explicit goal fundamental to Zen Buddhism, for example: to eliminate suffering. The *one way* to achieve freedom from *samsara* is by following the Buddhist path. This idea has a moral ring to it, different from the Jungian focus upon seeking wholeness and individuation.

I perceive Jung to be a true steward of the psyche, an ever-watchful guardian of the unqualified truth about humanity and human beings—who are a motley composite of diverse characteristics—those we extol and those we wish we could exterminate. The goal of wholeness sounds more approachable than eliminating all suffering. Jung's focus was the individuation process by which each person becomes more fully him- or herself, by dealing with *all* forces, positive and negative, light and dark, within the self and in the collective world. Thus, from a Jungian frame of reference, a defining purpose of our earthly existence might be the conscious acceptance of this totality rather than eliminating anything—and each individual has a unique path to follow toward individuation. This invitation differs significantly from following a path already established.[2]

In modern Western civilization, a conscious approach to healing by trying to illuminate one's inner landscape, including the dark, empty pitfalls of inner psychopathy, requires a shift in attitude. Our culturally prescribed method of problem-solving tends to be evidence-based and outcome-driven. Using my own experience as an example, this practical approach is one with which I have had to comply in nearly every job I ever held that involved a bureaucracy—including teaching, social services, and even as a psychologist and therapist, both forensic and private, when I had to bill an agency. There was typically an entity to which I had to submit documented results in order to get paid.

By contrast, resolving a problem by noticing an unconscious, relatively intangible inner process does not fit this model. For example, deliberately paying attention to the automatic rhythm of breathing to activate its healing potential is a strategy familiar in yoga but somewhat challenging to insurance companies, as such a process inherently eludes standardization—although health practices involving mindfulness, including breathing exercises, are increasingly mainstream. Nonetheless, whether we consciously work to heal our inner gaps—and regardless of the approach we choose to do so—life generally presents us with changes and challenges to face in this arena as we age anyway.

By the time we reach a certain point in life, roughly associated with chronological aging, but not exclusively, most of us accept an imperfect, paradoxical reality, surrendering to compromise and granting exceptions to our own rules. The biggest challenge we face may be to redefine success by learning to embrace our authentic personality, our personal history and its idiosyncratic circumstances, unimpeded by

---

2   Heide M. Kolb, October 29, 2011, "A Little Help from a Master: Jungian Reflections," *Heidekolb's Blog*, http://www.jungianwork.wordpress.com/tag/jungian-psychology/

regret about what evolved differently from the blueprint we imagined or how we hoped to be regarded by others.

This redefining process requires an honest tally of one's external scoreboard, which typically displays an assortment of perceived accomplishments and failures to reconcile, entailing introspection and probably some pain. We humans are obviously not all similarly inclined to plumb the depths of the psyche. However, I began to consider the idea of a common call to some version of reconciling our inner opposites, corroborated by my experiences in the world and with others in my private, academic, and professional life. While I have no way of knowing to what extent this discovery may have reflected an element of self-fulfilling prophecy, since I became sharply attuned to the subject and thus noticed it with heightened sensitivity, the idea was curious and interesting to me, leading me to suspect that understanding psychopathy within oneself is an integral part of a natural human urge toward inner reconciliation, even if we describe or approach the process differently.

Reconciling Our Inner Opposites by Seeking Eros

Psychopathy is typically understood as an expression of the darkest dimension of our shadow side, those aspects of our personalities that we prefer to avoid, project, and scapegoat, as opposed to considering what positive energy it may contain. While psychopathy, as defined here, is not unwanted inner *contents*, but rather an *absence* of content, a void without eros, this dimension of our personalities is similarly (and understandably) something we would rather escape or deny. Opening the door to our inner psychopathy is uncomfortable and ugly, but critical, since acknowledging its reality is fundamental to any potential to heal it. *Psychopathy* represents a sinister-sounding and powerful inner process of archetypal proportions. However, avoiding it does not rid us of it, so acknowledging the possibility of some version of psychopathy within us can disarm the amplified fear associated with it. More importantly, the temptation to consider it from a nonjudgmental or at least relatively objective perspective is intriguing because it suggests the possibility of freeing some untapped creative, transformative potential for healing held within its vacuous chambers.

The dark or hidden aspects within us may actually contain a treasure trove. One way Jung described this possibility was by drawing parallels to the ancient art of alchemy, which involved transforming base metal into gold. Jung found many symbolic equivalents between alchemy and the process of individuation, which he compared to transforming primitive, undifferentiated psychic material into an evolved, integrated, differentiated self. It may be difficult to envision what could be worthwhile about illuminating one's inner psychopathy, especially given our serial-killer associations with the term, but the idea that the darker dimensions of personality contain an indirect value is certainly not new. In the symbolism of the alchemical world, if the blackest material carries the potential to be transmuted into gold, certainly psychopathy qualifies as that matter, deep within the vast netherworld of shadow contents.

The persistence of our human quest for love when it is lacking reflects an innate yearning for healing through the power of eros—the natural panacea for psychopathy. Despite myriad variations on the theme, the human soul searches for healing. Uninvited memories or dreams may bring unrelenting reminders of whatever we would rather avoid. I hear somewhat similar descriptions of inner restlessness from many in both my personal and professional worlds. Part of this angst seems to stem from failure to make peace with the past, which can produce distraction or a sense of vague dissatisfaction: If we never fully accept and live life consciously in the present, we may opt instead for permanent, low-grade frustration and anxiety.

Certainly, frustration and anxiety are extremely common these days. Harboring what is unresolved becomes automatic when it remains unconscious, and hidden content can wreak havoc with one's peace of mind. That alone suggests the value of illuminating such material, even if doing so seems unbearable or impossible—especially since our efforts to avoid it may cause more problems than they appear to solve.

Our gaps, our inner psychopathy, can be gifts of guidance for inner healing—or they can seriously interfere with our ability to actualize the rich potential of our lives. These undeveloped aspects seem to manifest anyway, in relationships and in innumerable situations that arise without prompting. The circumstances of our lives change, but our own calling to individuation replays persistently despite our misgivings. That repeated beckoning can be comforting, like an inner caretaker, even if what emerges is not always comfortable.

CHAPTER 17

My Father/My Self:
Reflections on Final Reconciliation
and the Magic of Eros

Iturn again to an example of my father and my experience with him as an illustration of the natural human urge toward some kind of inner reconciliation, perhaps particularly as life is waning.

I will never know whether Albert had the opportunity or will to explore his own inner landscape or if he struggled consciously with unrest in his soul. My only barometer of such a condition is the state of my own soul, which was deeply impacted by him. It appears to me that his potential was never fulfilled, in terms of his personality, his creativity, or his relationships. His psychopathy interfered with his capacity for commitment and affected his connection to others, although it also meant that he was apparently unaffected by this detachment. The urge to avoid conscious responsibility regarding our inner states is rampant in the world—so in that respect he was no exception to the rule. However, he may have been pulled, or gently nudged, toward individuation and greater wholeness at the very end of his life, when I glimpsed him experiencing the conflicts in his character.

During his final weeks, the war in Albert's psyche produced a panoply of disturbing dreams and hallucinations, as he and his brain wrestled with Parkinson's. The untamed opposites within him were most evident during those episodes when he lost control of his body and his mind. In those rare scenes his emotions poured out of him with uncharacteristic abandon, such as I had never before witnessed in him, as though leaking without his consent, revealing a hidden cache of feeling: tearful hugs as we prepared final documents in his studio and again, weeks later, when I said goodbye to him at the board-and-care home where he stayed so briefly.

My father had never really been there for me throughout our lives, so even at the end of his life, I had some difficulty conceding that it was now my turn to be there for him. Only by letting go of my own reverence for order, my perceptions about fairness and need for logical consequences, could I offer him the kind of help that, by then, neither of us could deny he needed. Finally, despite the opposites within and between us, the healing power of eros was activated—for us both. His inner psychopathy, the long-buried gap in his soul, was flooded with the light of love, finally, with a transformative power that also pene-trated the dark recesses of my own empty places: I will never forget the tenderness of those unprecedented moments.

When my father reached the end of his life, he knew it, yet he resolved to carry on in some version of the same unique style he had established throughout it, with whatever means remained at his disposal. He dictated detailed grocery lists with scrupulous instructions about what specific types and brands of food to purchase for him. He created his own walker using materials from his studio, scoffing at the high-tech models offered by the hospital, and proudly demonstrating his alternative invention as he staggered painstakingly from his plastic chair in front of his TV to his small kitchen area. He hooted with triumph when we managed to get through his medical appointment with the Parkinson's specialist unscathed, in his perception. Albert enthusiastically countered each diagnostic impression and offer of inter-vention the doctor made with the tenacity of a tennis player parrying balls, until, exhausted, the doctor finally gave up and conceded that even though he obviously had the symptoms and could barely navigate himself, it was quite possible he had a "syndrome" of Parkinson's traits and not the full-blown condition. When I encouraged Albert to take his medication or submit to procedures to identify and manage his symptoms, he repeatedly refused, telling me dramatically, "I'm done; I've seen enough."

Although Albert almost aggressively avoided any serious intro-spection, and never expressed remorse or regrets, what he avoided or left unsaid came out of him anyway, in his deeply disturbing dreams, which occasionally morphed into waking hallucinations at the end of his life. I wonder if the reason that process was so very unconscious and externalized was because of the extent of his psychopathy. He certainly did not appear to be at peace with himself, his psychic gaps, or the universe.

Albert communicated no final insights and made no efforts at atonement. He did succeed in living life his way, but this boastfully healthy man who ran away from relationships whenever it suited him and without a backward glance, unexpectedly and ironically found himself at 80 years old, suddenly and radically decompensating with Parkinson's disease, of which there was no known family history, such that he was finally unable to walk at all, let alone run away as he had so many times in the past—both literally and figuratively.

Albert had always been a jazz lover and musician, and his passion for that music had accompanied and somehow represented his life story. As his life drew to a close, he stopped listening to music altogether, ignoring his treasured collection where it remained in a bookcase across the room in his small studio. He said he did not have time and it was too much work. I briefly considered taking the initiative to go ahead and play his music for him anyway, without his permission, but immediately thought better of the idea, knowing that doing so would have been a disaster, despite good intentions. Any gesture made without his approval was tremendously upsetting to him and inevitably shut down anyway, followed by his scathing wrath. Later, it dawned on me that in actuality, he may have known he would have been unable to handle the feelings generated by his jazz, and he feared losing control. That beloved music might have opened his heart and reminded him of his precious relationship to life and the last words never spoken, exposing him to a painful and stark reality, newly stripped of the carefully crafted philosophical illusions that had staunchly barricaded his fragile ego.

Albert's unwanted feelings emerged anyway, mercilessly, in visions and dreams. His hallucinatory experiences could not be attributed to medication side effects, since he had refused to take any. During the last months of his life, he was plagued with horrific nightmares, some featuring rats as big as humans attacking him where he lived, so unsettling he was afraid to go to sleep and spent nights sitting on his chair, collapsing onto his bed exhausted with the morning light. When the thin line between his daytime reality and his dreamtime blurred and the hallucinations ensued, he saw dead bodies everywhere and imagined he was trapped in the basement of his apartment complex, in a wheelchair unable to move. The trapped sensation agitated him so much that he woke up and rushed out onto his third-floor balcony, gesturing wildly and yelling below to anyone within earshot. These were the days when the police made several visits to his residence.

Albert's gaps were cleverly revealed by the creative universe in his final phase of life, perhaps best illustrated by a rare and unsettling experience of *abaissement du niveau mental*—French psychologist Pierre Janet's term, elaborated by Jung, meaning a lowering of consciousness that overlapped from his reality to mine—that occurred while I was attempting to help him relocate from the hospital to a board-and-care home.[1] As the ambulance bore him from the hospital to the facility, I rushed to his studio to gather some of his belongings to bring him. I was

---

1   Jung, *Archetypes and the Collective Unconscious*, 117.

leaving his place with my arms loaded and pushed the button to take the elevator to ground level, only it kept going, into the basement of his complex. The doors parted and there directly in front of me, wanly reaching a thin arm toward me, was a young woman literally covered in blood! She asked me for help and said she had cut herself—clearly an understatement. Catching my breath, I told her I would go for help, and did so. A short while later, when I was making my next trip down from Albert's studio, bearing another armful of his most treasured belongings, the elevator opened on the ground level and there she was again, like an ominous apparition, lying on the concrete just to the left side of the doors with the paramedics and the building manager looking on. Only later did it occur to me what a creative universe it was, that had provided such a perfect symbolic image of the *wounded anima*, there in my father's complex by the elevator, as he lay dying and literally in transit across town.

This story illustrates that what we do not deal with directly expresses itself somehow anyway—also reinforcing that it may behoove us to deliberately seek ways to bring unconscious material to light. As Jung stated, "That which we do not bring to consciousness appears in our lives as fate."[2]

One of my father's signature qualities was his adamant disbelief and distrust in anything he could not see. Intangibles were nonexistent to him, along with sentimentality and faith; all concepts of this ilk ended up in the same heap, described with disdain and dismissed. Toward the very end of his life, he cautiously disclosed that he had his own sense of spirituality, although he avoided that word to describe it. He felt he had a private understanding of belonging to something greater than his limited human existence, the parameters of which he could no longer avoid and was becoming increasingly aware of, despite the tenacity of his cavalier manner. He alluded to this newly conceded

---

2   C. G. Jung, in *Meeting the Shadow: The Hidden Power of the Dark Side of Human Nature*. Edited by Connie Zweig and Jeremiah Abrams (New York: Tarcher/Putnam, 1991), v.

awareness almost shyly, in a deliberate, no-nonsense tone, more like acknowledging a bigger picture, perhaps comparable to a large-scale architectural drawing—safe territory for him—rather than a state of enlightenment or transformation.

Albert's rigid denial of the reality of feelings augmented the barrier to our closeness. I did not know him to be sensitive or vulnerable, other than when he deliberately offered such information about himself to make a point or tell a good story, always after the fact. This style of communication contributed to my caution around him; if he had behaved otherwise, gentler and kinder, it would have been unsettling, maybe even experienced as invasive, after a lifetime—at least that portion we had shared—of verbal sparring and ready sarcasm, although I know I yearned for that gentle kindness in some small corner of my heart.

Perhaps we both softened a little during those last months while he was dying. Years earlier, when he had first begun showing signs of Parkinson's, his then-girlfriend of a few years had tried to coax him into a nursing home, a process into which she invested considerable detailed research, and then tried to demand my increased involvement. This seemed wildly inappropriate to me and only incited my anger; he adamantly refused any assisted living arrangement, not to mention the suddenly relevant factor that he had never really been there for me, so with a new level of unavoidable reality, I had difficulty conceding that now it was my turn to be there for him. She idealized him, as most of his partners had done, at least in that phase of their relationship. Even when I finally recited to her the litany of his abandonment and lack of support toward all of his past wives and various children, pointing out that we were not a "typical family," she responded by berating me and insisted passionately that yes, we were, and he "needed" me—even though he denied as much—so I should drop everything and rush to his aid. At the time she made her first demand, I refused, incensed at the very idea, let alone that she was the one suggesting it, whereas it would have been a different matter if he himself had made the overture. Eventually, she left the area, although apparently they parted on amicable terms.

During that last chapter of his life and our relationship, I think we began to be freer to just love each other, to admit as much. Despite our mutual efforts to preserve the barrier of sarcastic repartee that had always so characterized our interaction, at the end something deeper and more substantial prevailed anyway. Perhaps there was an unstated shared need for some kind of closure, a last chance for resolution of sorts, a careful truce after a lifetime of underlying values conflict: the tension between my intense need for him to acknowledge the error of his ways and to seek forgiveness, and his at least equally intense need to adamantly refuse both. Whether our final arrangement was motivated by his self-focused desperation or my inflated heroism is less relevant than the fact that finally, despite the opposites within and between us, the transformative healing power of eros was activated within and between us before it was too late.

The magic of love can be experienced in such unpredictable ways that sometimes evidence of its healing may not come clear until after the fact. For example, I really only recognized the consistent love that had flowed between my father and my children after he died. That recognition took me by surprise, with a meaning that was potentially transformative to my perceptions about him—and certainly relevant to my understanding of psychopathy on a continuum. Nothing else so clearly illustrated to me the disparate aspects of his character than the contrast between our patchy relationship and the easy, loving rapport he shared so spontaneously with his grandchildren.

My father abandoned five children from three different families he formed during his adult life, leaving me when I was 2 years old, and my two biological half-siblings when my brother was 3 or 4 and my sister was an infant. He raised my other two adoptive half-siblings through their growing-up years, leaving suddenly when my brother was in his early 20s and my sister was in her late teens. Such stark realities tend to dominate my perspective on his capacity for parenting, for obvious reasons, but like most things about him, there was another, opposite dimension. As my stepmother commented to me days before he died, when their two children were young, he was a wonderful, attentive, apparently devoted father. He could be playful, funny, genuinely loving, and spontaneously affectionate—in addition to being callous, unreliable, and self-focused. He was generally more interested in being entertaining than really providing consistently for anyone beyond himself, but his random gestures were noteworthy and imaginative when he was motivated. The patriarch, or *good father,* qualities within him appeared unpredictably. He demonstrated creative, uninhibited initiative in finding engaging activities for children, such as horseback riding lessons for my half-sister during elementary school when she had problems he was passionately devoted to resolving.

He produced unusual, generous gifts on occasion—but never if expected. When my son was 4 years old, Albert showed up with a child-sized, fully operable electric dirt bike for him one Christmas, which captured everyone's attention, along with our hearts. Although devoutly unpredictable as always, he always participated in my children's lives, with a constancy I barely noticed until after his death, as I reviewed family photographs that depict the unequivocal joy of their connection.

The contrast between the obvious eros energy displayed in many photo images I rediscovered of "Grandpa Albert" spanning decades and the darker aspects of Albert's personality illustrates the enigma that was him—and the premise that psychopathy exists on a continuum, along with the power of love.

CHAPTER 18

Psychopathy as Infidelity to the Soul: Implications for Healing

G ranted, the nature and severity of one's inner psychopathy and its possible manifestations vary considerably. If the more general applicability of psychopathy as a personality characteristic posited here is true, then obviously we do not all act on this aspect of ourselves, at least not in the ways we typically associate with psychopathic behavior, such as overt cruelty and violence, and we may not even be conscious of our own psychopathic niches, what Guggenbühl-Craig described as "lacunae—empty places—where each and every one of us is lacking in something."[1] Part of what I found myself exploring during my journey to reconceptualize psychopathy is how else it might manifest in us beyond our typical associations with the term, how we can become aware of it, and perhaps most importantly, why that would be helpful and what to do about it once we notice it.

Infidelity to the Soul

Intrapsychic psychopathy is a fundamental form of infidelity—to the self. Loss of soul connection, of connection to the self, is an abstract

---

1   Guggenbühl-Craig, *Emptied Soul*, 79.

form of psychopathy that triggers feelings of hopelessness, depression, and anxiety: symptoms that are now so widespread, they are less clinical than ordinary. The idea of living an authentic, genuinely satisfying life, cliché as that sounds, usually becomes increasingly relevant in our later years and poses a challenge that may remain unmet for many reasons.

We live in such an urgent, ruthlessly competitive material world. Significantly, the root of the word *material* is *matter*, derived from the Latin *mater*, meaning *mother*. However, our obsessive striving for material gain, our emphasis on monetary value, and our extreme cultural identification with the world of things also represent attempts at connecting to an archetypal symbol of the feminine essence, or soul. In a biological parallel, the presence of only female chromosomes when life first forms, before the male chromosomes enter, means that in a sense, we all begin life in the feminine. This sequence of the origin of a human life can be viewed as symbolizing the evolution of human consciousness and the journey to self, from an unconscious (feminine) state to one of awareness and differentiation. Human beings all have and need both masculine and feminine aspects. Primarily, we manifest and develop these aspects through relationships, but relationships also inevitably mirror our inner process. We humans are a competitive, materialistic race, but also capable of the inclination to differentiate and integrate our different aspects within, to grow, and to become as whole and fully functional as possible.

Illuminating our inner psychopathy can help us to know and accept the truth about ourselves more fully, enabling unexpected growth. The shift to valuing an inner focus offers opportunity, unlimited and potentially invigorating, carrying the hopeful possibility of discovering (or rediscovering) our true path, at any age, defined less by outer appearance and concerns about the reactions of others than by inner compass. The nature of this process defies a generic road map; the navigator is the self.

Implications for Healing

If psychopathy is a psychic gap, then the opposite needed for healing the gap would nurture the process of individuation through which the unseen inner world is slowly brought into conscious awareness, thereby closing the gap. The human psyche contains what Jung referred to as an "original propensity to wholeness," which involves unconditionally embracing—or at least tolerating—the totality of our being.[2] Discovering how to heal our gaps may not be as complicated or nebulous as it sounds.

The potential for healing may be activated by a first halting attempt to listen to an unmet need that has been split off, to connect with that need, and to tend it. Fidelity to the soul—allowing and honoring our true needs, aspirations, and convictions—heals the psychopath within. This path is clear when we are "following our bliss," as Joseph Campbell expressed it, but also in less obvious (often uncomfortable) ways, when life offers us glimmers of opportunity to admit who we are at a deep level.[3]

The concept of *living an authentic life* defies a broad definition because we all must seek our own *specific* version. Illuminating our psychopathy, those gaps in the deepest layers of the psyche, may help liberate us to find our most satisfying life path. Genuine fulfillment might manifest through deeply satisfying activities and accomplishments or merely appear as an attitude shift: developing a healing perspective, for example. However we experience our authentic life, attending to disturbance at the core of the personality, at the soul level, opens a portal to healing—inviting integration of our inner opposites, wholeness, and individuation—freeing us to discover our true destiny, to become more fully who we are.

2　Jung, *Aion*, 169.
3　Joseph Campbell, *The Power of Myth* (New York: Anchor Books, 1991), 120, 149.

The degree to which we do this kind of inner work is inevitably influenced by our unique personalities and experiences. Whether or not we consciously seek such change through therapy, analysis, or other approaches, what appears universally true is that it is unlikely to happen in a linear, predictable way and absolutely cannot be scheduled, plotted, or forced. This level of change involves more of a feminine process that is diffuse and vague, reflecting an openness at the unconscious level. In fact, trying to make it happen can backfire, with the best of intentions, leaving us frustrated, or worse. I am reminded of one of my favorite lines from *Alice in Wonderland*: "The hurrieder I go, the behinder I get."

My life has never fit neatly into the pictures I had in mind. In that regard I have not had a perfect life. Rather, the unique perfection of my own quirky story, my life's colorful, variegated tapestry, reveals itself to me periodically—not because things turn out the way I want them to or planned, necessarily, but because shifts in my perspective illuminate my life story in a different light. Looking back from the vantage point of accumulating years, most lives contain a motley combination of many interconnected factors, including those never chosen or anticipated, at least some of which we might rather have avoided. Accepting our inevitable vulnerability, the truth about ourselves, and the reality of our circumstances can be unsettling to downright daunting, depending on the twists and turns of fate and the nature of our hidden or surprise material—but denial rarely works and can lead to even harsher prob-lems than it is designed to evade. In worst-case scenarios, denial can so trap one in fear that it engulfs existence in a flood of delusion, regret, and bitterness—while missing the fertile opportunity for growth that lies in the very areas we wish most to avoid.

Often the aspects of ourselves that we find darkest and most intolerable are the very parts that are instrumental to healing and wholeness. This idea that, figuratively speaking, out of darkness comes light is fundamental to Jungian psychology and certainly to the premise of this writing, with reference to the gaps in one's psychic landscape, absent eros: our inner psychopathy. Once illuminated, made conscious, these psychopathic gaps also hold the potential for healing through love. When I have experienced leaps in consciousness and positive life changes, they have rarely arrived in the form or time frame I had in mind. Despite my best-laid plans and industrious efforts, providence unfolds anyway, with or without my permission. In this respect, even during my darkest hours, I can find solace in the knowledge that at least I am not alone—nor ultimately in control.

Disturbing as it may be to consider the idea of psychopathy beyond pathology, as a more universally applicable human personality trait on a continuum, cracking open the meaning can also be liberating. The timeworn biblical quotation that "the truth shall set you free" comes to mind. Suggesting that psychopathy may apply to us all in one degree or another affirms the range of opposites within each of us as a member of the human species—a powerful conceptual dimension of a Jungian orientation that holds particular personal value to me as well, in terms of helping me to understand my experience with my father. Aspects of myself that I experience as painful and ugly—but undeniably real— also make me undeniably human, rather than just an outsider with a dark secret. This awareness helps me to feel less alone in my struggle to integrate these features within, and to regard others with respect and compassion. As Guggenbühl-Craig wrote: "An appreciation for psychopathy can help each of us to reduce the damage we do to our own psychopathic side. Finally confronting and dealing with psychopathy gives us a fuller appreciation for what it means to be human."[4]

---

4   Ibid, 85.

CHAPTER 19

The Transformational Potential of Psychopathy

A human being is a part of a whole, called by us "Universe," a part limited in time and space. He experiences himself, his thoughts and feelings, as something separated from the rest, a kind of optical delusion of his consciousness. This delusion is a kind of prison for us, restricting us to our personal desires and to affection for a few persons nearest to us. Our task must be to free ourselves from this prison by widening our circle of compassion to embrace all living creatures and the whole of nature in its beauty. Nobody is able to achieve this completely, but the striving for such achievement is in itself a part of the liberation and a foundation for inner security.

—Albert Einstein, 1950

How can awareness of our inner psychopathy help us personally, professionally, and in relationships? Understanding one's inner workings requires energy and courage. Since the excavation process is often painful and the outcome is unpredictable—essentially beyond our control—it may seem pointless to try. However, bringing consciousness to this hidden dimension of our existence potentially affects every aspect of our lives and functioning. An attitude of tolerance, grace, and compassion within and between us invites eros and helps to heal our inner psychopathy—and the world.

Sometimes we lie, hurt, or abandon our true selves and each other. These are characteristics of psychopathy that are pervasive and timeless; ancient history and mythology are replete with examples of the same theme. The conflicts these traits cause within and between us represent the quintessential human struggle between the polarities of good and evil, played out in a wide continuum; the resolution is usually neither absolute nor permanent. Personality and experience, whether deliberate or destined, influence the nature and extent to which the hurt, spoiled, or empty aspects within us manifest—but these dark dimensions also represent our shared humanity and potential libera-tion, and may contain an opportunity for healing transformation. As Jung posited:

> When we must deal with problems, we instinctively resist trying the way that leads through obscurity and darkness. We wish to hear only of unequivocal results, and completely forget that these results can only be brought about when we have ventured into and emerged again from the darkness. But to penetrate the darkness we must summon all the powers of enlightenment that consciousness can offer.[1]

An inescapable reality is that our lifetime is precious and limited. A recent visit to the buried city of Pompeii brought that notion to the forefront of my thinking with dramatic impact. The once-living statues of these terrified, unprepared individuals, halted forever on an other-wise ordinary day in their incredibly sophisticated ancient communities, moved me deeply. One minute they were following their daily routines, putting bread in the oven, and the next they were memorialized in that mundane moment by a tsunami of molten lava. We are certainly bombarded with parallel examples of different magnitudes in our

---

1   Jung, *Structure and Dynamics of the Psyche*, 389.

modern world on a daily basis. This ancient ruin came to represent for me a quintessential template, a graphic reminder of how temporary life is and of the timeworn cautionary note to take nothing for granted, to make the most of the journey and discover what we can along the way—to heal ourselves and the world while we have the fleeting chance. As Jungian analyst and author Tess Castleman writes in *Threads, Knots, Tapestries*, "Truly, our lives are our best creative work."[2]

Ancient Greek philosopher Heraclitus wrote, "Ethos anthropoid daimon": a person's character is fated. This statement can be understood to mean that we are born predetermined, but it may also suggest that what we choose to do with our lives can affect our destiny and legacy, individually and collectively.

Living true to ourselves—living with soul—generally promotes some form of inner discovery and confrontation that fosters a reconciliation of opposites within us and a restoration of our gaps within. This process may or may not be readily observable. Sometimes a therapy client on probation or parole who has acted out psychopathy through criminal behavior, undergoes a meaningful therapeutic experience through which the person learns to identify the core emptiness within that underlies this conduct and to feel compassion toward this inner aspect. This painful awareness can lead to a newfound capacity for self-love, a shift that may be most evident through acts of compassion toward others.

An example of a subtler version of this process is a high-functioning therapy client who was proud of her strong thinking capacity, her logic, and her impeccable integrity. She described her parents as perfect. Through therapy, it became evident that counter to her appearance and her beliefs about herself, she harbored a harsh inner critic who felt mean and angry. Although she never expressed this side overtly to others, she

---

2   Tess Castleman, *Threads, Knots, Tapestries: How a Tribal Connection Is Revealed through Dreams and Synchronicities* (Einsiedeln, Switzerland: Daimon Verlag, 2004), 254.

suffered deeply as a result and felt that something inside her was missing. At long last, tearfully, she identified her unmet need for compassion—even compassion she intellectually discounted as unwarranted—that lacked expression. Once she understood and accepted this, she was able to begin feeling the softness she so lacked toward herself and others. Her experience exemplifies how illuminating inner psychopathy can potentially heal it through eros, with restorative self-love.

Awareness of psychopathy as a basic human pitfall can help reduce the damage we do toward ourselves or others in our own inevitable psychopathic moments. For those of us in the helping professions, this includes how we experience *and* how we impact our patients. For us all, whatever remains unconscious is more likely to be acted out in thoughtless, indirect, and destructive ways. That which is conscious has at least the potential to be changed or healed.

Psychopathy is at the edge of our conscious human nature, if not completely hidden, and yet our unloved or empty aspects are instrumental to the whole of our existence, along with those characteristics we prefer and choose to display. Our painful experiences of suffering and inferiority may also contain all of the invaluable elements for inner transformation: what the alchemists referred to as *gold*. Acknowledging and integrating these difficult inner contents is fundamental to individuation, to becoming who we truly are.

When we are living true to ourselves, things tend to fall into place, what Eastern philosophy might refer to as becoming one with the tao (*Tao Te Ching*) or harmonizing one's will with the eternal, natural order of the universe. Although our modern lives are inevitably filled with chores and distractions, this Eastern-influenced approach to life requires focusing upon attitude more than action, something we can choose no matter what our responsibilities are or how little time and energy we have to spare. This concept is expressed universally. The Viking rune for *breakthrough* or *transformation* refers to "living the ordinary life in a nonordinary way."[3]

---

3   Ralph Blum, *The Book of Runes* (New York: St. Martin's Press, 1982), 105.

Discovering what the self is seeking may simply require willingness and attention. Greek author and philosopher Nikos Kazantzakis provided an eloquent illustration of this kind of discovery in the *Last Temptation of Christ*.[4] In this reimagined version of the myth, Christ was attempting to live like everybody else: as a married man in a village. In Kazantzakis's description of an ephemeral waking dream, everything appeared normal to civilian Jesus—except for an ever-present black sprite, often clinging to a wall like a visiting lizard, that he could only partially ignore, like an inescapable reminder of the truth about his real life and destiny that were waiting, ultimately unavoidable. We all have a true self and the natural capacity to notice its emergence. An example of this phenomenon occurs whenever we discover some aspect of ourselves or our reality that seems incredibly obvious in retrospect, but that we had somehow managed to overlook—to compartmentalize into some dark corner of the unconscious—until bringing our conscious attention and a willingness to accept it become unavoidable for one reason or another. "To thine own self be true" is Polonius's last piece of advice to his son Laertes in Shakespeare's *Hamlet:*

This above all: to thine own self be true,
And it must follow, as the night the day,
Thou canst not then be false to any man.[5]

In a related approach to healing, Jung spoke of holding the tension between opposites to produce a transcendent function—an unanticipated, irrational solution (1960).[6] As noted previously, the transcendent function bridges the unconscious and the conscious. This process might be understood as getting in touch with the soul and connecting with eros, our own inner feminine experienced through feeling. As an inner source of guidance, eros cannot be planned or sought directly, but

---

4 Nikos Kazantzakis, *The Last Temptation of Christ* (New York: Simon & Schuster, 1960), 459–484.
5 William Shakespeare, *Hamlet*, Scene 3, 78–82.
6 Jung, *Transcendent Function.*

can be invited by turning our conscious attention to the relationship between our inner processes and outer experiences.

For example, the chaos inherent in the prison environment where I often work (outer experience) is also *prima materia* for examining my own relationship to that chaos (inner process): in the correctional system, among the inmates, and within myself. Professional ethics and legal mandates dictate how I conduct my clinical interviews in that setting and the questions I must answer in my evaluations. However, I realized over time that this framework does not preclude further effects of my work as a forensic evaluator—a role I certainly never anticipated. The deeper reasons for my contact and experience with a given individual, such as an inmate, are often convoluted or hidden from my immediate awareness, to be perceived and revealed after the fact, only over time or through my dreams. As a Jungian, I do not believe in coincidence; that I find myself working with this particular population has resonance with my inner process and somehow holds meaning for my life.

At a symbolic level I work to develop an understanding of *the prisoner* as an important inner archetype for me. On a more obvious level, I am aware of how my relationship with my father encouraged me to find humanity in unusual ways, people, and places. A similar kind of synchronicity is apparent as I reflect upon my career overall; unraveling the mystery of how I have found myself engaged professionally over the years can feel like a gift when the thread of meaning becomes evident, inevitably mirroring some aspect of myself, my history, or a calling from my unique inner *daimon*, my soul-companion and carrier of my destiny.[7] We often find ourselves connecting or working with others whose suffering resonates with our own—sometimes intentionally. For example, when individuals have been abused as children or addicted to drugs, they may find relief from traumatic memories by using their survival to help others similarly afflicted. Their own painful

---

7   Hillman, *The Soul's Code*, 8.

history thereby gains purpose, positively transforming the meaning of their suffering through potential healing for others. However, we may recognize such synchronicity only in hindsight.

This healing process of mining the deeper meaning of our life experiences at a symbolic level may also bring uncomfortable truth to light, requiring patience, persistence, and humility to keep it illuminated so that we learn whatever this painful realization can teach us. Of course, appearances can be deceiving, and often my conscious reasons for following a particular path have been only part of the story; years may elapse before I realize how a particular job or setting has served my individuation.

Healing Psychopathy Within

When we manage to summon healing energy within ourselves, our relationships with others are inevitably affected. It is common knowledge that our chosen friends and lovers both reflect and influence our own orientation and functioning, either deliberately or by default. As helping professionals we emphasize this reciprocal flow. We often advise patients to seek companions who represent and thereby reinforce the kinds of life choices they admire and emulate. The same kind of attentiveness and care can be applied to the task of relating to various aspects within the personality and psyche, including accepting our areas of emptiness or psychopathy, and drawing upon the innate human capacity to heal ourselves.

We spend so much of our lives focused on relationships with others, while sometimes ignoring the state of our own souls. The kind of loving attention we offer to others can also be directed inward, and some of the same benefits we experience in a positive mutual connection with a partner may be discovered independently. Being estranged from aspects of ourselves can leave us feeling lonely or incomplete, even when not alone. Self-acceptance can generate a comforting feeling of connection to humanity, the sense of belonging to an infinite family, while depending less on others and external circumstances to make us feel safe or worthy.

This idea parallels the adage that one is "never alone because God is there," but our definitions of God are so subjective and culturally prescribed, often subsumed by fundamentalist religions, that this terminology does not speak to everyone. Nonetheless, the need to feel that there is some purpose to our existence seems to be part of our shared human legacy. In our own unique ways, most of us seek a meaning to life we can believe in and the feeling of belonging to something eternal: that we matter. This faith ultimately entails a developed relationship with the self.

Cultivating a relationship with the self is a universal concept, although our ways of describing this process are as different as we are from each other, reflecting our tremendously diverse personal beliefs and cultural attitudes. Shifting from an emphasis upon interpersonal relationships to focus more on the inner process of one's relationship with the self is related to the Jungian concept of finding your own path toward individuation. This path is inherently different for each of us, and the details matter less than that it represents each individual's personal truth. Gauging whether one is following such a path is corroborated by feeling aligned and comfortable about choices, experiencing a form of liberating self-love: eros within. When we consciously allow the flow of eros within ourselves, for ourselves, we become receptive to our own creativity and to our ability to actualize our potential for an authentic life, despite the inevitable turmoil of challenges involved in our day-to-day dealings with family, lovers, friends, and work demands. Illuminating the self-sabotaging psychopathy within us may free us from self-imposed obstructions to our individuation, helping us to attain some degree of inner peace.

This kind of pursuit can be evasive and confusing, especially if we tend to be impatient and driven, since the endeavor is guided less by deliberate action than by an inner process of staying open to the whispers of the self. Listening for these "messages in a bottle" is counter to our typical way of accomplishing goals in this culture, where targeting intentions, making plans to follow, and striving hard for an outcome are all implemented from a steadfastly conscious vantage point. Instead, the most effective strategy here may be a kind of attentive *not*-doing that I think of as *active waiting*. By invoking this kind of tuned-in patience, when one finally takes action, it simply happens and may seem effortless. Active waiting may produce unexpected gold. Two examples of this approach are found in the wisdom of oracular writings from two extremely dissimilar cultures, which in itself reflects the universality of the concept: the ancient *Viking runes* and the highly structured sacred text of the *I Ching*.

The Viking Runes and the I Ching

Two very divergent sources of parallel wisdom and guidance, the Viking runes and the *I Ching*, both address our innate tendency toward healing and our capacity to access it by consciously allowing things to unfold rather than trying to force outcomes.

The runes were the letters with which the ancient Norse wrote until approximately 1,000 B.C.E., and their carved shapes can still be seen on rune stones across Scandinavia to this day. The runes also had oracular, mythological, and psychological import. The Viking letters of this 2,000-year-old runic alphabet represent most of life's major themes: joy, partnership, disruption, standstill, movement, defense, journey, fertility, growth, harvest, and the divine—all carved on a set of clay stones, with the 25th stone left blank to represent the unknowable. For example, *Othila*, the rune of acquisition and benefits, includes this instruction:

> Not rigidity but flow is the proper attitude at this time. And yet you must wait for the universe to act. When drawing this Rune, remember, we do without doing and everything gets done.[8]

---

8   Blum, 69.

Eihwaz, the rune of patience, counsels:

> Nothing hectic, no acting needy or lusting after a desired outcome. This Rune speaks to the difficulties that arise at the beginning of new life. Often it announces a time of waiting—for a spring to fill up with water, for fruit to ripen on the bough. Perseverance and foresight are called for here. The ability to foresee consequences before you act is the mark of the profound person. Avert anticipated difficulties through right action. Even more than we are *doers*, we are *deciders*. Once our decision is clear, the doing becomes effortless, for then the universe supports and empowers our action.[9]

The *I Ching* originated in ancient China and is the oldest Chinese classical text. Traditionally, the *I Ching* was thought to predate recorded history, and based on traditional Chinese accounts, its origins trace back to the third or second millennium B.C.E. The *I Ching* is a panoply of practical wisdom, pertaining to every conceivable life situation. "*I Ching*" means "Classic of Changes" or "Book of Changes." There are 64 different kinds of situations addressed in the *I Ching*. Each one is indicated by a hexagram, which is a symbol composed of six lines, each of which can be broken or unbroken. To obtain advice from the *I Ching* about one's current situation, one can consult it as an oracle. To decide which hexagram is related to the situation at hand, a random hexagram is obtained by throwing coins, although yarrow sticks were traditionally used. The random hexagram is considered not random at all, but to coincide in a synchronistic way with the situation.

A special friend and colleague of Jung's, Richard Wilhelm, translated the *I Ching* from Chinese into German in the 1920s, and his translations were later translated into English by Cary F. Baynes, an American who was another of Jung's close associates. Jung was deeply

---

9   Ibid., 78.

interested in the philosophy and implications of the *I Ching*.[10] The philosophy of the *I Ching*, or *Book of Changes*, includes a metaphor for the idea of *active waiting* comparable to that described in the Viking runes. Hexagram 5 of the *I Ching*, "Waiting (Nourishment)," is also quoted in Shinoda Bolen's *The Tao of Psychology: Synchronicity and the Self*:

> All things have need of nourishment. But the gift of food comes in its own time, and for this one must wait. This hexagram shows the clouds in the heavens, giving rain to refresh all that grows. . . . The rain will come in its own time. We cannot make it come; we have to wait for it. The idea of waiting is further suggested by the attributes of the two trigrams—strength within, danger in front. Strength in the face of danger does not plunge ahead but bides its time, whereas weakness in the face of danger grows agitated and has not the patience to wait. . . .

> Waiting is not mere empty hoping. It has an inner certainty of reaching a goal. Such certainty alone gives that light which leads to success. This leads to the perseverance that leads to good fortune and bestows power to cross the great water.

> One is faced with danger that must be overcome. Weakness and impatience can do nothing. Only a strong man can stand up to his fate, for his inner security enables him to endure to the end. This strength shows itself in uncompromising truthfulness (with himself). It is only when we have the courage to face things exactly as they are, without any sort of self-deception or illusion, that a light will develop out of events, by which the path to success may be recognized. This recognition must be followed by resolute and persevering action. For only the man who goes to meet his fate resolutely is equipped to deal with it adequately. Then he will be able to cross the

---

10 Jung, *Memories, Dreams, Reflections*, 373–377.

great water—that is to say, he will be capable of making the necessary decision and of surmounting the danger.[11]

Any kind of waiting presents an ominous challenge in our collective culture. Waiting is associated with failing to take matters in hand, to drive for goals as expected, and to succeed at achieving measurable outcomes in the shortest time frame possible: to wit, our popular definition of laziness. To wait requires stoic patience, counterintuitive in our fast-paced, driven society, where *im*patience is endemic. Laziness and impatience are closely related, however, although they may appear opposite in nature, because both tend to produce or protect inertia of many kinds, including at the level of the psyche, keeping us from moving forward in our own growth. Despite their polar opposite appearances, they are actually parallel strategies of avoidance. Active waiting involves holding quiet energy and an open attitude. Neither laziness nor impatience equates to active waiting, which is intrinsically conducive to unobstructed growth rather than predictable results.

We are naturally predisposed to grow, even in spite of ourselves. This healing tendency emerges in different ways. For example, we may attract partners who initially appeared strikingly similar to us but then, with the passage of time, turn out to embody all of the opposite qualities we have been trying industriously to ignore. However, as our mutual projections are withdrawn over time, we may eventually recognize in each other someone with whom we can truly resonate—whose very differences energize us toward our own individuation.

The material emerging in dreams that have repeating themes may offer another catalyst for growth. One function of dreams is to integrate the truth of our daily lives with other aspects of ourselves: unwanted characteristics or the ideal life we imagine ourselves destined for, but that eludes us. The unresolved haunts us one way or another. Depending upon how aware we are of our personal depths, this may be a conscious process or a relatively unconscious one.

---

11 Bolen, *Tao of Psychology*, 63, 64.

Our personal depths are often closer to the surface than we notice, for example, through self-talk, also known as internal monologue, inner voice, internal speech, or verbal stream of consciousness. These semiconstant internal conversations we have with ourselves at a conscious or semiconscious level can reveal a great deal, once we turn our full attention to their content. One's inner voice may promote an inflated or distracted attitude, reflecting a chattering, overstressed, too-busy mind. If one's inner monologue is discouraging and devaluing, ignoring it only exacerbates problems. Despite our own natural resistance, accepting the challenge of listening to and considering those inner voices invites the possibility of growth and healing. Refusing to listen can produce telling symptoms as well, often revealed psychosomatically. The body is a terrific messenger. One male patient who was struggling to maintain an unhappy relationship while avoiding his true feelings once told me that he felt as though all the "reins in his chest" were pulling back.

The conceptual roots for *quieting the mind* were based on the teachings of Lao Tzu, a Taoist sage and philosopher. By quieting the mind, one can self-calm. Consistent with meditation practice, that state of mind is where peace abides, and when we experience peace, we naturally experience joy and creativity and can readily access our own natural wisdom: our eros, our capacity for healing.

Jung and many authors of kindred spirit who followed him, from Joseph Campbell to Robert Johnson, urge us to *face our demons* and *own our own shadows*. Daily life is rife with opportunities to do so. Snapshot memories or random daydreams may emerge unexpectedly from our own depths. We can choose to pay attention and acknowledge those thoughts and feelings, even if they are painful or elusive. Being serious and patient while enduring uncomfortable experiences of reflection, rather than trying to avoid them, may free us to learn more about ourselves and face life with less fear.

Fearing pain keeps us on the move, addicted to activities or substances to distract us, whether drugs or alcohol, bad relationships, work, or other compulsions through which we seek numbness and ignore unwanted reality, even if we are unsure what we are avoiding. Such efforts never really work. At best, we survive while immobilized, to some degree, by our own doubts and fears, often suspecting that there may be dimensions to life we have not discovered and do not dare to try. Still, each in our own ways, we yearn for some kind of magical immortality, perhaps most universally accessible through a sense of spirit, of inner depth and connectivity that yields some awareness of life everlasting—even if only in the imagination. The following is widely attributed to R. D. Laing:

> The range of what we think and do
> is limited by what we fail to notice.
> And because we fail to notice
> that we fail to notice
> there is little we can do
> to change
> until we notice
> how failing to notice
> shapes our thoughts and deeds.[12]

Many of us feel culturally beholden to spend our lives preoccupied and forever distracted by the external, material trappings of existence as we know it, well beyond the obvious priority of meeting basic needs. We try to compartmentalize, institutionalize, and sanitize the eternal in hopes that we can make it manageable, that we can avoid what we cannot control or understand. Our expressions of spirituality are prone to becoming objectified and concretized, reflecting our collective consciousness: safely devoid of the very depth and mystery that constitute the essence of faith. Traditional religions are often discriminating and exclusive, unfortunately becoming another institutionalized means of dividing us from undesirable aspects of ourselves and each other,

---

12 Jack L. Seymour, Margaret Ann Crain, and Joseph Crockett, *Educating Christians: The Intersection of Meaning, Learning, and Vocation* (Nashville: Abingdon Press, 1993), 53.

rather than of liberating us to experience the fundamental unity of the universe, the *Unus Mundus*.

This kind of aggressive superficiality constitutes a culturally prescribed loss of soul: psychopathy manifested at the collective level. Such an attitude further reinforces our tendency to stringently avoid those dimensions of ourselves and our lives that are less than perfect in our own estimation. The reality of those rejected aspects—physical and otherwise—tends to become harder to ignore with aging, despite our most elaborate defenses. Consistent with this aversion, we over-value youth; our associations with that idealized image include perfect physical attractiveness, vitality, innocence, and endless possibilities. No wonder so many of us want to be young forever, or at least look that way. Extreme identification with youth has implications at the unconscious level as well as superficially, however, symbolizing all that we choose to leave unexplored, unresolved, and undeveloped—at a cost.

During one summer session at the Jung Institute in Küsnacht, I met Jungian analyst and activist Jean Shinoda Bolen. In that environment, running into remarkable individuals who listen to their inner voice was more the rule than the exception, unlike my earthly world back home. Although her training topic was something different, the essence of her presentation emphasized paying attention to the continuum of inner contents we all contain, and the need to have a sense of our true selves in this way. She talked about this awareness as including an acceptance of the connection between all living things. I have heard the concept of spirituality expressed in a plethora of ways, but for me, it refers to a universal need to belong to something lasting and meaningful. In *The Tao of Psychology*, Shinoda Bolen describes a dynamic I found related to my observations about psychopathy, including her reference to an inner wound:

> When the ego is cut off from experiencing the Self—or, put
> differently, when an individual lacks the inner sense of being
> connected to God or being part of the Tao—then a wound

exists that the person experiences as gnawing, pervasive, persisting insecurity. All kinds of defensive maneuvers, from smoking to amassing power, are unsatisfying efforts to feel better. The narcissism of modern times seems fueled by the feeling of being deprived and unnourished emotionally or spiritually, which is part of the same wound.[13]

I understood her ideas to suggest that a lack of spiritual affiliation leads to a prevailing sense of emptiness, and that the struggle to compensate for that emptiness within us and in our lives—our psychopathy within— may lead to desperate, extreme opinions or reactions. Certainly the current prevalence of extreme positions and violent behaviors, here and abroad, represents a kind of collective global psychopathy.

The life journey toward individuation can yield liberating self-love and enlightened regard for others, helping us to find our way in this seemingly tattered world with a hopeful perspective. In one of a multitude of perceptive statements by Jung expressing this concept of the meaning of our lives, he emphasizes the universal human quest to belong to a mystery greater than ourselves, the potential implications for life's meaning, and the relationship between this intangible value and the more superficial and temporary goals, attitudes, and distractions of our earthly existence:

The decisive question for man is: Is he related to something infinite or not? That is the telling question of his life. Only if we know that the thing which truly matters is the infinite can we avoid fixing our interest upon futilities, and upon all kinds of goals which are not of real importance. Thus we demand that the world grant us recognition for qualities which we regard as personal possessions: our talent or our beauty. The more a man lays stress on false possessions, and the less sensitivity he has for what is essential, the less satis-

---

13 Bolen, *Tao of Psychology*, 100.

fying is his life. He feels limited because he has limited aims, and the result is envy and jealousy. If we understand and feel that here in this life we already have a link with the infinite, desires and attitudes change. In the final analysis, we count for something only because of the essential we embody, and if we do not embody that, life is wasted. In our relationships to other men, too, the crucial question is whether an element of boundlessness is expressed in the relationship.[14]

Seeking self-realization behind our carefully crafted personas and daring to delve into the masked material can make us feel frightened, unpopular, unattractive, and worse. This material is often held hostage in the unconscious, yet it is inseparable from the whole self, despite our best efforts to quarantine it. Ironically, our fear and avoidance of the aspects of ourselves we reject preclude us from fully owning the potent, transcendent contents contained therein: what alchemists refer to as hidden gold.

Final Reflections on Albert

The hidden gold in the psychic cavern of my father's abandonment became evident after his death, when my struggle to understand him and our relationship inspired me to acknowledge and then find meaning in that suddenly permanent emptiness, a development I could never have planned and certainly would never have written voluntarily into my life script. Nonetheless, our story—of his life and our relationship— was the *prima materia* of my thinking about this gradated definition of psychopathy. The concept and practice of illuminating that inner gap—not just his psychopathy but my own—has proven instrumental to my individual healing process and to my hope that these ideas about a revised definition of the characteristic may prove useful well beyond my individuation. As such, this writing closes with final reflections

---

14 Jung, *Memories, Dreams, Reflections,* p. 325.

upon my father and me, with which I offer a final illustration of how the potential for healing inner psychopathy might appear.

In the end, although I deeply regret the gaps in my time and relationship with Albert, I am tremendously glad I knew him. I still feel his presence. I can easily imagine his characteristic responses, although I am sure if he were here, he would argue, with a scoff, that I have absolutely no idea. My mother often stated that he would have been very difficult to live with, had I had the opportunity growing up, and from my experience with him as an adult, I surmise that she is correct. For this reason, I suppose the fact that he was out of my life for as long as he was, and the ways in which I did not know or count on him, protected my love for him while keeping me at a safe distance. Part of the impact of his psyche on my own psyche has been the mystery of his unavailability, which caused me pain—and also triggered my imagination. The fantasies I created to fill the void of my own sadness about his absence when I was a child, spurred by photos and stories, became entrenched memories and impressions, creating a forever internalized image. Insulated from the sharper edges of reality, I was freer to continue loving him—and to discover love's potential for healing.

Raging at my father for his lengthy abandonment was on my list of intentions, at least intellectually, but by the time the opportunity actually felt ripe in terms of our relationship and logistics, there were other urgent priorities: He was fading fast, in and out of dementia. There was his daily-life business to wrap up before it was too late, and we were in survival mode. If I was avoiding a confrontation, I did not do so consciously. The kind of intense anger at him that others suggested to me was warranted for his abandonment never quite surfaced, although I was aware that the anger must have been there—or, perhaps more aptly and significantly, should have been.

In retrospect, my experience of this justifiable feeling—righteous indignation and intense outrage at Albert's abandonment—was notably absent: a kind of empty space within me, *absent eros*. From the vantage point of this writing, such a gap appears to have been a form of self-abandonment: an aspect of my inner psychopathy. I had no premeditated plan to heal this psychopathic gap with love, but in our final days together, loving Albert and feeling his love for me in return were more important to me than expressing my anger at him for having abandoned me during my growing-up years—and there was simply not time for both. That anger became unnecessary in the final hour, or at least less necessary than everything else with which we were dealing. At this point, my anger over his abandonment feels no more or less important than the many other conversations I never got the chance to have with him, about which I continue to reflect.

I revisited my experience of Albert's physical absence during my childhood with renewed clarity after he died. During these two deeply impactful periods of my relationship with him, the *idea* of him informed my feelings more than the reality of who he was in totality, which remains an enigma in so many ways. Perhaps I felt safest with him after his death, when I reviewed the time we did share and realized the nature of our connection in ways that were never obvious before. Since his passing, I feel a softening in my attitude and increased confidence in my perceptions about him, relieved of the irritation and frustration his physical presence inevitably generated—and the unavoidable truth of his coldness. I am released to simply love him and feel less burdened by his psychopathic gaps; after all, he has always spent more time in my imagination than keeping me company otherwise. My memories of him flourish. I miss him. This time the abandonment is bottomless, but simultaneously I feel closer to him than ever, with an unprecedented wholeness of perspective. He would probably dismiss this with his typical half-snicker and comment disparagingly in a withering tone, loaded with disdain, that I am being "sentimental."

Our own psychopathy may be most evident when we examine those people and ideas we judge most harshly, since what we find most intolerable within we tend to project elsewhere—which is also why, as we heal within, we bring positive change to the world. Love, like psychopathy, has a gradated definition, and the presence of one aspect does not preclude the other, but love holds the potential to positively transform our inner emptiness with caring, meaning, and purpose. In symbolic terms, illuminating psychopathy within—those empty places in the soul where the light of love has yet to enter—may also invoke one's healing inner muse. The healing remedy for psychopathy within might appear in the form of creativity inspired by eros.

My dream of attaining the ideal, consistently loving and reliable father is forever broken. His death and dying brought me one of my darkest hours, but in the wake of grief and loss emerged these ensuing memoirs, myths, and musings about psychopathy—certainly his least appealing but ultimately most challenging character quality. My amplified awareness of the opposites in Albert's character and in our relationship produced no finite resolution.

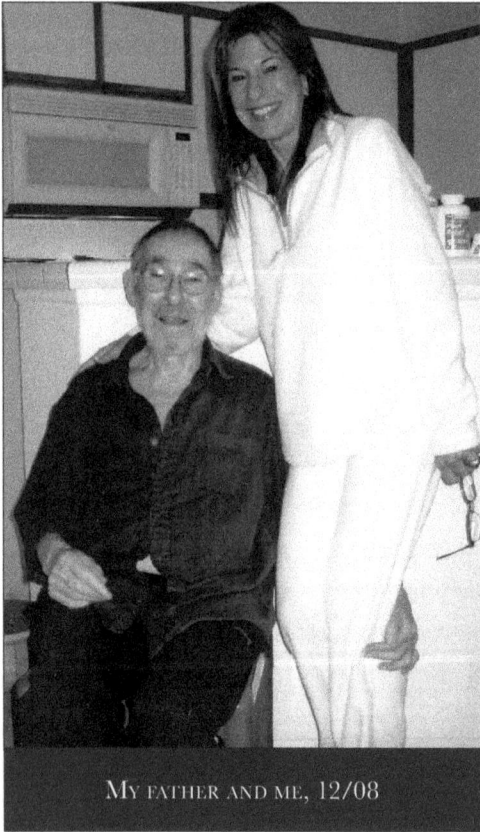

MY FATHER AND ME, 12/08

Holding the tension of these opposites ultimately led me to a deep unveiling I recognized as the transcendent function at work within me. That experience inspired me to question the meaning of psychopathy in ways I had never contemplated—and to consider the potential for healing it, through eros.

272

Bibliography

American Psychiatric Association. *Diagnostic and Statistical Manual of Mental Disorders, Fourth Edition, Text Revision (DSM-IV-TR)*. Washington, DC: Author, 2000.

Beebe, John. *Integrity in Depth* (Carolyn and Ernest Fay Series in Analytical *Psychology*). New York: Fromm Psychology, 1992.

Black, D., and L. Larson. *Bad Boys, Bad Men: Confronting Antisocial Personality Disorder*. New York: Oxford University Press, 2000.

Blum, R. *The Book of Runes*. New York: St. Martin's Press, 1982.

Bly, Robert. *Iron John*. New York: Vintage Books, 1990.

Bolen, Jean Shinoda. *The Tao of Psychology: Synchronicity and the Self* 2nd ed. New York: HarperCollins, 2004.

Campbell, Joseph. *The Masks of God: Occidental Mythology*. New York: Penguin Books, 1976.

———. *The Power of Myth*. New York: Anchor Books, 1991.

Castleman, Tess. *Sacred Dream Circles: A Guide to Facilitating Jungian Dream Groups*. Einsiedeln, Switzerland: Daimon Verlag, 2009.

———. *Threads, Knots, Tapestries: How a Tribal Connection Is Revealed through Dreams and Synchronicities*. Einsiedeln, Switzerland: Daimon Verlag, 2004.

Castaneda, Carlos. *The Teachings of Don Juan: A Yaqui Way of Knowledge*. Berkeley and Los Angeles: University of California Press, 1969.

Cavalli, Thom F. *Alchemical Psychology*. New York: Tarcher/Putnam, 2002.

Claremont de Castillo, Irene. *Knowing Woman: A Feminine Psychology*. Boston: Shambhala, 1973.

Cleckley, Hervey Milton. *The Mask of Sanity*. St. Louis, MO: Mosby, 1988 (1976).

Edinger, Edward. *The Aion Lectures*. Toronto: Inner City Books, 1996.

Freud, Sigmund. "Dostoevsky and Parricide." *Standard Edition of The Complete Psychological Works of Sigmund Freud, Vol. 21.* London: Hogarth Press, 1928, pp. 175–196.

Guggenbühl-Craig, Adolph. *The Emptied Soul: On the Nature of the Psychopath.* University of Dallas, Irving, TX: Spring, 1999.

———. *Eros on Crutches: Reflections on Psychopathy and Amorality.* University of Dallas, Irving, TX: Spring, 1980.

Hare, Robert. *The Hare Psychopathy Checklist—Revised.* Toronto: Multi-Health Systems, 1991.

———. "Psychopathy: A clinical construct whose time has come." *Criminal Justice and Behavior* 23 (1996): 25–54. doi: 10.1177/0093854896023001004

———. *Without Conscience: The Disturbing World of the Psychopaths among Us.* New York: Guilford Press, 1999.

Haule, John Ryan. *Divine Madness: Archetypes of Romantic Love.* Boston: Shambhala, 1990.

Henderson, Joseph L. "Ancient Myths and Modern Man." In C. G. Jung, *Man and His Symbols.* London: Pan Books, 1978.

Hillman, James. "Anima II." *Spring* (1974): 113–146.

———. *Anima: An Anatomy of a Personified Notion.* Woodstock, CT: Spring, 1985.

———. *The Soul's Code: In Search of Character and Calling.* New York: Warner Books, 1996.

Hopke, Robert H. *A Guided Tour of the Collected Works of C. G. Jung.* Boston: Shambhala, 1999.

Johnson, Robert. *Owning Your Own Shadow.* San Francisco: HarperCollins, 1991.

Jung, C. G. *Alchemical Studies. Vol. 13. The Collected Works of C. G. Jung* (2d ed.). Princeton, NJ: Princeton University Press, 1983/1942.

———. *The Archetypes and the Collective Unconscious. Vol. 9i. The Collected Works of C. G. Jung* (2d ed.). Princeton, NJ: Princeton University Press, 1968.

———. *The Development of Personality. Vol. 17. The Collected Works of C. G. Jung* (2d ed.). Princeton, NJ: Princeton University Press, 1954.

————. *C. G. Jung Speaking: Interviews and Encounters.* Edited by William McGuire & R. F. C. Hull. Princeton, NJ: Princeton University Press, 1977.

————. *Memories, Dreams, Reflections* (Rev. ed.). Edited by Aniela Jaffé. New York: Random House, 1989/1961.

————. *The Practice of Psychotherapy. Vol. 16. The Collected Works of C. G. Jung* (2d ed.). Princeton, NJ: Princeton University Press, 1966.

————. *Psychiatric Studies. Vol. 1. The Collected Works of C. G. Jung* (2d ed.). Princeton, NJ: Princeton University Press, 1970.

————. *Psychological Types. Vol. 6. The Collected Works of C. G. Jung, Vol. 6,* (2d ed.). Princeton, NJ: Princeton University Press, 1974.

————. *The Structure and Dynamics of the Psyche. Vol. 8. The Collected Works of C. G. Jung* (2d ed.). Princeton, NJ: Princeton University Press, 1981.

————. *The Symbolic Life. Vol. 18. The Collected Works of C. G. Jung* (11th ed.). Princeton, NJ: Princeton University Press, 1976.

————. *Synchronicity: An Acausal Connecting Principle.* Princeton, NJ: Princeton University Press, 1993/1952.

————. *The Transcendent Function. Vol. 8. The Collected Works of C. G. Jung* (2d ed.). Princeton, NJ: Princeton University Press, 1960.

————. *Two Essays on Analytical Psychology. Vol. 7. The Collected Works of C. G. Jung* (2d ed.). Princeton, NJ: Princeton University Press, 1966.

————, M.-L. von Franz, J. L. Henderson, J. Jacobi, & A. Jaffé. *Man and His Symbols.* New York: Dell, 1964.

Kazantzakis, N. *The Last Temptation of Christ.* New York: Simon-Schuster, 1998.

Magid, K. *High Risk: Children without a Conscience.* New York: Bantam Books, 1987.

Martens, W. H. J. "The hidden suffering of the psychopath." *Psychiatric Times* 19 (2002): Issue 1. http://www.goertzel.org/dynapsyc/2003/psychopaths.htm.

Neumann, E. *Depth Psychology and a New Ethic.* New York: Harper Torchbooks, 1969.

Rinpoche, S. *The Tibetan Book of Living and Dying.* New York: HarperCollins, 2002.

Samuels, Andrew. *Jung and the Post-Jungians.* New York: Routledge & Kegan Paul, 1985.

Sanford, John A. *The Invisible Partners: How the Male and Female in Each of Us Affects Our Relationships.* New York: Paulist Press, 1980.

Trent, M., and J. McCormick. *The psychopathic style* [A documentary]. Dallas: Intra Muros, 2004.

Ulanov, Ann, and Barry Ulanov. *Transforming Sexuality: The Archetypal World of Anima and Animus.* Boston: Shambhala, 1994.

van der Post, Laurens. *Jung and the Story of Our Time.* New York: Vintage Books, 1975.

von Franz, Marie-Louise. *Alchemy.* Toronto: Inner City Books, 1980.

von Franz, M.-L. *The Problem of the Puer Aeternus.* Toronto: Inner City Books, 2000.

Zoja, L. *The Father: Historical, Psychological, and Cultural Perspectives.* London & New York: Routledge, 2001.

ODILON REDON (1840–1916), CENTAURE LISANT (CENTAUR READING)] (PLEASE SEE NOTE ON P. 283)

Index

A

R

S

T

About the Author

Eve Maram is a clinical and forensic psychologist and a Jungian-oriented psychotherapist in private practice in Orange, California. She is currently pursuing Jungian analytic training through the Inter-Regional Society of Jungian Analysts (IRSJA), C.G. Jung Institute of Santa Fe, New Mexico.

www.ingramcontent.com/pod-product-compliance
Lightning Source LLC
Chambersburg PA
CBHW040139270326
41928CB00022B/3261